DATE DUE

DEC 12 '73			
MAR 18			

Unquestioning Obedience to the President

Books by Leon Friedman

The Wise Minority
Obscenity (editor)
The Justices of the United States Supreme Court
    (editor and contributor)
Argument (editor)
The Civil Rights Reader (editor)
Southern Justice (editor and contributor)

Books by Burt Neuborne

Uncle Sam Is Watching You (contributor)
The Rights of the Poor (contributor)

UNQUESTIONING OBEDIENCE TO THE PRESIDENT

The ACLU Case Against the Illegal War in Vietnam
by Leon Friedman and Burt Neuborne

Introduction by
Senator George S. McGovern

W · W · NORTON & COMPANY · INC ·

NEW YORK

FIRST EDITION

Library of Congress Cataloging in Publication Data
Friedman, Leon.
  Unquestioning obedience to the President.

  Includes bibliographical references.
  1. Berk, Malcolm A.   2.   Orlando, Salvatore, 1948–
3. War and emergency powers—U.S.   4.   Vietnamese
Conflict, 1961–   —U.S.   I.   Neuborne, Burt,
1941–   joint author. II. Title.
KF5060.F7   342'.73'062   76-169044
  ISBN 0-393-05462-4 (cloth edition)
  ISBN 0-393-05470-5 (paper edition)

Published simultaneously in Canada
by George J. McLeod Limited, Toronto

PRINTED IN THE UNITED STATES OF AMERICA

1 2 3 4 5 6 7 8 9 0

Contents

Acknowledgments

This book contains the legal documents in two related cases challenging the constitutionality of the Vietnam war. Legal briefs are generally joint endeavors in which a single lawyer may prepare a first draft that is subsequently edited and re-edited by the team working on the case. Although initially we prepared most of the legal materials reproduced in this book, we wish to acknowledge the important contributions made by each lawyer who participated in the enterprise. These include Norman Dorsen, Melvin Wulf, Marc J. Luxemburg, Mark Alcott, Theodore C. Sorensen, Kay Ellen Hays, Lawrence Velvel, Peter Smith, Alfred Lawrence Toombs and Steven J. Hyman.

In the interests of conciseness and clarity, it has often been necessary to omit certain portions of the documents relating to this case. In most instances, deletions have been indicated by ellipses. Where the deletion occurred in the original document, we have indicated it by asterisks. Occasionally, however, where repeated use of ellipses and asterisks would render the materials difficult to read, they have been omitted. We have, of course, refrained from deletions which might affect the basic meaning of the documents involved.

There are many additional debts of gratitude that we wish to acknowledge. The New York Civil Liberties Union under Aryeh Neier (who subsequently became Executive Director of the American Civil Liberties Union) and under Ira Glasser financed the litigation, and its staff made important contributions throughout. The research work of Edwin Oppenheimer and Arthur Eisenberg was extremely important, as were the efforts of Toby Jo Platt and Phyllis Applebaum. Richard P. Cecil first suggested the idea for this book and assisted in its organization. Above all we must thank Malcolm Berk and Salvatore Orlando for their courage in bringing the cases to court.

—LEON FRIEDMAN
BURT NEUBORNE
New York, N.Y.
September 1971

Introduction

The Vietnam war must be considered one of the great disasters in American history. It would have been a serious mistake from an international point of view even if the American people had been fully informed of every step in the escalation of the war and even if Congress had unanimously approved the commitment of our army to Southeast Asia. The proportions of the blunder are magnified because neither one of these conditions occurred. Instead, the American people and the United States Congress have been deceived by the highest officials in the government, including even the president of the United States. And one of the most important powers granted by the Constitution to Congress—the power to declare war—has been usurped by the president. These actions amount to an affront to the Constitution without equal in this century. The Congress must carry a heavy burden of responsibility for permitting its war power to be eroded.

The deception of the American people and Congress has been clearly revealed in the Pentagon papers first disclosed to the public by *The New York Times* in June 1971. The papers show, for example, that the United States planned to attack

North Vietnam long before the Gulf of Tonkin incident and the ensuing resolution. In a memo to President Johnson dated December 21, 1963, Secretary of Defense Robert S. McNamara suggested a covert program of CIA and U.S. military plans for operations in the north. He wrote:

> They [the plans] present a wide variety of sabotage and psychological operations against North Vietnam from which I believe we should aim to select those that provide maximum pressure with minimum risk.[1]

Beginning in February 1964, the United States had begun operation 34A, which included flights over North Vietnam by U-2 spy planes, parachuting sabotage and psychological-warfare teams into the North, commando raids from the sea to blow up rail and highway bridges, and the use of PT boats (manned by South Vietnamese) to bombard North Vietnamese coastal installations.

By May 1964, Executive planners had already made preparations for more direct attacks on the North by American planes. Assistant Secretary of State William Bundy actually drafted the key language of the Gulf of Tonkin Resolution in May 1964 —two months before the Gulf of Tonkin incident took place. We now know that American destroyers were in the gulf gathering information for 34A operations when the alleged attacks by North Vietnamese PT boats occurred. American bombers were able to retaliate so quickly after the Tonkin incident because targets had been selected months before as part of the enlarged operations plan.

The Pentagon documents also show that, as early as September 1964, plans had been made to bomb North Vietnam—precisely at the time when top administration officials were ridiculing Senator Goldwater for advocating that same course. A "scenario" was prepared to provoke the Vietcong into actions that would justify the bombings. An assistant secretary of defense, John McNaughton, suggested to McNamara on September 3, 1964, that further military steps be taken, which he described as

> an orchestration of three classes of actions, all designed to meet these five desiderata—(1) From the U.S., GVN [Government of

[1] *Pentagon Papers* (New York: Bantam, 1971), p. 273.

South Vietnam] and hopefully allied points of view they should be legitimate things to do under the circumstances, (2) they should cause apprehension, ideally increasing apprehension in the D.R.V. [Democratic Republic of Vietnam, i.e., North Vietnam], (3) they should be likely at some point to provoke a military D.R.V. response, (4) the provoked response should be likely to provide good grounds for us to escalate if we wish, and (5) the timing and crescendo should be under our control, with the scenario capable of being turned off at any time.[2]

Actual events followed McNaughton's plan quite closely. In September and October 1964, air strikes by South Vietnamese planes on Laos infiltration routes increased, as did coastal raids on the North. American destroyer patrols resumed in the Gulf of Tonkin. The Vietcong then attacked the American airfield at Bienhoa in November 1964. Within thirty days, although no public announcement was made, American planes were attacking the Ho Chi Minh Trail in Laos. In January 1965, the Vietcong scored an important victory at Binhia over South Vietnam troops. In early February, a United States military advisers' compound at Pleiku was attacked. American jets then commenced their first attack on targets in North Vietnam. Within a week a sustained bombing campaign was in operation.

Such provocation brings to mind all too clearly the plan for a simulated Polish attack on German forces which enabled the Nazis to invade Poland and launch World War II. Most Americans would not have believed this kind of cynical manipulation was conceivable by our national leaders.

Congress was a primary target of the pattern of deception practiced by the Executive department. To cite just one example, during the debate on the Tonkin Gulf Resolution I asked Senator Fulbright whether American ships were involved in military operations off the coast of North Vietnam on July 30, 1964, just prior to the alleged North Vietnamese PT-boat attack on our destroyers. Senator Fulbright said, in all good faith, that he had been assured by the administration that American vessels were not involved in those harassment operations. Secretary of Defense McNamara told the Senate Foreign Relations Committee meeting in secret session on August 6, 1964, ". . . our Navy

[2] *Ibid.*, p. 356.

played absolutely no part in, was not associated with, was not aware of any South Vietnamese actions, if there were any. . . ." The truth is that this program, though manned by South Vietnamese, was planned and financed by our government. Senator Fulbright had been told a lie, but his assurances were the decisive factor that led me, for one, to support the Gulf of Tonkin Resolution in spite of my expressed apprehension.

The period of congressional deception by the Executive department lasted from early 1964 until the summer of 1965, when American ground troops began to arrive in force in Vietnam. At that point a new relationship between the president and Congress was created, lasting from May 1965 until the middle of 1969. This second phase consisted of congressional acquiescence in military actions in Vietnam. Once the president had secured the Gulf of Tonkin Resolution and commenced the rapid escalation of the war, he thought he would have no difficulty in persuading Congress to pay the increasing bills for the war.[3] He knew that Congress would find it impossible to deny funds for military supplies needed to supply and protect troops in the field. Whatever their views might have been before troops were committed to battle, members of Congress could hardly refuse to equip fighting men engaged in actual hostilities.

This view was expressed in many of the early congressional debates on military-spending bills. In a Senate debate in February 1966 on the first large-scale request for money for Vietnam —$3.4 billion in additional defense authorization funds and $12.3 billion in additional appropriations—Senator Richard Russell, chairman of the Armed Services Committee, said:

[3] In reponse to a letter asking for specific amounts spent in Vietnam, the Defense Department sent me the following information:

The following are the estimated Department of Defense expenditures in support of Southeast Asia:

	Billions
Fiscal year 1965	$ 0.1
Fiscal year 1966	5.8
Fiscal year 1967	20.1
Fiscal year 1968	26.5
Fiscal year 1969	28.8
Fiscal year 1970	23.2

See 117 *Cong. Rec.* S.4478 (daily ed., April 1, 1971).

Members of the Armed Forces are in southeast Asia under orders. From all reports, they are giving a splendid account of themselves. I am proud of them. Although many have volunteered for this duty, others are there not by choice. They nonetheless are doing their best. An unreasonable delay in approving this bill or a close vote on it is hardly the way to demonstrate appreciation for their sacrifices in our behalf. If we try to view our position on this bill through their eyes, I hope the Senate will not let itself be misunderstood.[4]

Senator Leverett Saltonstall, the ranking Republican on the Armed Services Committee, took the same position:

The purpose is to provide the necessary funds for our forces and the South Vietnamese who are fighting in that country at the present time. It does not concern whether we are right or wrong in our policies in so fighting. We are supporting our boys, and that is the purpose of this authorization bill which will lead to appropriations.[5]

An exchange between Senators Aiken and Stennis confirmed this point of view:

MR. AIKEN: Does the Senator from Mississippi interpret the approval of this request for supplemental appropriations as either approving or disapproving our policy in South Vietnam?

MR. STENNIS: Frankly, I think it is neither approval or disapproval of our policy. We are already committed. We have already gone in. We have already put the men on the ground. They must have support; $1.2 billion of the funds in the bill is for military construction items. It is to take care of the men and materiel that we already have there, that are on the way, or that are expected to be sent there.

This Bill merely presents the question of supporting our men. . . .

MR. GORE: I shall support the pending bill. I shall do so because, whether wisely or unwisely, as has been said here, our troops are committed to battle there. They are there on orders, not of their choosing, but on orders of the Commander in Chief.[6]

---

[4] 112 *Cong. Rec.* 3136 (February 16, 1966).

[5] 112 *Cong. Rec.* 3138 (February 16, 1966).

[6] *Ibid.*, 3139, 3140 (February 16, 1966).

I made the same point during the debate:

> I quite agree with the Senator from Georgia that our forces are
> committed and, therefore, must be adequately equipped. I was in
> Vietnam and visited some of them in November and December.
> They are the finest group of military men we have ever sent over-
> seas. There is no question in my mind about their competence,
> their dedication and their capacity. In every sense of the word,
> they are a superb group of men, and I personally want to see
> them have all the equipment they need for the defense of their
> lives.[7]

Later congressional debates echoed the same sentiments. An
effort was made in March 1967 to urge the president to initiate
a peace conference, with a view toward a negotiated settlement
in Vietnam. Senator Mansfield introduced an amendment to
the Armed Forces Supplemental Authorization Bill declaring
congressional support of efforts to end the war. But no teeth were
put into this statement of policy, and the war continued to
escalate.

Congress was never consulted, of course, about any significant
steps in the escalation. Representative George E. Brown of
California complained openly about the way the Executive
department was hiding its plans from Congress while asking it
to pay the billions required for continued hostilities. He said on
March 1, 1966:

> Last year when the President asked this Congress for $700 million
> in supplemental defense appropriations, many of my colleagues
> made similar statements as they voted for that modest sum. At
> the very moment we were voting, operations were being con-
> ducted that required many times that amount of additional fund-
> ing. Plans were then in existence, and were announced within a
> few weeks, to triple our military manpower in Vietnam and to
> expand our military construction program in Vietnam many
> times over. In addition, those plans, since carried out, have been
> doubled again before the year is out. Not once has Congress been
> asked to vote on these decisions prior to their being taken.[8]

By early 1968 it was apparent that permitting the president
a free hand in conducting our foreign and military policy in

[7] 112 *Cong. Rec.* 3447 (February 18, 1966).
[8] 112 *Cong. Rec.* 4465 (March 1, 1966).

Vietnam could lead only to further disaster. The Democratic primaries in New Hampshire and Wisconsin indicated that many people had rejected the Vietnam policies of the Johnson administration. The cessation of the bombing of North Vietnam in March 1968 and the start of peace talks in Paris, coupled with the tragedies and turmoil of the election year, made it difficult for Congress to reassert its power immediately. However, by 1969 a series of steps were taken by Congress to assume a greater measure of responsibility and control over American foreign affairs, as intended by the Constitution.

This third stage of the relationship between the President and Congress over Vietnam began with the passage of the National Commitments Resolution on June 25, 1969. By a vote of 70 to 16 the Senate resolved:

> That (1) a national commitment for the purpose of this resolution means the use of the armed forces of the United States on foreign territory, or a promise to assist a foreign country, government, or people by the use of the armed forces or financial resources of the United States either immediately or upon the happening of certain events, and (2) it is the sense of the Senate that a national commitment by the United States results only from affirmative action taken by the executive and legislative branches of the United States Government by means of a treaty, statute, or concurrent resolution of both Houses of Congress specifically providing for such commitment.

The resolution made clear that the Executive cannot bypass congressional authority to declare war or the Senate's power to ratify treaties. The president cannot sign executive agreements in lieu of a treaty, and he cannot rely on vague and undefined "inherent" powers to wage war. The Senate put the president on notice that any national commitment of the United States must be accomplished by constitutional means.

On August 30, 1969, soon after the resolution was passed, Senator John Sherman Cooper introduced an amendment to a military authorization bill forbidding the use of American combat troops in Laos. His amendment was quickly adopted in the Senate. Later in the year a substitute amendment introduced by Senator Frank Church forbade the use of any military funds "to finance the introduction of American ground combat troops in Laos or Thailand." Congress approved the amendment in December 1969, and it was signed into law on December 30. This was the first time since the Vietnam war began that Congress asserted its constitutional prerogative to decide where and when America should go to war. It did so through its unquestioned control of the purse strings.

Unfortunately, the first Cooper-Church Amendment did not mention Cambodia. This was not a deliberate oversight. Congress cannot be in the position of trying to guess what country the president might want to invade and of passing a resolution forbidding that step before the event occurs. Despite the fact that the president did not have any constitutional authority to invade or attack Cambodia or any other nation in the world, President Nixon ordered American troops into Cambodia in April 1970. This time Congress acted swiftly to insure that American troops be withdrawn and forbidden to return to Cambodia. Senators Church and Cooper introduced legislation forbidding the use of any funds to pay for the introduction of American troops into Cambodia as fighting men or as advisers. That amendment passed the Senate by a vote of 58 to 37 on June 30, 1970.

At the same time, I introduced a broader resolution with the co-sponsorship of Senator Mark Hatfield and other Senators, including Charles Goodell, Harold Hughes, and Alan Cranston. That "amendment to end the war" would have forbidden the use of any military funds for Vietnam after December 31, 1970, except to arrange for the withdrawal of American forces, the termination of hostilities, and the release of all prisoners of war. It was our intention that Congress should reclaim its proper role in the constitutional scheme of deciding issues of war and peace and should make explicit decisions on the questions which were exclusively within its province—on the kinds of military power available to the president and when and how they should be committed to war.

The amendment was debated throughout the summer of 1970. Modifications were made to permit the maintenance of 280,000 troops in Vietnam by April 30, 1971, and complete withdrawal by December 31, 1971. In case of immediate danger to American troops the deadline could be extended. Nevertheless the McGovern-Hatfield amendment was defeated on September 1, 1970 by a vote of 55 to 38. Many of those who voted against the amendment seemed to feel that the president's negotiating position in Paris should not be undercut by restrictive legislation. Senator Everett Jordan of North Carolina said that the amendment would "limit . . . the president's options . . . in [his] efforts for a military scaledown and an acceptable peace settlement." But he added, "Even without the amendment I think Congress has already made clear its desire for a settlement of the Vietnam issue and its intention of taking a part in that settlement." [9]

While the McGovern-Hatfield debate continued over the summer of 1970, the Senate quietly repealed the Gulf of Tonkin Resolution, the result of the first deception practiced upon the Senate by the Executive department. By a vote of 81 to 10, the Senate corrected its earlier mistake. Later in the year the House concurred, and on January 12, 1971, repeal was enacted into law. As Senator Fulbright explained:

> One of the most unheralded events of American constitutional history occurred on January 12, 1971, when President Nixon signed into law a bill, which, among other things, repealed the Gulf of Tonkin resolution. With that tarnished, contested and thoroughly unlamented act of Congress went the last compliance with that clear provision of the Constitution which says that the power to initiate war belongs to Congress, not the President.[10]

Congress returned to the McGovern-Hatfield Amendment in its new session in January 1971. The amendment once again set December 31, 1971, as the cutoff date for funds for the Vietnam war, but permitted the president to continue to provide for the safety of American forces during their withdrawal from Vietnam. The cutoff date was also dependent on satisfactory arrangements being made for the release of American prisoners. Once again the Senate rejected the amendment, but by a closer vote of 55 to 42 on June 16, 1971. The next day a similar amendment was rejected by the House by a vote of 254 to 158.

Immediately after the negative vote on the amendment, Sena-

9 116 *Cong. Rec.* S. 14851 (daily ed. September 1, 1970).
10 117 *Cong Rec.* S. 887 (daily ed. February 5, 1971).

tor Mansfield introduced a new proposal to establish a final
date of withdrawal of American forces nine months after passage of the law, subject to the release of American prisoners of
war. The amendment would not cut off funds but urged the
president to take the necessary steps to implement that policy.
The Senate quickly passed the Mansfield proposal by a vote of
57 to 42. As of this writing, the final fate of the amendment is
in doubt.†

In one sense, all these actions by Congress should have been
unnecessary. The Constitution does not impose upon Congress
the obligation of stopping a war once it has been illegally
started by the president. The responsibility is the reverse: no
war can legally begin or continue unless Congress explicitly
approves such a step. One of the great tragedies of the Vietnam
war has been that there has never been a clear-cut, up-or-down
vote by Congress on the war. Congressman Donald Riegle complained on the floor:

> Everyone in this Chamber knows that we have not had one vote
> on the war in Vietnam in either the House or the Senate in the
> last 10 years, and I mean a direct 'yes' or 'no' vote on the war
> in Vietnam. We even hide the money for the war in Vietnam in
> the Defense appropriation so that we do not have to have a
> specific vote on the issue.[11]

Without such a "yes" vote by Congress, made in an explicit
and unambiguous manner, any large-scale military action taken
by the president alone is unconstitutional. No one can read the
record of the debates leading up to the establishment of the
Constitution without being aware of the very strong convictions
of the delegates to that convention that the war power should
reside in Congress when it comes to the question of whether we
go to war or whether we end it. The war power that the president has relates entirely to his function in commanding the
troops once they are committed by the act of Congress, or once
committed to meet an emergency situation or to repel an attack.

† A modified form of the Mansfield amendment passed Congress in November
1971 (*Editor*).
[11] 117 *Cong. Rec.* H. 3442 (daily ed. May 4, 1971).

It does not justify the kind of authority that the Executive branch has claimed in connection with the long, drawn-out struggle in Indochina. All the constitutional debates point to the conclusion that the power to determine the purposes for which American military forces will be used resides in the Legislative branch, whose laws must be faithfully executed by the president. The commander-in-chief clause merely entitles the president to the supreme command and tactical control of those forces when they are engaged in activities authorized either by enacted laws or by the Constitution itself. It can be read no other way.

Those who contend now for inflated presidential powers can cite no textual support for their thesis. They make but one assertion—that the president holds full control over the use of the armed forces in pursuit of American security interests by reason of "practice" or "tradition," most of that tradition in the last few decades.

I fail to see how such foggy precepts can allow us to alter, without amendment, the terms of the Constitution itself. The truth is that Congress has acquiesced in Executive actions because it either supported them or lacked the will to assert its opposition. In most instances in which the president has acted alone, he probably could have obtained congressional authority had he asked for it. The trend which has concerned us has developed because Congress had not really disagreed with the Executive and has thus felt no need to assert its own views. It is a serious perversion of the Constitution to suggest that congressional inaction signals the loss of congressional power and the gross expansion of executive authority.

The logical import of the presidential powers claimed would be to destroy the constitutional scheme so painstakingly constructed by the framers. It would establish virtual one-man rule over the most momentous decisions any government is ever called upon to make—the decisions of war and peace. Considering the breadth of security interests claimed or potentially claimed by the Executive, it would leave the president free to engage in any conflict, large or small, short or indefinite, anywhere in the world. Under the new assumption of executive power, it is hard to envision a conflict for which congressional authority would be required.

The Congressional attempts to alter our military course in Vietnam and the legal attempts to have the courts determine the legality of the war (described in the following pages) are two complementary paths designed to re-establish the constitutional equilibrium contemplated by the framers of the Constitution. The issue is not an abstract legal problem but one which affects the most vital interests of the people of this nation.

Continued conflict cannot redeem the terrible price we have paid in Indochina. The quest for a military solution can only bring more pain for both Americans and Asians. We must abandon that hopeless course, and instead move to end this foul war quickly, and above all to grasp its lessons.

The Vietnam experience must have a profound effect on our perception of America's role in the world, of the limitations of force as an instrument of foreign policy, and of the futility of involvement in internal disputes which we can neither understand nor influence.

But beyond that, it must lead to a renewed understanding of our own institutions. Henceforth we must never forget that a responsibility of decision on questions of war and peace is inherent in the congressional office. Each member of the Senate and each member of the House of Representatives should come to recognize that the Constitution requires him to exercise his independent judgment on such issues, and that it does not allow him to yield up his authority to the president on such grounds as party loyalty, courtesy, or deference to the Executive. Each member has an obligation to decide whether Americans' lives will be risked, lost, or spared.

The constitutional scheme was devised to impede war and to facilitate peace. If it impels us toward re-establishment of that sound principle, and if we begin living by its substantive lessons, then we will be pursuing the single hope we have of redeeming our sad endeavor in Indochina.

—George S. McGovern
U.S. Senate

Unquestioning Obedience to the President

PART ONE

The Legal Background

This is the story of the legal attempt to end the war in Vietnam.

Under the American system, the government's obligation to act under the law, rather than above it, is policed by the federal judiciary. This book chronicles an attempt to persuade the federal courts to measure the Vietnam war against the Constitution they are sworn to uphold.

De Tocqueville wrote over one hundred years ago, ". . . scarcely any question arises in the United States which does not become, sooner or later, a subject of judicial debate." The reason for such judicial omnipresence, he said, is that "armed with the power of declaring the laws to be unconstitutional, the American [judge] perpetually interferes in political affairs. He cannot force the people to make laws but at least he can oblige [the government] not to disobey its own enactments, or to act inconsistently with its own principles." Of all the political problems that have arisen in this century, the Vietnam war shows the American government acting most "inconsistently with its own principles," that is, in most flagrant violation of the basic tenets of the Constitution. The special task of lawyers has been to enlist the judicial power to re-establish the constitutional equilibrium.

Our military involvement in Vietnam became an issue of national concern in early 1965 when American planes began bombing North Vietnam and American combat units landed in force in the South. From that moment, senators, congressmen, lawyers, and many millions of Americans began to express their doubt not only about the wisdom of our military moves in Vietnam, but about the legality of allowing the president to send troops and planes to fight in a war never authorized by Congress. It was true that Congress had passed the Gulf of Tonkin Resolution in August 1964, but it was viewed only as an expression of congressional support for the president's limited response to what then seemed like an unprovoked attack on American ships in international waters. President Johnson himself said that "the United States intends no rashness and seeks no wider war," and many senators and congressmen stated that they did not intend the resolution to be "an advance declaration of war." † Since the Constitution declared flatly that Congress and Congress alone had the power "to declare war," how could the president justify launching and waging, on his own authority, the longest and costliest war in our history?

So long as the president had to answer only congressional critics and newspaper editorials, he did not worry too much about the constitutional justifications for his actions. Thus, at one time President Johnson claimed that the Gulf of Tonkin Resolution was "not . . . necessary to do what we did and what we are doing." At other times, the State Department claimed that the resolution was the "functional equivalent" of a declaration of war. Later the State Department under President Nixon wrote to Congress that the administration "has not relied on or referred to the Tonkin Gulf Resolution . . . as support for its Vietnam policy." Although the war had been waged offensively for years, with steady military escalation reaching its peak in early 1969, Presidents Johnson and Nixon both insisted that the war was "defensive" in

† See p. 148 below, Statement of President Johnson, 110 *Cong. Rec.* 18132. Statement of Representative Morgan, 110 *Cong. Rec.* 18539.

nature and the Executive department had "inherent authority" to defend American troops in the field.

Critics of American policy in Vietnam could point out these inconsistencies to the public. But many members of the legal profession thought it was necessary to pin down the Executive's position in court, where he could not answer with political rhetoric or take contradictory and irrational positions plainly contrary to the facts of what had happened in Vietnam. If the judges were not satisfied with the president's explanation, theoretically they could order the war stopped, or at least require that Congress be meaningfully involved in any future decision to continue the fighting.

Prior to Korea and Vietnam, no president had committed American troops to prolonged combat without meticulously complying with the letter of Article I, Section 8, clause 11, of the Constitution, which unequivocally names Congress as the ultimate arbiter of war or peace. Thus, until Korea, few occasions arose for direct judicial inquiry into the legality of an American war. Indeed, the challenge of an "unconstitutional" war had been hurled only once —in connection with misrepresentations by President Polk which led to the declaration of war against Mexico—by a then little-known congressman from Illinois, Abraham Lincoln.

In 1951, after presidential initiation of the Korean police action without congressional authorization, the first attempt to secure judicial review of the constitutionality of an undeclared war foundered on a technicality. The plaintiff, a draftee who had refused to report for induction, had not actually received orders to go to Korea. Therefore, the court held, his interest in challenging the legality of the Korean war not sufficiently direct to warrant judicial action.†

Identical technical defects, called in legal jargon "lack of standing," similarly frustrated early attempts to secure judicial review of the war in Vietnam. The early Vietnam cases also arose primarily as abortive defenses to indictments charging failure to report for induction. Thus, David Mitchell, one of the early draft-resistance leaders, asserted the illegality of the Vietnam war as a

† See *United States* v. *Bolton,* 192 F.2d 805 (2d Cir. 1951).

defense to his criminal prosecution in 1965. The courts refused to consider the issue, stating: "Had [Mitchell] been inducted, he might never have been sent abroad, much less to Vietnam. Until inducted and ordered to Vietnam, his claim . . . is premature." †

However, even soldiers with orders to go to Vietnam found it virtually impossible to induce a court to hear their claims. In the summer of 1966, three young soldiers, Dennis Mora, James Johnson, and David Samas, stationed at Fort Hood, Texas, refused to go to Vietnam and were court-martialed for disobeying orders. The "Fort Hood Three" then went into federal court, challenging the legality of their shipment orders. The United States Court of Appeals for the District of Columbia rejected their contention that the war was illegal, invoking the doctrine that this was a "political question" which the courts could not examine:

> It is difficult to think of an area less suited for judicial action than that into which [the soldiers] would have us intrude. The fundamental division of authority and power established by the Constitution precludes judges from overseeing the conduct of foreign policy or the use and disposition of military power; these matters are plainly the exclusive province of Congress and the Executive. [*Luftig* v. *McNamara,* 373 F.2d 664 (D.C. Cir. 1967)]

The court added, in a contemptuous aside, "The only purpose to be accomplished by saying this much on the subject is to make it clear to others comparably situated and similarly inclined that resort to the courts is futile, in addition to being wasteful of judicial time, for which there are urgent legitimate demands." ‡

In November 1967, the Supreme Court, with Justices Douglas and Stewart dissenting, refused to review the Court of Appeals decision. However, Justice Stewart's dissenting opinion brilliantly

---

† Mitchell also claimed that the war was an "aggressive war" being waged by the United States in violation of various treaties to which we were a signatory. When he appealed his case to the United States Supreme Court, they refused to hear the case. But Justice William O. Douglas dissented, writing that "these are extremely delicate and sensitive questions . . . we have here a recurring question in present-day Selective Service cases." 386 U.S. 974, 975.

‡ One of the three judges who joined in the *Luftig* opinion was Circuit Judge (now Chief Justice) Warren E. Burger. The complete opinion in *Mora* can be found at 387 F.2d 862 (D.C. Cir. 1967).

enunciated the legal issues raised by the war, and together with Justice Douglas's dissent in David Mitchell's case, formed the starting point for future analysis of its legality. Justice Stewart wrote in *Mora* v. *McNamara,* 389 U.S. 934 (1967):

> There exist in this case questions of great magnitude. Some are akin to those referred to by MR. JUSTICE DOUGLAS in *Mitchell* v. *United States.* But there are others.
>
> I. Is the present United States military activity in Vietnam a "war" within the meaning of Article I, Section 8, Clause 11, of the Constitution?
>
> II. If so, may the Executive constitutionally order the petitioners to participate in that military activity, when no war has been declared by the Congress?
>
> III. Of what relevance to Question II are the present treaty obligations of the United States?
>
> IV. Of what relevance to Question II is the Joint Congressional ("Tonkin Gulf") Resolution of August 10, 1964?
>
> (a) Do present United States military operations fall within the terms of the Joint Resolution?
>
> (b) If the Joint Resolution purports to the Chief Executive authority to commit United States forces to armed conflict limited in scope only by his own absolute discretion, is the Resolution a constitutionally impermissible delegation of all or part of Congress' power to declare war?

Despite Justice Stewart's dissent, subsequent attempts to challenge the war's legality in the courts also failed, because of the reluctance of the judiciary to pass on what many judges considered a "political question". Thus, Chief Judge Charles Wyzanski of Massachusetts, a widely respected federal judge, refused to rule on the war's legality because he believed that it raised a "political question," outside the power of the federal courts.

It thus became apparent that the real obstacle to securing judicial review of the Vietnam war was not the technical "standing" issue which had frustrated earlier cases, but rather a philosophical dispute as to whether judges had any business at all in passing upon an issue as politically sensitive as war or peace.

During the years of Justice Frankfurter's intellectual primacy on the Supreme Court, the political-question doctrine had acted as an instrument of judicial paralysis, compelling the judiciary to refrain from deciding issues which were thought more properly determinable by Congress and the president—as the "political" branches of government. The political-question doctrine reached its zenith in 1946 when the Supreme Court declared that the federal courts had no role in reviewing flagrantly malapportioned state legislatures.† Seventeen years later, however, *Baker* v. *Carr,* the historic "one-man–one-vote" case, the Supreme Court repudiated the extreme view of the political-question doctrine espoused by Justice Frankfurter, and formulated the following guidelines for the doctrine:

> Prominent on the surface of any case held to involve a political question is found a textually demonstrable constitutional commitment of the issue to a coordinate political department; or a lack of judicially discoverable and manageable standards for resolving it; or the impossibility of deciding without an initial policy determination of a kind clearly for nonjudicial discretion; or the impossibility of a court's undertaking independent resolution without expressing lack of the respect due coordinate branches of government; or an unusual need for unquestioning adherence to a political decision already made; or the potentiality of embarrassment from multifarious pronouncements by various departments on one question.‡

In recent years, the doctrine has fallen upon hard times. The Supreme Court repudiated the principle in the cases of Adam Clayton Powell and Julian Bond when it refused to defer to the "political" branch and rendered independent constitutional determinations.§

Despite its weakened condition, however, the political-question doctrine remained a formidable procedural obstacle to judicial

---

† *Colegrove* v. *Green,* 328 U.S. 549 (1946).

‡ 369 U.S. 186, 217 (1962).

§ Both Powell and Bond challenged the right of the legislature to bar them from their seats. In each case the legislature argued that the suits raised "political questions" which could not be examined by the courts. The Supreme Court rejected that contention and decided in favor of Powell and Bond. See *Bond* v. *Floyd,* 385 U.S. 116 (1966) and *Powell* v. *McCormack,* 395 U.S. 486 (1969).

review of the war in Vietnam. It is easy to understand why a judge would be reluctant to rule on the legality of any war. It is, of course, well established that courts should not interfere with presidential conduct of foreign relations. Nor, ordinarily, should they rule on the deployment of troops abroad in a noncombat situation. Nor should they rule upon the propriety or wisdom of basic national-defense policy. To many judges, the issue of the Vietnam war's legality posed similar taboos.

However, as Justice Stewart's dissenting opinion revealed, the legal issues raised by the war in Vietnam had nothing whatever to do with the wisdom or propriety of the war, but rather focused solely upon whether the president could wage a major war in Vietnam without the authorization of Congress—a classical judicial question, calling for the traditional process of constitutional interpretation. Such a question did not involve the political wisdom of the war or the capacity of the president as commander-in-chief to command the troops once he had been properly authorized to do so. A soldier who had been sent to Europe as part of our NATO forces might not be able to challenge his orders, since there was no danger to his life involved, and no breach of any constitutional duty of the president could be called into question. But a soldier with orders to go to Vietnam could complain both that the Constitution was being violated and that the violation endangered his life. The federal courts were instituted to hear precisely those kinds of complaints. If they did not, who would?

In 1952, when President Truman seized the nation's steel mills in the midst of the Korean war, pursuant to his alleged "inherent" authority as commander-in-chief, the Supreme Court had repudiated his actions, despite charges that they raised unreviewable "political" questions.† Inasmuch as the courts had rejected the president's contentions that he could seize American property pursuant to his powers as commander-in-chief, it seemed obvious that the courts should review his power to seize the lives of fifty thousand young Americans and untold numbers of Vietnamese pursuant to some equally tenuous constitutional authorization.

Nevertheless, no court would consider the merits of a challenge to the constitutionality of the Vietnam war until the summer of

† *Youngstown Sheet & Tube Co.* v. *Sawyer,* 343 U.S. 579 (1952).

1970, when the *Berk* and *Orlando* cases were commenced. Two events of considerable import preceded and undoubtedly influenced the *Berk* and *Orlando* breakthroughs.

First, in April 1970, in Massachusetts, persistent opposition to the continuation of the war culminated in the passage of a statute directing the state attorney general to challenge the war's legality on behalf of Massachusetts residents ordered to Vietnam. The passage of the Massachusetts act, and the interest which it stimulated in legal circles, set the stage for a new and intensively researched attempt to secure judicial review of the war.

Then, in May 1970, President Nixon's decision to invade Cambodia stimulated strong antiwar sentiment throughout the nation. The dangers of untrammeled presidential power in the area of war and peace were acutely revealed by Cambodia, and the prospects for judicial review of presidential warmaking increased accordingly.

Meanwhile, an active political campaign was being waged in New York State for the Democratic nomination for United States senator. Candidate Theodore C. Sorensen had his staff examine the question of whether New York State should pass a law similar to the Massachusetts statute providing for a court test of the war. One of his lawyers discovered that New York already had such a law, Section 5 of the New York Civil Rights Law, dating from 1787, forbidding the shipment of New York soldiers out of the state, except in cases specifically provided for in the federal Constitution. Sorensen's campaign office put out a press release pointing out the existence of the old law. Immediately his office was deluged with calls from soldiers asking for legal assistance to block their Vietnam orders.

One of the most insistent was Malcolm Berk, a young resident of Queens, who had orders to report for shipment to Vietnam on June 7, 1970. He spoke to Mark Alcott, a lawyer who was the director of research for the Sorensen campaign. Alcott told him of the dangers of bringing such a lawsuit—Berk would be marked as a troublemaker in his outfit, the chances were practically nil that the court would even hear the case, and so on. Nevertheless, Berk wanted to start an action. He felt it was important to press a test case on the war and asked for Sorensen's and Alcott's help. They agreed to take the case. Other lawyers were called in: Marc Lux-

emburg, who was active in the Lawyers Committee to End the
War in Vietnam; Peter Smith, a lawyer working on the Sorensen
campaign; and Kay Ellen Hays, another Lawyers' Committee
member.

The decision to take Berk's case was made on June 1. After
working all night Tuesday and into Wednesday morning, Berk's
formal challenge to the war was filed on Wednesday afternoon
and set for a preliminary hearing before Judge Orrin G. Judd, a
widely respected District Court judge, on Friday, June 5, 1970.
The relevant portions of Berk's complaint follow:

Complaint, Berk v. Laird, District Court

United States District Court
Eastern District of New York

Malcolm A. Berk,

            Plaintiff,

    against

MELVIN LAIRD, Individually,
and as Secretary of Defense of
the United States, STANLEY
S. RESOR, individually, and as   COMPLAINT
Secretary of the Army of the
United States, and COL. T. F.
SPENCER, individually, and as
Chief of Staff, United States
Army Engineer Center, Fort
Belvoir,

            Defendants.

    Plaintiff, MALCOLM A. BERK, by his attorneys for his com-
plaint in this action, respectfully alleges:

First Claim for Relief:

1. This is an action to enjoin defendants from ordering or otherwise causing, compelling or requiring plaintiff, a citizen of the United States and of the State of New York and a Private First Class in the United States Army, to comply with certain orders he has received directing him to remove himself from the State of New York and proceed to Fort Dix, New Jersey for dispatch to Cambodia or Vietnam or other Areas of Indochina for active military service. Jurisdiction over this claim is based on 28 U.S.C. § 1331(a) † on the pendent jurisdiction of this Court, on Article I, Section 1 of the Constitution of the State of New York, and on Sections 2 and 5 of the Civil Rights Law of the State of New York,

. . .

3. The plaintiff is a citizen of the United States and of the State of New York, a resident of the County of Queens, State of New York, and is a Private First Class in the United States Army. He is currently at home on leave, after 11 months of service.

4. The defendant MELVIN LAIRD is the Secretary of Defense of the United States, and on information and belief, is a resident of the State of Maryland.

5. The defendant STANLEY R. RESOR is the Secretary of the Army of the United States, and on information and belief, is a resident of the District of Columbia.

6. The defendant COL. T. F. SPENCER is an officer of the Army of the United States and is the Chief of Staff of the Army Engineer Center at Fort Belvoir, Virginia, and on information and belief, is a resident of the Commonwealth of Virginia.

. . .

8. Section 5 of the Civil Rights Law of the State of New York provides:

† Subsequent challenges to the legality of the war have alleged Title 28 U.S.C. Section 1361 as an additional basis for federal jurisdiction.

"No citizen of this state can be constrained to arm himself, or to go out of this state . . . without the grant and assent of the people of this state, by their representatives in senate and assembly, except in the cases specially provided for by the constitution of the United States."

9. Article 1, § 8 of the Constitution of the United States provides that:

"The Congress shall have Power . . . To declare War, grant Letters of Marque and Reprisal, and make Rules concerning Captures on land and Water;

"To raise and support Armies, but no Appropriation of Money to that Use shall be for a longer Term than two Years;

"To provide and maintain a Navy;

"To make Rules for the Government and Regulation of the land and naval Forces;".

. . .

12. The Army of the United States and other branches of our military forces are currently engaged in military activities in various areas of Indochina. These activities involve armed conflict with the citizens or armies of other countries, and have resulted in destruction and devastation of large areas of Indochina, and in the death of more than 40,000 American citizens in the Army and of more than 600,000 citizens of other countries who may or may not have been actual combatants.

13. At no time has the Congress of the United States issued a declaration of war or otherwise authorized the current United States military activities in South Vietnam or other areas of Indochina.

14. The United States Army has no right to engage in any of the aforementioned activities in the absence of a declaration of war or other authorization by Congress pursuant to the Constitution.

. . .

20. The executive department and defendants are acting in excess of their lawful authority as set forth in the Constitution of the United States, and the order issued to plaintiff violates his

rights under the Fifth, Ninth, Tenth and Fourteenth amendments to the Constitution.

. . .

WHEREFORE, plaintiff respectfully demands judgment . . . against the defendants and against each of them and for an order.

(iii) declaring that defendants and each of them are without authority to order plaintiff to comply with the aforementioned orders of April 29, 1970, or any other orders of like tenor; and

(iv) permanently enjoining defendants from ordering plaintiff to comply with the aforementioned orders of April 29, 1970, or any other orders of like tenor;

Dated: New York, N.Y.
       June 3, 1970

Judge Judd, confronted with Berk's challenge to the war in Vietnam, initially reacted in the traditional manner by declining to reach the merits of Berk's contentions, on the ground that they probably raised a nonjusticiable political question.

During the oral argument that followed, Theodore Sorensen and Judge Judd debated the point. Extracts from the formal transcript follow:

Extracts from Oral Argument, Berk v. Laird, District Court

June 5, 1970

MR. SORENSEN: Let me simply say, your Honor, that we are out to look at the broader context in which this argument is brought. The chief constitutional issue in the United States today is the constitutionality of the President's powers with respect to the conduct of the war. The Cooper-Church Amendment to which the U.S. Attorney referred is an attempt by the legislative branch to assert authority under the constitution. I feel that we ought to at least examine thoroughly whether the authority of the judicial branch should not also be asserted.

To say that this is a political issue—that it is not a justiciable case—is to say that there is no such thing as an unconstitutional war; that there is no restraint on the exercise of the powers of the President who wishes to send American forces into combat anywhere in the world.

THE COURT: The District of Columbia Court of Appeals, with Judge Burger concurring, says it is difficult to think of an area less suitable for judicial decision.

MR. SORENSEN: But in the *Youngstown* case the Court was willing to exercise restraint upon the executive branch for the very reason that the founding fathers put a checks-and-balances system together.

THE COURT: But that did not involve a war problem.

MR. SORENSEN: In part.

THE COURT: Indirectly, yes. All right. Go ahead.

. . .

MR. SORENSEN: There are very serious issues raised here; both of us ought to have an opportunity to document in some detail the threat to the plaintiff's rights. And I would hope that a stay could be issued which would assure a thorough explanation and a thorough exploration of those rights.

It seems to me that whatever the Congress may be doing, whatever the President may be indicating, the courts of the United States have an obligation to rule on serious constitutional questions of this kind.

. . .

MR. NEAHER [United States Attorney]: What I am saying is that, as Mr. Sorensen has made very clear, what he wants decided is, really, the larger legal question, as he terms it, although in the Government's view we think the question will ultimately turn out to be political, as your Honor pointed out at the outset, and it is for that very reason, in the nature of the question involved, that it seems to me it would be impractical to keep a man indefinitely to stay the normal enforcement of a military order pending the resolution of such a question.

As you pointed out, I am sure the Court would be deluged by similar requests. It would open a Pandora's box, and the ingenuity of counsel representing people who for one reason or another wish to refrain from military service would know no bounds in extending this beyond every scope conceivable at the moment. This is far enough, as I see it.

. . .

THE COURT: Let me say what I think, with the modification that the argument this morning has brought up—and I will put this in the record to include some findings of fact so that it can be reviewed if need be.

We are faced this morning with a complaint by a soldier who enlisted in the United States Army for a period of—expiring, I think, on June 27, 1972, who asked for a declaratory judgment that there is no authority in the President of the United States to send troops into Cambodia.

The issue today is his request for a temporary restraining order and a preliminary injunction against being sent to South Vietnam next week, which is anticipated after he reports as ordered on June 7th to Fort Dix.

. . .

[THE COURT:] Reading the cases [*Mitchell* and *Bolton*], while they have not decided this issue, they are predominantly opposed to court interference with the conduct of military operations.

In the First Circuit, Judge Wyzanski refused to receive evidence in a criminal case concerning the illegality of the Vietnam war, saying it was a politial question. . . .

. . .

The Court of Appeals of this Circuit in an appeal from a decision of this Court attacking the shipments to Korea as being an undeclared war, said that it must be raised by someone ordered to Korea. But that was cited later, saying that the Court should not examine the purpose for which the Executive employs the armed forces abroad.

. . .

The Court of Appeals for the District of Columbia, as I mentioned before, refused to grant a declaratory judgment with an injunction against sending a man to Vietnam, saying the use and disposition of the military powers are exclusively provisions of Congress and the Executive under the division of powers.

. . .

There are cases [that say] that the question may still be open.

Judge Medina, in *United States* against *Mitchell* a few years ago, held that it was proper to exclude evidence on the illegality of the Vietnam War, but that the question might be attacked after the individual had qualified. That might be by review of orders attempted to be made across the sea.

Now, there have been dissents by Judge Douglas and Judge Stewart in a couple of the Supreme Court cases where Judge Douglas thought it was quite important to review the question of the legality of the Vietnam War. But in this state of the authorities, a District Court should not on quick decision without the benefit of full argument enter any decision.

I am aware of the limitations of the political question doctrine. I have read the *Youngstown* case. I can draw various inferences from the *Powell* case. At any rate, that shows that the United States Supreme Court is not afraid to act and declare the illegality of actions of Congress.

But with the specific case before me today, I conclude that the validity of the cause of an action for declaratory judgment presents difficult questions on which I believe there is less than an even chance for the plaintiff to succeed, even in establishing the right to review in this case.

I think the risk of danger to the efforts of the—the military efforts of the United States is much greater than the risk that this particular plaintiff will run. And, therefore, I deny the motion for a preliminary injunction.

One of the spectators in the courtroom listening to Sorensen's argument was Edwin Oppenheimer, a law clerk at the New York Civil Liberties Union and staff coordinator for the Union's Selective Service Panel. Although Oppenheimer was an apprentice lawyer—he could not take the bar examination until he had clerked for four years—he had become an expert on court procedures relating to military cases. He offered his assistance to help Sorensen prepare an immediate appeal to the Second Circuit

Court of Appeals. The appeal papers were submitted on Friday afternoon to Judge Henry Friendly, a circuit judge of the Court of Appeals. Judge Friendly refused to issue a temporary stay of Berk's orders, but he did set the case for a full hearing before the Court of Appeals on June 17, 1970. He also asked the government, "if practicable," to keep Berk in the jurisdiction until the hearing was held. The government would not promise to do so.

Faced with the fact that Berk had orders to go to Vietnam on Sunday, June 7, 1970, Peter Smith, a young lawyer working on Sorensen's campaign, flew to Washington on Saturday morning, to see whether a justice of the United States Supreme Court could be persuaded to keep Berk in the country pending his appeal. The papers were submitted to Justice Byron White, thought to be one of the more conservative justices of the Court. Surprisingly, Justice White signed a stay, ordering that Berk temporarily remain within the country. It follows:

Stay Order, Berk v. Laird

UPON CONSIDERATION of the application of counsel for the petitioner.

IT IS ORDERED that the deployment of the petitioner beyond the continental borders of the United States be, and the same is hereby stayed pending the filing of a response by the Solicitor General and of the further order of the undersigned or, Mr. Justice Harlan or the Court.

> Byron K. White
> Associate Justice of the Supreme
> Court of the United States

Justice White's stay was of dramatic psychological importance in continuing the legal fight against the war. His action suggested that yet another justice of the Supreme Court had joined Justices Douglas and Stewart in recognizing that substantial legal questions were raised by the war in Vietnam. Wide newspaper coverage of Justice White's stay, coupled with a continued national uproar over the Cambodian invasion, gave new hope to the antiwar elements of the legal community.

One of the first results of Justice White's order was the filing of new legal actions challenging the war's legality. The most important new suit was brought by Salvatore Orlando, of Rockville Center, New York. Orlando had enlisted in the army on November 11, 1965, and reenlisted on May 8, 1968. He became an aviation-ordnance repairman and spent a year in Thailand. When the army reassigned him to do routine supply work in the United States, he volunteered for Vietnam, hoping to get back into aviation repair. His wife learned what he had done in February 1970, and pleaded with him to withdraw the request. Orlando did so by writing to General Westmoreland, but, nevertheless, new orders were cut directing him to Vietnam in June 1970. The combination of the Cambodian invasion and Berk's success in having his orders stayed prompted Orlando to call a lawyer, Alfred Lawrence Toombs, who had handled many draft and military cases. Toombs was asked to start a new proceeding on Orlando's behalf. The necessary legal papers, identical to those in the Berk case, were filed on June 11, 1970. The case was assigned to Judge John Dooling, one of the most able federal judges on the Dictrict Court level. Immediately he scheduled a hearing on the case for June 12, 1970.

At the outset Judge Dooling indicated that he felt Justice White's stay had put a different complexion on cases attacking the Vietnam war. Some excerpts from the transcript of proceedings follow:

Proceedings, Orlando v. Laird, District Court

THE COURT [Judge Dooling] : So I must say that I was, as I think all of us were, surprised by Justice White's action after there had been so many denials of stays by so many of the Justices, other than Mr. Justice Douglas. . . .

. . .

. . . my own sense of the whole thing is that there must be something here that Mr. Justice White, who is, I would certainly think in popular reading one of the swing justices and not one of the either-end justices, that there is something that he is concerned about that has not been apparent before.

Now I have myself denied this kind of relief on the theory that you don't know that you are being asked to do anything in Vietnam that a man of honor would not do, and you don't really, until the order is issued, know that you are required to do something wrong.

. . .

When the Supreme Court concluded that it would not—apparently concluded that it would not—consider the legality of our participation in the Vietnam military action, that decided all other questions for us.

Now that is why—and I thought I had caught the sense of the Supreme Court, I might say as much by—well, far more by what it did not say and did not do than by what it did do, I thought I caught the sense of it about right. That is why it surprised me so to learn that Mr. Justice White thought that these cases coming up from our State, that is, this case coming up from our State, presented something suddenly different. . . .

Well, I will tell you very frankly what I would feel good order in this District required. . . . [Unless] I have some kind of informal assurance from Mr. Morse [United States Attorney] or his colleagues that nothing would be done until there is a further order from a court of competent jurisdiction. I would issue such an order [keeping Orlando in New York] because frankly, my feeling is the same as Judge Friendly's, that something new and mysterious has been injected into this picture.

. . .

MR. MORSE: Now, if your Honor please, the Government is prepared to take a position, but before I take a position with absoluteness there is a motion, in fact I would like to call one witness to put something on the record which I think is important.

May I do that?

THE COURT: Certainly.

MR. MORSE: Mr. Orlando, will you take the stand, please?

. . .

Was it against your conscience to serve in the Armed Forces in Indochina at the time that you——

THE COURT: In Indochina?

Q   In Indochina at the time that you signed this affidavit on June 11, 1970, which is quite recently.

A [ORLANDO]   Yes.

Q   Yes?

A   Yes, I didn't want to go, I didn't want to go to Southeast Asia.

Orlando was then cross-examined concerning his reasons for bringing the lawsuit. His responses exemplified the disillusionment with the war in Vietnam which had spread throughout the country.

Q   Was that always your position?

A   Was that always my position?

MR. HYMAN [Orlando's co-counsel]: Objection, Your Honor.

A   Well, let's put it this way: No, it wasn't. As time went by, my opinion of the war went on.

Q   I see.

When would you say your opinion of the war changed?

A   When President Nixon ordered them into Cambodia, it changed a whole lot.

Q   Prior to that, what was your view?

A   Prior to that, I thought that President Nixon was taking the men out of it. He couldn't withdraw all the men at once, a little at a time.

I thought it was the right thing; but when he invaded Cambodia, I think he made a mistake because they are going to come back with a bigger attack. They have to make points for themselves now.

Q   I see.

Did you ever volunteer to go to Vietnam?

A   Did I ever volunteer to go to Vietnam?

Q   Yes.

A   Yes, I did.

Q   When did you volunteer to go to Vietnam?

A   In, let's see, November 11, '69.

Q   Did you ever write a letter to General Westmoreland?

A   I sure did. . . . When I had volunteered for Vietnam I had a moment of haste and I changed my opinion. I didn't want to go, and I wished he would help me out.

Q   You told General Westmoreland that you didn't want to go to Vietnam?

A   I believe I did. I believe that was in the letter, yes.

THE COURT: That he did or did not?

THE WITNESS: I did not want to go to Vietnam any more. I changed my mind; I didn't want to go. And I was trying to explain to him how my feelings were at the time of the Company that I was in. I was not working in my position. I was not getting ahead in the army.

When I did write this letter my opinion of Vietnam was that Nixon was doing the right thing at the time. He promised to bring out so many men in a certain period of time. It was great. It was the best thing that could be done.

I can say you can't withdraw all of them at one time, it was impossible, too much going on.

Okay?

When he went into Cambodia, and when he started to make wider the war, that is all he is doing, he is widening the war, I felt, I can't see any use to go now and die because they are—to die over something I don't feel is right any more.

Q   It is true, is it not, that the reason you don't want to go to Vietnam is that you disagree with the President's decision about the war, or widening the war, and not because of moral scruples?

A   No, no.

When I did write this letter, I sort of wanted to go to Vietnam but I was unhappy. I was unhappy in the situation which the army placed me, which they breached a contract that I had. I had a written contract. They breached the contract. And my wife, my wife is a nervous woman, she gets very nervous and she shakes all the time and everything else, thinking about me going to Vietnam, and what I wrote him this letter thinking that he could help me out. . . .

Q   Isn't it true that the motivation in bringing this action is that you personally don't want to go to Vietnam, but it is not a moral question; isn't that true?

MR. HYMAN: I object to that.

THE COURT: We have here this question of paragraph nine [of the affidavit] and this man's very complex attitude towards a very complex matter.

Now I think we have got to listen to him.

We are a lot of lawyers around here, our business is talk. We are good at it, or we ought to be good at it. His business is not talk.

Mr. HYMAN: I appreciate that, Your Honor.

MR. MORSE: Yes, Your Honor.

THE COURT: So we are going to have to listen hard because he is trying to explain to us something that great novelists have failed at.

This is a complex frame of mind. Let the man have his say—

MR. MORSE: Yes, Your Honor.

THE WITNESS: My feelings, my feelings changed. I feel I am a human being, I have a right to change my mind from now and then.

At one time I believed in the war—in the army we don't call it war—conflicts or misunderstandings; we never mention the word "war" because we don't feel it is a war.

But at times, we sit down, we discuss, we talk to the officers and in the service to the high non-com officers, and my feelings changed.

I talked to my friends who came back from Vietnam. They told me what was going on and my feelings changed.

Right now I think that too many lives are being wasted, too many young men.

BY MR. MORSE:

Q   You volunteered, though, to go to Vietnam?

A   At the time, yes, I did.

Q   Why did you volunteer to go to Vietnam?

A   Because I was unhappy in this position that the army placed me, very unhappy, very, very unhappy.

Here I am an E-5, doing a job that privates coming into the company could do. I was issuing pants; I was issuing clothes. That is all I was doing.

I am getting pro pay. I am making pretty good money out of your taxes, and this was a private's job, anybody could issue a pair of pants and saying, What, medium, and give a pair of medium pants. I didn't want this.

Q   At the time you volunteered to go to Vietnam, were you concerned with moral scruples of the war, and if so, how, in your own words?

A   To be honest, at the time I felt a little different about the war. At the time, I thought the war was—well, I say again the war, the conflict, it was a conflict, and we were stopping the Communists from taking over more land, more land in Asia where there is more than half the population of the world, and at the time, I thought it was the right thing, but I don't think it is any more.

Cambodia itself, that is what I'm trying to say, has changed my mind, but they are not sending me to Cambodia, they are sending me to Vietnam, then who knows, when I get there they might throw me into Cambodia, that is part and parcel, because they have done it already. But Cambodia is not going to wind up the war, they have hurt the Communists in a bad way and the Communists are not going to sit down taking it, they have China behind them, and I know it, they are going to come back with a big attack. I don't see why I should go over there and die.

I would like to state because I have already been in Asia, I have been in Thailand for a year when the Government was telling all the people in the United States that there were no people in Laos, and we were sending over—I mean I don't know, well, they were talking about it and they were sending men in, they would send a hundred men in there with blue jeeps, in civilian clothes, and swearing that no people were there, and I was one of the people who was sending them in, and I wouldn't doubt that the Government has to do certain things behind people's backs, they have to make certain maneuvers—

Q   The executive has to—

A   (continuing) To keep peace at home you have to say certain things.

Q   Do you know whether or not—

A   No, I don't know, I am not there.

Q   Do you know whether any uniformed military personnel such as yourself are now being sent into—

THE COURT: Now, now look, Mr. Morse, what he has said is that on that issue he was in a position to know what was going on when weasel-worded statements were being made to the public that produced a quite contrary impression: now he may be wrong about it, we don't know, but I don't think that would help us any, that knowledge.

Q   Do you have any knowledge of any one or more crimes that might be committed if you were sent to Cambodia as compared to what might have been committed in the past in Vietnam?

A   I wouldn't know, I wouldn't know until the time comes, I don't know what is going to happen, I don't know what they are going to put me to or what kind of battle might come up at the time when that position might happen.

Q   You have no knowledge whether or not you will be requested to commit war crimes?

A   I do know that as soon as I get there I'm being issued an M-16 and 90 rounds, and they don't, they are not issuing blanks, that means, that means that they expect me at the right time, when the time happens, to use that weapon, otherwise they wouldn't be issuing it to me, it's as simple as that—

Q   If you had gone—

A   They are asking me to kill by giving me that weapon in Vietnam.

Q   Does the Cambodian issue make it a war crime?

A   I'm not saying that, I am just saying that they moved into Cambodia and I feel that something is bad is going to happen, I got a feeling that they are going to come back strong and I don't want to be there when it happens. I can't see what there is much to get killed over there, I can't see dying for those Southeast Asians, the entire lot of them don't like Americans, at any one time they stab you in the back, I can't see that kind of people, I can't see myself dying for them.

I was sworn in to protect my country and fight the enemies against my country, and I don't feel like Vietnamese is an enemy against my country at the present time, no, I don't, I feel they are fighting for something they believe is right, just, that what the Vietnamese are fighting is right.

BY MR. HYMAN:

Q   Do you believe that your rights are in violation as a result of being ordered—

THE COURT: Are being violated.

Q   Are being violated?

A   Yes.

Q   Will you describe to the Court the way in which you believe they are being violated?

A   Well, I feel I am being forced to go to Southeast Asia for a second time into a combat zone, this time to use a weapon if I had to, and I mean—and I am scared that after I have seen so many other things on the news and everything that I might have to kill somebody that shouldn't have to be killed, and that would be on my conscience, and I just can't see my killing anybody. I have never done it before and I don't ever want to do it.

Q   Would you explain to the Court why you believe as a matter of conscience that service in Indochina would be against your beliefs?

A   Well, at the time when I wrote, when I wrote the letter I started talking—and I won't mention any names, because he is making a career out of the army—one of my friends, he was in the Infantry, and he told me some of the things that he had done to the North Vietnamese when they caught them—

MR. MORSE: If Your Honor please, I will object to hearsay testimony, as to what someone said. It is irrelevant and I see no purpose whatsoever in going into what some unidentified person said.

I object to his testimony as to what an unidentified person told him of what is done to the North Vietnamese.

MR. HYMAN: Your Honor—

THE COURT: No, I don't think it proves that any more than any of these things that we have been hearing prove anything. But unfortunately, we all live in this atmosphere, we hear rumors about what is going on in Vietnam, contradictions, charge, counter-charge, explanation, re-explanation, rescission of explanation, reconciliation of explanation, and it is all part of that turmoil that is going on at the moment.

BY MR. HYMAN:

Q   Mr. Orlando, will you explain to the Court as you are doing the manner in which you believe that your conscience will be violated and the basis upon which you have formed these beliefs that it would be violated by being sent to Indochina.

A   He told me when they were out on patrol, when they used to catch them, they couldn't take them with them—

Q   Catch who?

A   Catch North Vietnamese, that sometimes they cut off an ear or two ears and just leave them tied to a tree, the North Vietnamese or tied them upside down and pour water down their nose, and that started changing my mind—

Q   Talk a little slower.

A   What really started to change my mind, he was from the Infantry, I wasn't too worried about that, but when I started talking to people that was in Aviation, well, mostly when they got there and they couldn't fill the job, they made them—in other words, they would send them to Supplies, Aviation Supply, and then they worked as a door gunner, a door gunner, and I just couldn't see me climbing up on a helicopter and shooting, and he told me that when they used to get shot at, they just would see a movement, and even though they didn't know what it is they would just shoot at it anyway, and that's when I started to say that ain't for me.

Q   Was there ever any mention about innocent civilians in these discussions?

A   Well, yes, but it was at times when, I heard, that, you know, how a man is—I don't know how to express it, I don't know how to say it, when they get frustrated, I guess, and you know, a woman, say, is working out in the rice paddies and sometimes they—well, they see a woman and they go over them, they pull out these—whatever they are, automatics and they have to kill them, stuff like that, and sometimes a baby with them, and the baby gets killed, too.

Q   What are your beliefs in regard to this after hearing these stories?

A   Well, if that is true, I just, I couldn't do it myself, I would have to—in that case it would be the first time I disobeyed an order because I wouldn't shoot if I was a door gunner unless possibly they were shooting at me, it's either them or me.

Q   Have your beliefs changed from now to what they were in November, 1969?

A   Oh, yes.

Q   In what way have they changed?

A   In a big way, at the time I thought that the capitalist states were right to be in Vietnam, all they were doing was trying to stop the Communists from taking over Southeast Asia, but then after I found out what was actually going on and found out more about the war, I was more interested in it, my views of the war started changing, because like I said, I was in Thailand, I was there, we wasn't in combat, but we seen the Queen's Cobras—I don't know, can I say, can I mention names of the Army we sent there, you know, we trained?

Q   Go ahead.

A   We had the Thai army also for combat and we gave them weapons and carbines and we trained them for combat and sent them, the Queen's Cobras, we sent them to Vietnam, and all the time the people, the way they just lived, and this made me sick.

Q   And what are your views with regard to the Cambodian incursion or invasion?

A   I think it widened the war myself.

Q   Are you willing to serve in that kind of war?

A   I am not willing to serve. If I had to go, I mean if I was forced to go I would go because I don't want to go to jail.

Q   Is it your desire to bring this action in this court at this time?

A   Yes, I want, I want to try to stop from going there, from any of this happening.

[JUDGE DOOLING:] I see no reason to suppose that Mr. Orlando would think any differently from any other human being, and might well be sensitized to every bit of information, rumor, untruth that he heard about Vietnam, and I daresay in view of what he has said here that he has perhaps a more specific appreciation than any of us in this room about the disparity between what seems to be said about official action and the translation of whatever reality that refers to into human acts in Southeast Asia.

I would find unsurprising, and I do find essentially correct, Mr. Toombs' expression of Mr. Orlando's present attitude. We are not dealing with frames of mind that are, for some, elitist notions which [are] capable of studying the expression of its own emotion; we are dealing with a man whose emotions have all of the complexity of human emotion and not any elitist abstraction into forms that can conveniently fit ideas of unmixed conscientious objection.

I think such to me edifying candor of expression as we have heard from this man, with all of its unselectedness, is novel and true; it is all in there, every bit of it is in there—the resentment of the treatment of the army, remorse at having gone behind his wife's back to write that foolish letter of November; a sense of regret and inadequacy of his letter to General Westmoreland; a simple human feeling that the last thing in the world he wants to do is to get into Vietnam; and along with all of that, and in his total candor of expression not selected out and highlighted as sole resplendent and central pious emotion, an essentially moral revulsion from the kind of thing that what he has heard makes him feel he may be getting into.

I am sure that others, under other circumstances, would have expressed these facts very differently, would have been schooled so that lawyers and judges would be able to fit into their convenient categories matters that would not make life difficult and embarrassing and human and would so have narrowed the case so that it could not be used as precedent in any other very numerous class of situations.

But perhaps this man's education will never make him equal to that kind of intellectual essay. But I don't think that should deprive him of his right to be a moral man by his own moral lights, and whatever the complexity of the manifold of emotion and thought of which his moral revulsion is an element.

In view of the posture of these cases in this Circuit, and of the posture of the Berk case in the Supreme Court of the United States, and in view of the Order to Show Cause that has been presented, the temporary Order [keeping Orlando in the United States] will be signed [and the case scheduled for a speedy hearing].

PART TWO

The Court Opens
Its Doors

While Orlando prepared for his hearing before Judge Dooling, Berk's lawyers, reinforced by attorneys for the New York Civil Liberties Union, prepared an expedited appeal to the United States Court of Appeals from Judge Judd's initial refusal to review the war's legality. The basic issue before the Second Circuit in this first Berk appeal was the threshold question of whether judges were barred from passing on the legality of the Vietnam war by the political-question doctrine. A section from *Berk's* brief, discussing that point, follows:

Appeal Brief, Berk v. Laird, Second Circuit Court of Appeals

The Questions Presented by This Appeal Are Justiciable, Not "Political"

The Supreme Court in *Youngstown Sheet & Tube Co.* v. *Sawyer*, 343 U.S. 579 (1952) enjoined the Secretary of Commerce from seizing and operating a number of the nation's steel mills. The President sought to sustain his power to act in that instance squarely on the war power, asserting that steel was essential to the war effort then being conducted in Korea. Nonetheless, the Supreme Court decided that under the Constitution the question of whether the steel mills should be seized was committed to Congress. That Court granted the very kind of injunction appellant seeks here, based on its view that the Executive had exceeded its constitutional powers. The only substantial difference between that case and this one is that in *Youngstown* the court was dealing with the use of steel, and here we are dealing with human lives.

Should this Court refuse to rule on the questions presented by appellant, it will not only ignore the clear mandate of *Youngstown,* but it will also be denying its power to determine the constitutional limits upon the war powers allotted to the Executive. This Court must realize that a decision by it, abstaining from ruling upon these, the most burning constitutional questions of our time, will mean in effect, that a citizen of the United States cannot, at any time, seek a judicial determination upon the activities of the Executive with relation to the war powers, even when he alleges such activities have exceeded the constitutional limits afforded that branch of the government.

Furthermore, the fear expressed both by the Court below and Judge Friendly in chambers, that the issuance of a preliminary injunction would prompt a deluge of applications for injunctive relief misconstrues the gravamen of the nature of this proceeding. By abstaining from a ruling upon the merits of the issues raised by appellant, the Court will insure exactly the result which it seeks to avert. Servicemen will continue to petition the courts of this Circuit seeking a judicial determination upon these issues as long as hope for success on the merits exists.

Appellant is not seeking a determination as to the advisability of the decision of either the President or Congress in engaging the United States in the war in Vietnam. What appellant is seeking, however, is a determination as to whether the President has exceeded his constitutional authority. While this Court may not decide whether this nation should be involved in Vietnam, clearly it may determine who, constitutionally, may make that decision.

The question of which branch is, in fact, to analyze the alleged power of the Executive vis-a-vis the evident power of the Congress in declaring war, is itself a question constitutionally committed to the courts, and only to the courts. This postulate is obvious from a mere cataloguing of the questions which would be involved in any decision of the merits herein—questions formulated by Justices Stewart and Douglas in *Mora* v. *McNamara,* [see pp. 27 above]

. . .

The cases since 1803 have clearly demonstrated that this Court has the power and responsibility to determine and construe the authority of the various branches of the Government. *Marbury* v. *Madison,* 5 U.S. (1 Cranch) 137, 176 (1803). The courts have consistently considered issues involving the nation's war powers and have made determinations relative to those issues [citation of cases omitted].

Indeed, in [the *Mitchell* case], this Court took care to point out when appellant introduced evidence regarding the legality of the war in Vietnam that the Congressional power to raise and support armies and to provide and maintain a navy was a matter quite distinct from the use which the Executive may make of those who had been found qualified and who had been inducted into the Armed Forces.

Baker v. *Carr,* 369 U.S. 186 (1962) tells us that ". . . it is error to suppose that every case or controversy which touches foreign relations lies beyond the judicial cognizance" (*id.* at 211).

The District Court rested his decision on the conclusion that the applicable cases "are predominantly opposed to court interference with the conduct of military operations." This conclusion was erroneous.

Two such Second Circuit cases cited by the District Court— *United States* v. *Bolton,* 192 F.2d 805 (2d Cir. 1951), and *United States* v. *Hogans,* 369 F.2d 359 (2d Cir. 1966)—support rather than cast doubt upon the justiciability of the current case. These were criminal actions against draftees who refused to be inducted into the Army on the ground that no war had been declared. This Court held that the defendants had no standing to challenge foreign military operations since they had not been ordered abroad. But this Court said, in *Bolton:*

> Any question as to the legality of an order sending men to Korea to fight in an "undeclared war" *should be raised by someone to whom such an order has been directed.* 192 F.2d at 806 (emphasis supplied).

Appellant here is thus in precisely the position that this Court recognized gives right to a judicial review of executive action under the war power.

An additional case cited by the court below on the issue of justiciability was *Luftig* v. *McNamara.* . . . In *Luftig,* the court, in effect, held that the constitutional question of the authority for declaring war was nonjusticiable and within the realm of the "political-question" doctrine. But *Luftig* is contrary to *Youngstown,* and *Luftig* stands alone. As one scholar has noted, "in the entire history of this country [only the *Luftig* case] can surely be said to have held, at least by implication, that the question of which branch of government has the power to declare war is a political question rather than a justiciable one.''

In view of the overwhelming number of cases that have examined the type of issue here claimed to be ''political'' and is ''non-justiciable,'' it is clear that the District Court's conclusion that the cases are predominantly opposed to justiciability was erroneous.

Justice Douglas has noted:

> There should not be the slightest doubt but that whenever the Chief Executive of the country takes any citizen by the neck and either puts him in prison or subjects him to some ordeal or sends him overseas to fight in a war, the question is a justiciable one. To call issues of that kind "political" would be to abdicate the judicial function which the Court honored in the midst of the Civil War in the Prize cases. *Drifka* v. *Brainard,* 21 L.Ed. 2d 427, 429 (1968) (in chambers)

The government answered this argument in the same way it had done in the past: it argued that the whole issue of the Vietnam war was a political question which Congress and the president must work out between themselves. While the United States attorney never explicitly suggested that the president had inherent authority to wage a major war, he argued that Congress and not the courts must determine whether the constitutional line had been crossed by the president. In any event, the government's answering brief said, Congress had approved the war by the Gulf of Tonkin Resolution and "had reaffirmed that approval by its repeated appropriation of the billions of dollars necessary to support those military actions."

The oral argument before the Court of Appeals was heard on Wednesday morning, June 17, 1970. The courtroom was packed with interested lawyers, members of the press, and many young members of the peace movement. Three lawyers presented the case for Berk: Sorensen, who presented the background to the cases; Norman Dorsen, who offered a superb argument on why the court should examine the issues; and Leon Friedman, who discussed the merits of the action.

Two days later, on June 19, 1970, the Court of Appeals issued its opinion. Relevant portions of the court's decision follow.

Decision, Berk v. Laird, Second Circuit Court of Appeals

* * * [T]he issue on this appeal is not whether the courts are empowered to "second-guess" the President in his decision to commit the armed forces to action, but whether they have the power to make a particular kind of constitutional decision involving the division of powers between legislative and executive branches. See, e.g., *Youngstown Sheet & Tube Co.* v. *Sawyer,* 343 U.S. 579 (1952). The appellees' position is essentially that the President's authority as Commander in Chief, in the absence of a declared war, is co-extensive with his broad and unitary power in the field of foreign affairs. See *United States* v. *Curtiss Wright Export Corp.,* 299 U.S. 304 (1936) ; cf. *Johnson* v. *Eisentrager,* 339 U.S. 763, 789 (1950) (dictum). If this were the case, Berk's claim would not be justiciable because the congressional power to "declare" a war would be reduced to an antique formality, leaving no executive "duty" to follow constitutional steps which can be judicially identified. See *Powell* v. *McCormack,* 395 U.S. 186, 516–18 (1969) ; *Baker* v. *Carr,* 369 U.S. 186, 198 (1962). However, the power to commit American military forces under various sets of circumstances is shared by Congress and the executive. History makes clear that the congressional power "to declare War" conferred by Article I, section 8, of the Constitution was intended as an explicit restriction upon the power of the Executive to initiate war on his own prerogative which was enjoyed by the British sovereign. Although Article II specifies that the President "shall be Commander in Chief of the Army and Navy of the United States" and also vests the "executive power" in him and requires that he "take Care that the Laws be faithfully executed," these provisions must be reconciled with the congressional war power. See generally Note,

Congress, the President, and the Power to Commit Forces to Combat, 81 Harv. L. Rev. 1771 (1968); Velvel, *The Vietnam War: Unconstitutional, Justiciable and Jurisdictionally Attackable,* 16 Kan. L. Rev. 449 (1968). Since orders to fight must be issued in accordance with proper authorization from both branches under some circumstances, executive officers are under a threshold constitutional "duty [which] can be judicially identified and its breach judicially determined." *Baker* v. *Carr, supra,* 369 U.S. at 198.

Even if it possesses this general attribute of justiciability, however, a claim still may not be decided if it involves a political question, as that term is defined in *Baker* v. *Carr, supra,* at 217. The challenge framed at this point by the appellant—"which branch has the power to decide if an order has been issued in violation of the Constitution"—may not be answered by stating that courts alone inevitably pass upon allegations of constitutional violations, as Berk seems to suppose. If the issue involved in this case is "political," Congress and the executive will "decide" whether there has been a usurpation of authority by the latter, through political means.

The political question doctrine itself requires that a court decline to adjudicate an issue involving "a lack of judicially discoverable and manageable standards for resolving it," *Baker* v. *Carr, supra,* 369 U.S. at 217. If the executive branch engaged the nation in prolonged foreign military activities without any significant congressional authorization, a court might be able to determine that this extreme step violated a discoverable standard calling for *some* mutual participation by Congress in accordance with Article I, section 8. But in this case, in which Congress definitely has acted, in part expressly through the Gulf of Tonkin Resolution and impliedly through appropriations and other acts in support of the project over a period of years, it is more difficult for Berk to suggest a set of manageable standards and escape the likelihood that his particular claim about this war at this time is a political question. It may be that he will be able to provide a method for resolving the question of when specified joint legislative-executive action is sufficient to authorize various levels of military activity, but no such standard has as yet been presented to us, although we do not foreclose the possibility that it can be shown at the hearing on the permanent injunction. Even if a distinction can be drawn between offensive and defensive conflicts and if some rather explicit congressional authorization is required for the former, there still remains the problem of determining whether a broad approving resolution followed by non-repeal meets the proposed criterion of "explicit" approval. * * *

Finally, even if Berk is able to show that his claim does not raise an unmanageable political question, he will be required to show the district court that congressional debates and actions, from the Gulf of Tonkin Resolution through the events of the subsequent six years, fall short of whatever "explicit approval" standard he propounds. This will involve a multitude of considerations concerning which neither the district court nor this court has been adequately informed, and we cannot, in good conscience, now say that the appellant has shown probability of success on the merits if this stage is reached, although once again we do not foreclose the appellant from seeking to establish his claims.

In summary, the appellant raises a claim which meets the general standard of justiciability set out in *Powell* v. *McCormack, supra,* and *Baker* v. *Carr, supra,* but must still be shown to escape the political question doctrine. Even though he has perhaps raised substantial questions going to the merits, neither the likelihood of success nor the balance of equities inclines so strongly in his favor that a preliminary injunction is required. * * * As to the latter, we add to the considerations mentioned by the district court the fact that Berk did enlist a year ago presumably fully aware of the Vietnam conflict. The parties have expressed their readiness to proceed immediately, so that additional risks to which Berk might be subjected during the very brief interval before the district court acts are highly speculative. Nor do we see any necessity for Berk's physical presence at or in preparation for the district court proceedings. Berk's absence would not moot the underlying action. The facts concerning Berk on which the action is predicated are undisputed and there remain only the basic legal and constitutional issues and facts relevant thereto. * * *

By opening the door to further judicial explorations into the legal issues raised by the war in Vietnam, the Second Circuit, for the first time, allowed the constitutionality of an undeclared war to be presented to a federal court. It was now the responsibility of the attorneys for Berk and Orlando to evolve and to enunciate the "manageable judicial standards" with which to measure the legality of the Vietnam war.

PART THREE

The Legality of the War

Once the Court of Appeals had opened the door, the first judge to pass on the legality of the war was Judge John Dooling. Judge Dooling, appointed to the bench in 1961 by President Kennedy, had been a highly successful Wall Street lawyer. His career on the bench was marked with distinction, and he was generally regarded as being among the most able and scholarly of the district judges. Judge Dooling scheduled his hearing on the war for June 26, 1970.

In addition to the *Orlando* hearing before Judge Dooling, the attorneys looked forward to presenting the *Berk* case to Judge Orrin G. Judd pursuant to the Court of Appeal's instructions in the first *Berk* appeal. Judge Judd, also a highly able attorney prior to his appointment to the District Court in 1968 by President Johnson, was regarded as an ideal judge before whom to present the issues of the war, despite his initial reluctance to rule on the war's legality. Judge Judd scheduled his hearing for mid-July.

In preparing for the hearings before Judge Dooling and Judge Judd, three issues appeared to be of critical importance in evolving the manageable judicial standards demanded by the appeals court in *Berk*.

First, it was vital to demolish the contention that the president possessed "inherent authority" as Commander-in-Chief to wage war in Southeast Asia.

Second, the assertion had to be countered that Congress, by appropriating money to pay for the war, impliedly authorized its prosecution.

Third, the assertion that the Gulf of Tonkin Resolution was the functional equivalent of a declaration of war had to be dealt with.

The president's-inherent-authority argument was based, in large part, on President Johnson's assertion that American history sanctioned the Commander-in-Chief's right to wage prolonged combat operations without explicit congressional authorization. Thus, the first task was the preparation of a historical analysis of past American military operations to rebut the myth of presidential omnipotence. The historical analysis which follows, was submitted to Judge Dooling as an amicus brief on behalf of the NYCLU's parent body, the American Civil Liberties Union.

ACLU Amicus Brief, Orlando v. Laird, District Court

The Constitution Requires that Explicit Congressional Approval Be Given to the Maximum Commitment of American Military Resources to Armed Hostilities

It can be shown at the trial of this case, both through the introduction of Congressional records and the testimony of historians that, prior to the Korean conflict, each maximum commitment of American military resources to armed hostilities received the *explicit* approval of the Congress.

Thus it is possible to distill from the American historical

experience the standard which Congress has inevitably followed before committing this nation's military resources to prolonged and bloody combat.

The War of 1812 was authorized by an explicit Congressional declaration of war, dated June 18, 1812. . . .

. . .

The Mexican War of 1846–1848 was authorized by an explicit Congressional declaration of war, dated May 13, 1846. . . .

The commitment of the nation's military resources to the Civil War was authorized by a joint resolution of Congress, dated August 6, 1861.

. . .

The Spanish-American War was authorized by a joint resolution of Congress, dated April 20, 1898, which ripened into a formal declaration of war on April 25, 1898. . . .

The First World War was authorized by an explicit Congressional declaration of war, dated April 6, 1917. . . .

The Second World War was authorized by an explicit Congressional declaration of war, dated December 8, 1941 (Japan) and December 11, 1941 (Germany and Italy). . . .

Thus, given the traditional Congressional response to the commitment of American military resources to a prolonged and bloody struggle, [Orlando] could contend that nothing short of a formal declaration of war satisfies the strictures of Article I, Section 8 of the Constitution. However, it is not necessary to rely upon so formalistic an argument. [Orlando] need only urge this Court to distill from the legislative materials accompanying this nation's entry into every prolonged and bloody military struggle in its history prior to Korea the principle that Congress must, in some explicit form, manifest its unequivocal will to embark this nation upon major armed hostilities as a constitutional precondition to involving this nation in war, whether it be *de jure* or *de facto*.

The legislative materials from which this constitutional standard may be distilled are supplemented by those instances where Congress has authorized the Executive to involve the nation in military hostilities of a secondary nature, involving a less than maximum commitment of the nation's military resources to armed hostilities.

Even in these "secondary military commitments," falling far below the level of commitment reached in the Vietnamese conflict, explicit Congressional manifestation of its unequivocal will to embark the nation upon a lesser level of military conflict was forthcoming.

The naval war with France, waged from 1798–1801, was authorized by explicit Congressional resolution. 1 Stat 561; 1 Stat 572, extended 2 Stat 39 (April 22, 1800); 1 Stat 574; 1 Stat 578; 1 Stat 743; *Bas* v. *Tingy,* 4 Dall. 37 (1800); *Talbot* v. *Seeman,* 1 Cranch 1 (1801).

The naval war against Tripoli (1802) was authorized by explicit Congressional resolution. 2 Stat 129.

The naval war against Algiers (1815) was authorized by explicit Congressional resolution.

The 1914 invasion of Mexico was authorized by explicit Congressional resolution. *Congressional Record,* vol. 5, pt. 7, 63rd Cong., 2d Sess. p. 6988.

Apart from Korea and Vietnam, no Executive has led this nation into prolonged and bloody armed hostilities without the explicit, unequivocal, authorization of Congress. Apart from the aberrations of Korea and Vietnam, the Executive commitment of armed forces abroad has involved, almost exclusively, short term commitments of small numbers of men to either protect American lives and property or to inflict minor reprisals in response to direct attacks upon Americans. In no event can such Executive action serve as a meaningful precedent for full scale war.

An analysis of the instances in which the Executive has committed armed forces abroad reveals the following categories:

(a) Short Term, Limited, Punitive Actions Against Politically Unorganized Bandits Preying Upon American Citizens

    (1) expeditions against pirates based in Sumatra in 1832, 1838 and 1839

    (2) expeditions against pirates based in the Fiji Islands in 1840, 1855 and 1858

    (3) an expedition against pirates on Drummond Island in 1841

    (4)   an expedition against pirates based on the Coast of West Africa in 1843

    (5)   an expedition against Formosan pirates in 1867

    (6)   an expedition against alleged pirates in Greytown, Nicaragua in 1854

(b)   Short Term, Limited, Border Incursions in Pursuit of Bandits Raiding the Borders or Shipping of the United States

    (1)   expeditions into Spanish Florida against marauding Seminole Indians from 1816–1818

    (2)   expedition against smugglers on Amelia Island in 1817

    (3)   expeditions against Cuban pirates in 1822, 1823, 1824 and 1825

    (4)   expedition against pirates based in the Greek Islands in 1827

    (5)   expedition into Mexico in pursuit of Cortino bandits in 1859

    (6)   expedition into Mexico in pursuit of Pancho Villa in 1916

(c)   Short Term, Limited, Punitive Responses to Unauthorized Attacks Upon American Vessels by Subordinate Officials of Foreign Governments

    (1)   naval engagement against Japanese feudal Prince Nagato in 1863

    (2)   retaliatory shelling of Prince Nagato's stronghold in 1864

    (3)   troops landed in Yokohama in 1868 to protect American citizens against local officials

    (4)   shelling of forts in 1871 maintained by Korean feudal lords

(d)   Short Term, Limited, Landing of Troops to Protect American Citizens Abroad from Temporary Threat of Mob Violence

    (1)   expeditions landed in Woosung and Shanghai to quell riots in 1859

    (2)   troops landed in Alexandria to protect American consulate in 1882

    (3)   troops landed in China to protect Americans from warlord depredations, 1911–1933

    (4)   troops landed in Argentina to quell riots during civil war of 1852

    (5)   troops landed in Uruguay to quell riots in 1855 and 1858

    (6)   landing of troops in Nicaragua and Colombia to protect Isthmian residents in 1903

    (7)   landing of troops to quell riots in the Dominican Republic in 1904

    (8)   landing of troops to restore order in Hawaii in 1874 and 1893 and in Samoa in 1899

    (9)   landing of troops in Lebanon in 1958 to protect American lives and property

    (10) landing of troops in the Dominican Republic in 1963 to protect American lives and property

(e)   Short Term, Limited, Punitive Expeditions to Redress the Maltreatment of American Citizens Abroad

    (1)   rescue of citizens held prisoner on Falkland Islands in 1831

    (2)   rescue of American citizen kidnapped by Austrian navy in 1853

    (3)   punitive assault upon Imperial forces in Shanghai during Taiping Rebellion in 1854

    (4)   razing of Canton barrier forts in 1854

    (5)   rescue of Ion Perdicaris from Moroccan bandits in 1904

    (6)   commitment of troops to rescue foreign legations in Peking during Boxer Rebellion in 1900

(f)   Short Term, Initial Intervention to Protect American Lives Followed by Prolonged Peaceful Occupation to Protect American Property

    (1)   occupation of Haiti, 1915–1934

    (2)   occupation of Dominican Republic, 1916–1922

    (3)   occupation of Nicaragua, 1912–1928; 1928–1933

    (4)   occupation of Cuba, 1906–1909.

No rational parallel may be drawn between the limited, short-term commitment of small numbers of men for short periods of time to achieve a definite objective invariably related to an attack upon American lives and property, and the maximum commitment of the nation's military might to an endless war on the mainland of Asia. The fact that the Executive has engaged in the former without Congressional authorization cannot justify his current attempt to wage total war in the absence of explicit, unequivocal Congressional approval.

Whenever military operations remotely resembling in scope the commitment of our men and resources to Korea and Vietnam have been contemplated, the Executive has inevitably sought the explicit and unequivocal assent of Congress. Given the existence of Article I, Section 8 of the Constitution he could do no less.

Once the historical perspective had been established that explicit congressional authorization was required to engage in a war, argument on whether Congress had, in fact, authorized the Vietnam war by appropriating money to pay for it or by passing the Tonkin Gulf Resolution was presented to both district judges. The briefs and arguments contained elaborate analyses of the legislative history of congressional appropriations for Vietnam, together with a detailed chronology of American involvement.

Extracts from Brief, Berk v. Laird, District Court

Plaintiff suggests the following standard in accordance with the Second Circuit's dictates:

I. The Executive department can commit the military forces of the nation into armed hostilities abroad without explicit Congressional approval in the following instances:

A. to repel sudden attack upon the United States, its territories, possessions, military forces or vessels;

B. to protect American citizens or property from temporary threat of violence or, by limited use of force, to redress maltreatment of American citizens abroad;

C. to pursue politically unorganized pirates, bandits or similar groups attacking American citizens or property;

D. in an emergency to protect American interests where prior Congressional approval would not be feasible because of the need for immediate action and/or secret planning. However, ratification and further authorization by Congress of Executive action must take place as soon as possible after the need for immediate action and/or secret planning has passed.

II. A. Explicit Congressional approval either through a declaration of general war or limited war or by treaty, law or resolution explicitly authorizing the use of military forces is necessary to permit the Executive to commence armed hostilities abroad in the following instances:

(1) to attack or to commit an act of war against any organized state or the forces thereof except in the instances outlined in Section I above;

(2) to come to the aid of any sovereign nation to protect such nation from internal or external attack, except in the instances outlined in Section I;

(3) in all instances other than those outlined in Section I.

B. Congressional approval need not be prior in time to Executive action taken under this section (except as noted in Section III below) but such ratification or further authorization must take place within a reasonable time after such action is commenced.

C. In no event can appropriations or other acts in and by themselves be considered adequate Congressional approval unless they explicitly and by their own terms authorize, sanction and/or direct military action.

III. Prior explicit Congressional approval either through a declaration of general war or limited war or treaty, law or resolution explicitly authorizing the use of military forces is necessary to permit the Executive to commence armed hostilities abroad in the following instances:

A. to initiate and carry on hostilities of the highest magnitude, involving the commitment of large numbers of troops, great amounts of military equipment, or the nation's most powerful weapons, unless emergency Executive action is necessary, in which case explicit Congressional approval must be obtained as soon as practicable;

B. in the event military hostilities commence at a low level of magnitude by Executive action alone or under limited Congressional authorization, it is necessary to obtain prior explicit Congressional approval before hostilities can be escalated into military action of the highest magnitude, unless emergency Executive action is necessary, in which case explicit Congressional approval must be obtained as soon as practicable.

. . .

Prior Explicit Congressional Approval

A. Wars of the Highest Magnitude

Justice Joseph Story has explained why the power to declare war was granted to the legislature rather than the Executive:

> . . . the power of declaring war is not only the highest sovereign prerogative, but it is, in its own nature and effects, so critical and calamitous, that it requires the utmost deliberation, and the successive review of all the councils of the nation. War, in its best estate, never fails to impose upon the people the most burdensome taxes, and personal sufferings. It is always injurious, and sometimes subversive of the great commercial, manufacturing, and agricultural interests. Nay, it always involves the prosperity, and not unfrequently the existence, of a nation. It is sometimes fatal to public liberty itself, by introducing a spirit of military glory . . . It should therefore be difficult in a republic to declare war; but not to make peace. The representatives of the people are to lay the taxes to support a war, and therefore have a right to be consulted as to its propriety and necessity. J. Story, *Commentaries on the Constitution of the United States* §1171 p. 92 (5th ed. 1891).

Although the founding fathers could not foresee the changes that have taken place in world politics since 1787 or the new technology in weaponry and communications, the dangers of war that Justice Story described are still with us, and indeed are even greater now than in the eighteenth century. Granted the fact that international politics is much more complex and the Executive must act quickly to meet rapidly developing dangers, the decision to go to war in its fullest sense still imposes the greatest burdens on the people, curtails their liberties and threatens their existence in the most literal way. [. . .] Therefore, it is as important today as in 1787 that Congress explicitly make the decision to initiate a war of the highest magnitude prior to the commitment of large numbers of troops or the use of our fleet, thousands of planes or our sophisticated missiles.

It will not be difficult to determine those situations which constitute wars of the highest magnitude. The measuring rods are the amounts of money spent on the war, the number of troops utilized, the extent of weapons used, the nature of the military operations, and the duration of open hostilities. By any of these standards, the war in Vietnam must be considered a war of the highest magnitude requiring explicit Congressional authorization.

The authorization must be at least as explicit as the National Commitments Report suggested:

> . . . in considering future resolutions involving the use or possible use of the Armed Forces, Congress—
> (1) debate the proposed resolution at sufficient length to establish a legislative record showing the intent of Congress;
> (2) use the words "authorize" or "empower" or such other language as will leave no doubt that Congress alone has the right to authorize the initiation of war and that, in granting the President authority to use the Armed Forces, Congress is granting him power that he would not otherwise have;
> (3) state in the resolution as explicitly as possible under the circumstances the kind of military action that is being authorized and the place and purpose of its use; and
> (4) put a time limit on the resolution, thereby assuring Congress the opportunity to review its decision and extend or terminate the President's authority to use military force. (at p. 33.)

Every other major war in our history excepting the Korean war has been sanctioned by an appropriate and explicit Congressional Act.

Thus the explicit Congressional authorization required to commence hostilities must be given prior to the time that major armed conflicts commence, with the exception of a true emergency such as an atomic attack on the United States. If the Executive alone can commit substantial troops to combat, he effectively deprives Congress of any role in the war-making Process: the greater the *fait accompli* and the more American troops involved, the stronger is the pressure on Congress to "protect our boys" and support the effort. However, a flat rule declared by the federal courts that prior Congressional approval of such a final and possibly fatal step in Constitutionally necessary would go a long way toward re-establishing the balance anticipated by the framers and required by domestic politics and the pressures of world affairs.

B. Escalation from Low Level of Hostilities

Since it is clear that Congress should and must act before significant hostilities commence, it follows that any escalation from a lower order of conflict to a major war requires the same type of explicit Congressional authorization. The requirement of Congressional action can be completely undercut by a series of moves each raising the level of conflict by several degrees until it reaches a maximum stage with no explicit legislative approval. For example, a President may be able to send military advisors to a foreign country. If they are shot at, they may respond without Congressional authorization. But before the President sends numerous divisions and planes to the area to defend the advisors, he must come to Congress for authorization. Otherwise the Executive can bootstrap the nation into any war by sending one American soldier into hostile territory. If that soldier is shot at, then can the President take it on himself to begin an atomic attack in his capacity as Commander-in-Chief?

The Vietnam war escalated in precisely this context. No one doubted that the President could authorize his destroyers to fight back against North Vietnamese torpedo boats which fired on United States Naval vessels in the Gulf of Tonkin. Armed with the Gulf of Tonkin Resolution, the President could perhaps have attacked selected targets from which the torpedo boats allegedly came. Perhaps he could have done more to meet that threat. As Commander-in-Chief and with Congressional authorization for acting against the immediate danger, the President had wide powers to act. But what he could not do was to launch the longest war in our history. At some point between August 1964 and April 1970 when plaintiff Berk received his orders to go to Vietnam—and at this stage it is not necessary to determine the precise point (perhaps when the first large scale landings of American troops occurred)—Congressional authorization was Constitutionally required. Since it was not given, any military orders issued pursuant to that course of action are invalid.

Extracts from Oral Argument, Berk v. Laird, District Court

July 22, 1970

MR. NEAHER [United States Attorney]: I have read the plaintiff's brief with care, and I must say that I feel that their position is summed up on page 57 about as succinctly as it can be done. And that is, they say that Congress was constitutionally required to authorize the Vietnam war, that that authorization was not given, and ergo the military orders to this plaintiff are not valid.

. . .

This president, facing this situation and committed to a policy of withdrawal from Vietnam, was exercising his commander-in-chief's judgment to do what he thought was necessary to protect the troops which were now committed to his care, and which he found in perilous combat conditions.

That is what we are trying to say.

We are not trying to say that he had assumed or we were clothing him with a power that is, as such, that of Congress to declare and wage war.

. . .

THE COURT [Judge Judd]: That means your argument is that even if the war is illegal, that the president still has power as commander-in-chief—

MR. NEAHER: To extricate the troops from a perilous situation.

THE COURT: That is a fallback position; right?

MR. NEAHER: That is a fallback position; right. I am dealing now with their stated standards of what Congress must do. And their stated standard implies very clearly to me that they are satisfied that Congress need not make a declaration of general—of general war or limited war, but is free to act in another way, by treaty, law or resolution, provided it does so in an explicit fashion.

And I am saying that in our position . . . that all these conditions were met.

Number one, we have a treaty, SEATO, a treaty by which the United States said it was committing itself to come to the aid of any signatory or other Power that would be affected by the treaty in that region of the world if that Power were attacked or—

THE COURT: Well, the argument will be that SEATO was subject to Constitutional procedures in the United States and therefore still required a declaration of war.

MR. NEAHER: I understand that. But what I am saying is they say "By treaty."

Of course, a treaty, as such, would not necessarily involve the House of Representatives. It would only involve the Senate, normally.

That wouldn't quite fill the bill.

Then they say, "Law" . . . we, or "Resolution," sir. Now, Resolution is the Tonkin Gulf resolution.

Now, I am saying we have satisfied each of the things they want.

THE COURT: In other words, you are not disclaiming reliance on the Gulf of Tonkin resolution, are you?

MR. NEAHER: No, I am not disclaiming reliance on it. It was a fact. The fact that it is now repealed by one House of Congress, not yet by the other, doesn't cause it to disappear from the scene. It was there when this thing started.

Now, I call attention to the fact in our little distillation that the very next [Congressional] act, the 1965 supplemental appropriations act, was a special appropriation measure; not the general appropriation act at all, but a supplemental appropriation.

And the quote there is, "allowing $700,000,000," not a small sum of money, to be transferred in connection—upon—"for transfer by the Secretary of Defense upon determination by the president that such action is necessary in connection with military activities in Southeast Asia."

Even the area was spelled out broadly here. There was no focusing on just Vietnam.

And without—I am boring your Honor because you can read as well as I can speak. Each of these acts which we have excerpted, as you go through here, contain the specific reference. The next time it was not $700,000,000. It was one billion seven hundred million.

It is just simply incredible to believe that these congressmen did not know what they were doing and did not sanction what was being done. . . .

MR. FRIEDMAN: In presenting our view of manageable standards, we are not writing upon a clean slate. The standards we suggest were followed by both Congress and the presidency for about 170 years.

Although we have no court decision, president after president went to Congress to ask for their specific authorization before he dared commit an act of war against another state.

For 170 years no president said, "I am going to initiate a war and if Congress does not like it, then they can refuse to pass an appropriations bill next year." . . .

MR. FRIEDMAN: We are not saying you need a formal piece

of paper [that says "we declare war"]. That is misconstruing our standard.

What we are saying is that you need an explicit grant of authority to the president to initiate hostilities.

[As for the Gulf of Tonkin resolution], if one looks at legislative history and looks at the words of the statute and looks at what the president said . . . one sees exactly what Congress had in mind. They were directed to that problem in the Gulf of Tonkin.

The contemporaneous statements of all the senators and congressmen at the time of the Gulf of Tonkin Resolution belie any notion that they were authorizing a major land war.

THE COURT: Has anyone declared war in Vietnam?

MR. FRIEDMAN: I do not believe so.

The declaration of war we agree is a kind of archaic relic, but the purpose of the declaration clause is not archaic.

Since Congress is going to authorize the money to fight that war, since it lays a great burden upon the people, since it curtails their liberties as we know from all the other wars, the people's representatives must specifically sanction that kind of hostility.

In our standard we lay out various areas [in] which the president does not need the approval of Congress. There is no question that the debates of the Constitutional Convention indicated he could repel attack.

. . .

The president has the right to protect American citizens abroad. A citizen does have a right to protection in cases of any problem that must arise. This has strong historic tradition. To attack pirates or bandits or unorganized bodies throughout the world, there is no question that a president can fight an aggressive war against groups of that kind. In an emergency, we do not dispute the fact—such as in the Cuban missile problem, there was a problem the president had to act quickly on.

As we said in reference to our standards, we are not trying to answer every conceivable problem that could arise. Obviously, there are a lot of problems that we could not think of and that the Court could not think of and that the Government could not think of.

When we get to this kind of extreme, when we get to a war of such high magnitude, the Constitution requires Congress to act specifically and explicitly to ratify what the president has done and authorize him to continue it. . . .

MR. SORENSEN: May it please the Court, it is now clear from this discussion today, as well as the briefs, that the key issue in this case is Did Congress explicitly authorize the massive combat effort undertaken by this nation in Vietnam?

By that, we are not saying ''Was there a formal declaration,'' because it had been our position from the outset that no formal declaration of war was required.

Do these appropriations measures constitute an authorization of war? Even authorizations by ratification, are they sufficient to legalize an unconstitutional war, when the Congress could easily have passed a more direct statement authorizing that war?

[The appropriations bills] refer in a general way to Southeast Asia, which includes Burma. It surely does not include Burma. They talk about ''in connection with military activities'' or ''in support of South Vietnam and the free world's forces in South Vietnam'' or ''to meet the needs of the free world's forces in Southeast Asia.''

I have examined over the years a great many appropriations bills in which that kind of general language frequently appears. The same kind of language refers to the support of American military forces elsewhere.

There is no claim that authorizes the United States to go to war against East Germany or Soviet Russia. Korea has language very much like this—''in connection with military activity.'' . . . It does not give authorization to start a new war in Korea.

The fact that one appropriation, by itself lacks Constitutional power, does not mean that by combining several inadequate appropriations together, you could somehow find a Constitutional validation.

Appropriation bills, which have been cited by the government, are not authorizations for anything, and certainly not authorizations for a massive land war.

To say that a request for $700,000,000 in 1965 constitutes authorization for the expenditure of 30 billion dollars a year in 1968 and '69 makes no sense.

Interesting enough, the Government in its brief does not cite a single quotation from any member of Congress, from either House, to support the assertions that these appropriation bills were intended to authorize a massive combative effort in Vietnam.

That is clear from our brief, and I am sure your Honor will know that anyway. These appropriation bills have been supported over the years by some people who favored the war in Vietnam, some people who opposed the war. They voted for appropriations bills, because it contained military salaries, provided for medicine, housing, transportation and food.

The bulk of that defense department appropriation is not being spent on Vietnam. . . .

I searched the record in vain and I searched the Government's brief in vain for any indication on the part of any members of Congress that the contrary was intended. They stated on Page 13 of their brief: "Plaintiff apparently believes that Congress did not mean what it said."

We have looked at what Congress had said and it appears that the Government would like this Court to believe that Congress meant what it did not say.

Extracts from Oral Argument, Orlando v. Laird, District Court

June 26, 1970

PROF. VELVEL [Orlando's co-counsel] : . . . If your Honor please, we think that in accordance with the Second Circuit's opinion in *Berk,* it is possible to show—and we shall show—an entirely manageable judicial standard for deciding when a war is legal under the United States Constitution. It is a standard which will have the——

THE COURT: Do we beg the question? We keep using the

word "war." What we are talking about is what we are doing in Vietnam, Cambodia, Thailand, Laos—whatever it is we are doing.

PROF. VELVEL: If you are suggesting that there may be a question whether what is occurring is a war, then I would have to say that no matter how often we call an apple a tomato, it is still an apple.

. . .

In order to understand our standard as to military activity, it is simply necessary to keep in mind what the only purpose was of the framers for putting the declaration of war clause into the Constitution. They were very much afraid of the Executive power. We pointed out in our brief—I will not read it here—that Justice Story indicated the great fear that the framers had of unchecked executive power, and Judge Story—and the records of the Constitution have pointed out the specific fears that were relevant in the framers' minds as to the Executive's getting us into a war; they were very much afraid of giving the Executive the power to get the nation into a war. They had seen what would happen if he had that power; they had seen what wars can do to a nation. They knew that a war can do away with liberty. A war will hurt a nation's economy. People die. There is the whole gamut of problems associated with war, and it was very familiar to the framers. They specifically decided that this nation should not undertake those risks, those problems, those dangers unless the Congress first makes the decision to do so.

. . .

They recognized, of course, that the President can repel an attack. But they thought that aside from repelling an immediate attack, the decision on whether or not this nation shall engage in a war belongs to Congress.

. . . As they have in other specific authorizations in the course of history, [Congress could] attach certain conditions to the specific authorization [of war], they might say that only 200,000 men of the Army shall be used in the fighting and that they shall be used only in North Korea and South Korea, the land and water and air confines of North and South Korea but not in China, for example, and that this authorization is good for only a certain period of time, such as six months. They don't necessarily have to attach these conditions, but they can.

The point that we are getting at is that it is a very manageable jurisdictional standard to say that the Congress must specifically and explicitly and consciously authorize the use of military force, and [only] when it does that is the President under the constitution, empowered to use military force against another country.

. . .

I point out, your Honor, that the appropriations paragraph is not and was never intended by the framers to be a way of legalizing certain illegal activities. All it is is a check on those illegal activities.

Let me present a very rough analogy, if I may. It is not a perfect analogy but it makes the point.

Suppose a policeman were to see somebody committing a crime, and, rather than stopping that man—and he has the power to stop the man—and this is all flowing from the appropriations power—he doesn't stop him, but he helps him. He gives him his gun. Does that make it legal? Of course not.

Appropriations may be used to help the President do something illegal, but that doesn't make it legal. Appropriation is only a check; it is not a way of authorizing him to do something. It is not a legalization or authorization for the President's doing as he wishes.

. . . Under the Constitution Congress had the power to declare war. And to get into a war you must have a majority in favor of getting into that war.

Why is this situation? If the President can get us into a war and then argue that the war is legal unless Congress cuts off the funds, the situation is that one man can get us into a war, and, instead of the majority—instead of the burden of obtaining a majority being upon those who want to get into a war it is upon those who want to get out of the war.

I pointed out to your Honor that nowhere in the Constitution would any people dream of such a theory. Suppose the President were to seize the steel mills—he has done this—and he were to say that this is now the law unless you can get a majority of the legislators to cut off funds. . . .

. . .

THE COURT: And I think the Court of Appeals . . . [said] that we have a case—that at least we are agreed on: that we have a lawsuit. So the first and greatest hurdle is over. We have a lawsuit. We are properly here.

The next question that the Court says we have is, Have we got a manageable standard by the definition of *Baker* versus *Carr* by which to determine the authority, if any, or the want of authority that underlies the acts with which we are here concerned?

As I understand it, you say, Yes, because of the overwhelming importance of the power with which we are concerned, the power to commit men to their death in combat, which is plainly lodged in the Congress. The standard is the clear, the simple, and the necessary standard of explicitness; that that is authorized which is authorized; that which is not authorized is not authorized. Point to the authorization, and the authorization must be an authorization of what is done and not laws which either pay for it or sweep up after it is done.

Is that your manageable standard?

PROF. VELVEL: Yes, sir. . . .

MR. FRIEDMAN [. . . appearing for ACLU]: The point is that the President obviously had a great deal of authority to meet any kind of emergency, and no one would dispute that. But at some point between the Tonkin resolution and the present, some six years have passed and we are now in the longest war in our history, one that has involved the largest commitment of our resources . . . and we have had nothing remotely resembling congressional authorization for it. . . . It seems to me in that kind of situation . . . we are not dealing with various intermediate levels of military activity—that is, whether it is an immediate armed attack on one of our frigates on the high seas, or piracy—pirates coming up from Cuba to attack some of our ships, or such situations as arose in Spanish Florida, when there were excursions by Indians into Georgia and the surrounding territory—that is not the situation at all.

Your Honor, we can show through historians or through situations which occurred historically . . . , that there are various levels of military activity and it is possible to discern joint

Legislative-Executive mixes that can justify that level of military activity. But when you get to the end—when you get to a No. 1 magnitude level of military activity such as World War I and World War II and the Vietnam War, then you must have the kind of explicit congressional authorization called for by the Constitution.

Your Honor said it before: Passing laws to pay for or clean up the débris is not that kind of authorization.

. . .

MR. FRIEDMAN: . . . I think it does fit into the constitutional argument also for the very reasons that Justice Story offered as to why a declaration of war is necessary and applies— that is, when we say a specific congressional authorization is necessary.

No. 1 is that it means a very significant marshaling of all of the resources of the country for a new adventure. War is the greatest adventure that a nation can go into, whether we call it a war or a military activity of any kind.

No. 2—There is a great danger of the curtailment of personal liberties in that time of crisis and the people's representatives should make that decision—not the President.

No. 3—The existence of the nation is endangered—and why should the President make that decision? The people's representatives in solemn conclave assembled are the ones to make that kind of decision.

Robert Morse, the Assistant United States Attorney, came back to the question the Court of Appeals had decided against the government in the *Berk* case: he still insisted that the legal issues of the war were political questions that the courts could not examine. In other words, no matter how flagrant the Executive's action, the courts owed the duty of "unquestioning adherence to a political decision made" by the President, as the solicitor general later wrote in his brief in *Massachusetts* v. *Laird.*† Judge Dooling showed his unwillingness to accept that argument.

---

† In the summer of 1970, Massachusetts tried to bring an original action in the Supreme Court to defend the rights of Massachusetts soldiers ordered to

MR. MORSE: So I submit to your Honor that your Honor must look at the Berk case, look at the standards, and I think the conclusion is clear that what Prof. Velvel has done with all his articulateness and all his precision is to prove to this Court that various levels of military activity in a modern day and age, where the government in its Executive branch and Congressional branch in whom jointly and severally reposes the entire question of foreign military action—that where that situation arises and that test arises, it is in effect a political question. Where majorities and minorities and Congress have disagreed, that is a political question. It is for them to have that disagreement.

The test, in the absence of a confrontation between the President and the Congress in which there is a paralysis, and where the courts must judicially determine where the manageable standards are—that a battalion with or without air support does constitute a war as compared to a conflict having 100,000 men, 200,000 men—the test is, Must the President of the United States define the latitude and longitude in modern warfare as to what he may or may not do? Must he be bound, that the enemy or the potential enemy know under what circumstances he may or may not move?

Is it necessary, so to speak, in an unfortunate situation—and one cannot tell what future situations may arise—must the President at this stage in this particular situation be defined and determined to tip his hand at this time when the war is being wound down?

Is this Court to determine prospectively what a President may do in a foreign situation not yet in existence?

go to Vietnam. The government's answering papers, prepared by the Solicitor General, claimed that congressional duty to participate in the warmaking process could not be judicially identified and the breach of that duty could not be judicially determined. (Both positions were rejected by the Court of Appeals in the *Berk* case.) The Supreme Court refused to accept the Massachusetts case by a vote of 6 to 3 in November 1970, with Justice Harlan joining Justices Douglas and Stewart, who wished to take the case. Massachusetts had to return to the District Court of Massachusetts to begin the case at the same level that Berk and Orlando had done. On June 1, 1971, the District Court dismissed the action on political-question grounds. Massachusetts appealed to the First Circuit Court of Appeals and is awaiting its decision.

THE COURT: I don't think anyone has suggested that the Court should do anything. But they have suggested the Congress should.

MR. MORSE: Is it necessary for the Congress to declare and to announce a war or at various levels of military——

THE COURT: Their answer is "Yes—when time permits."

MR. MORSE: I say, your Honor, that the circumstances, as we visualize them now, indicate that that is not only moot and academic but cannot be judicially determined.

Who is to determine whether time permits? Can we determine in 1970 that time permitted in 1965?

THE COURT: I think the question first and foremost is, Is this action in fact authorized?

MR. MORSE: I think, your Honor, that where the President of the United States——

THE COURT: Because I don't think anybody is arguing that whoever is President at a particular time has the power to declare a war. He has not.

MR. MORSE: Correct.

THE COURT: And there is no such contention, nor could there be. But the question is, really, Has the activity in Cambodia, Thailand, Laos, South Vietnam, and the adjacent coast been authorized by law?

MR. MORSE: The answer to that is a firm and clear Yes, in my opinion, for a number of reasons. Primarily the reason is that were the Congress of the United States—and our brief covers this in detail——

THE COURT: In effect it says that the failure of the Congress to repudiate the administrative action, given the difficulty of effective repudiation of Executive action of this kind, cannot be argued to amount to authorizing it, even when accompanied by a course of appropriations, amendments to draft laws, et cetera, which in other context might arguably support it or support such an argument, because, given the importance of the power of exercise, the ease of obtaining authorization, one cannot argue that such action can be implied but must be—such authority can be impliedly given because it should be explicitly given . . . Nothing worse or better can be done with a nation than to commit it to hostilities that can lead—and everybody would say—to us all being bombed off the face of the earth one night or midday or morning, and to commit yourself to what may seem like a modest little war in Southeast Asia, the next thing that happens is an incursion into China. The weather is bad; the radio is balled up. China has a bomb—a nice dirty one. They set it off. Somebody else sets one off. We are all dead in our beds.

Well, those things are perhaps 'way down the road, or perhaps they won't happen until they happen over Jerusalem. What they are saying is, ''What's so hard about any President of the United States going to Congress and saying, 'The national interest requires this military action. I request its authorization'?''

Nothing hard about asking for it; nothing hard about getting it if it is in fact in the national interest.

The Congress and the President by such concurrent action manifestly have the express power to do that and to do it at any level of activity.

Why the absence of it? What possible justification is there for either (a) an absence of such action; or (b) an implication of such action in the absence of taking it when neither necessity nor wisdom counsels such an implication? That is their argument.

MR. MORSE: May I respond?

THE COURT: You'd better—not in this court. It doesn't make much difference what happens here. But someone is bound to ask the question, the Supreme Court of the United States, perhaps. If it occurred to me it will occur to one of them.

It soon became apparent that the legislative history of Congressional appropriations of funds for Vietnam would be of critical importance in the cases. Accordingly, Edwin Oppenheimer prepared a detailed analysis of the background surrounding the passage of the various appropriations acts, which was submitted to Judge Judd.

Affidavit, Berk v. Laird, District Court

. . .

. . . An appropriation bill ordinarily is not considered by Congress until the program or activity is to be funded has been previously authorized by specific legislation. Thus spending by the government consists of a two step process: the passing of an authorization bill and then an appropriation bill.

. . . The substantive legislative committee which has authority over the subject matter involved originates an authorization bill. For example, the Armed Services Committee would introduce authorization bills for military expenditures. However, the Appropriations Committee (divided into separate subcommittees dealing with each substantive field) introduces appropriation bills.

. . . Both the House and the Senate have produced an elaborate body of rules and precedents to govern the relationship between the appropriations committees and the substantive committees in order to prevent the appropriations committees of either House from engaging in substantive legislation through appropriation bills. For example, House Rule 21, Section 2 states that "No appropriation shall be reported in any general appropriation bill or be in order as an amendment thereto, for any expenditure not previously authorized by law. . . ." This provides the formal basis in the House upon which a separation of tasks between the Appropriations Committee and the substantive committees, such as the Armed Services Committee, is maintained. With the exception only of "retrench expenditures," the Appropriations Committee is not to legislate substantively in an appropriations bill and under Section 4 of House Rule 21, the substantive committees cannot appropriate money.

. . . The Senate, which considers the appropriation bill after it has been passed in the House, also has similar expectations and rules regarding the role of its Appropriations Committee. The substantive committees of the Senate also expect that the Senate Appropriations Committee will not make decisions as to the substantive policy of the programs and purchases which it is funding. Rather, it is expected to determine the amount of money realistically needed to fund the authorized expenditures in an economical way. Senate Rule 16 is comparable to House Rule 21 in that it too forbids substantive legislation in an appropriation bill.

. . . Congressmen and Senators follow the rules on limiting debate on appropriations bills. For example, Senator Stephen Young commented during debate on the Supplemental Defense Appropriation Bill of 1967 (P.L. 90-8):

> MR. YOUNG: If the Senate adopts the policy of determining war policy on an appropriation bill, would it not be a precarious situation, sometime in the future, when we might be engaged in another war, soldiers would be reluctant to enlist because they would not know whether they would be supported financially with adequate equipment and supplies which they would need to fight a war? 113 *Cong. Rec.* 7189

This position was clearly articulated by Congressman Donald Edwards during the debate over the Supplemental Defense Appropriations Act of 1966 (P.L. 89-374). During that debate, Edwards declared:

. . .

> I will vote for H.R. 13546, the supplemental southeast Asia appropriations measure before this House today. I will do so because I feel it is unwise to decide policy issues through the appropriations process. It is the job of the authorizing committees to oversee the administration of duly authorized funds.
>
> My vote for this appropriation means two things. It does not alone mean that I do not believe it is proper to express any policy preferences in an appropriations measure. It also means that an appropriations measure should not be used by anyone else to express their policy preferences. My vote today is not an endorsement of our past policy in Vietnam. It is merely a certifi-

cation of prior House action on authorization measures. 112 *Cong. Rec.* 5820

. . . However, it is not clear that even authorization bills constitute an exercise of the Congress' powers under Article I, Section 8 with respect to the declaration of war. Generally defense authorization bills cover the number and kind of missiles, planes and naval vessels which the Department of Defense is authorized to procure and the total amount of money it is authorized to spend on such items. They rarely express any policy determinations such as how or where the weapons are to be used. In fact, Senators or Congressmen often object to the use of military authorization bills for this purpose. For example, Senator Richard Russell, then Chairman of the Senate Armed Services Committee, said during the debate on the Armed Forces Supplemental Appropriation Authorization of 1967 (P.L. 90-5) :

> . . . It was a very undesirable approach to the whole subject. I do not favor statements of policy on authorizing legislation or appropriations. As a general rule, it is a very bad practice.
>
> I have no particular quarrel with the language of this substitute, but I have very grave doubts about the propriety of attaching it to an authorization bill. It ought to be considered separately. 113 *Cong. Rec.* 4938

Senator Norris Cotton of New Hampshire spoke in the same vein :

> (W)e are passing an authorization bill for the money to maintain our forces and to put arms and supplies in the hands of our men that we have sent to Asia. I think it is not only inappropriate but also it is doing them a wrong to again, after all of our protestations of anxiety to meet anyone, anywhere to bring about peace, to attach any kind of amendment to it. . . . I find myself compelled to vote against any of the amendments and any of the declarations of policy that are sought to be attached to a simple authorization bill for an appropriation. 113 *Cong. Rec.* 4941

Senator Tower of Texas commented during the same debate :

> What we have done in the Senate today points up the inadvisability of debating policy when we are passing on the matter of providing the money to provide our American fighting men

with the hardware and the resources they need to fight a war.
113 *Cong. Rec.* 4949

. . . This affidavit sets out substantial portions of the legislative history of the authorization and appropriations bills passed for the Vietnam war

. . . Since 1964, when the United States' involvement in Vietnam increased to more than adviser level, there have been eighteen laws passed by Congress relating to military expenditures for our armed forces: eight authorization bills and ten appropriations bills.

. . .

. . . Of the eighteen bills passed, five contain no reference to Vietnam. The other acts merely authorize or appropriate money to be spent for our forces in Vietnam but by their terms they do not explicitly authorize or empower the Executive to carry on hostilities in Vietnam. The first act passed (P.L. 89–18) specified:

> For transfer by the Secretary of Defense, upon determination by the President that such action is necessary in connection with military activities in southeast Asia, to any appropriation available to the Department of Defense for military functions, to be merged with and to be available for the same purposes and for the same time period as the appropriation to which transferred, $700,000,000, to remain available until expended.

The next (P.L. 89-213) provided:

> For transfer by the Secretary of Defense, upon determination by the President that such action is necessary in connection with military activities in southeast Asia, to any appropriation available to the Department of Defense for military functions, to be merged with and to be available for the same purposes, and for the same time period as the appropriation to which transferred, $1,700,000,000, to remain available until expended.

The third law (P.L. 89-367) said:

> Sec. 401. (a) Funds authorized for appropriation for the use of the Armed Forces of the United States under this or any other Act are authorized to be made available for their stated purposes

in connection with support of Vietnamese and other free world forces in Vietnam, and related costs, during the fiscal years 1966 and 1967, on such terms and conditions as the Secretary of Defense may determine.

Later laws (except for P.L. 90-5 discussed below) carried forward the language noted above
. . . it is not clear from the legislative history of the various laws to what extent they were considered ratification of Presidential action in Vietnam or authorization for future action.

. . .

On May 4, 1965, President Johnson asked for $700,000,000 for additional Vietnam military costs through June 30, 1965. In the House, many Congressmen qualified their vote for the measure:

> MR. KASTENMEIR: . . . I am sure Congress will support this measure, in some cases because of agreement with its implicit policy—in others because of an unwillingness to be placed on record as denying funds for elements of the Armed Forces abroad including "equipment, aircraft, and ammunition."
>
> In this situation, however, it must be clear that this vote cannot be construed as an unqualified endorsement of our policies in either southeast Asia or in this hemisphere. A vote for these funds does not expunge the grave reservations many in this country have over these policies. 111 *Cong. Rec.* 9527.

Mr. Lindsay said:

. . .

> My vote . . . is not to be construed as an approval of the administration's whole policy in Vietnam; nor does it imply the endorsement of a blank check for the unexamined spending of more and more millions, the unilateral commitment of more and more of our Armed Forces and the expansion of the ground and air conflict into a major war, without allies and without the exercise of great diplomacy.
>
> I hope the President will recognize that many of us who vote in favor of this resolution do so in the hope that it will contribute, not to the widening of an unwanted war, but to the pursuit of an honorable peace. 111 *Cong. Rec.* 9530

Mr. Reuss commented:

> . . . Mr. Chairman, I shall vote for the resolution and the
> appropriation today because I believe that the troops we have
> committed in southeast Asia deserve the support—the supplies,
> the equipment, and the facilities—which the President has told
> us they need. That is what my vote today covers. It is not a vote
> for enlarging the present conflict in South Vietnam, or a vote of
> satisfaction with things as they are. 111 *Cong. Rec.* 9538

>   . . .

In the Senate there were similar comments: Senator Aiken
said:

> I suppose that there may be different reasons for voting to
> approve the request of the President. Does the Senator from
> New York accept the statement that he would be voting to en-
> dorse the mistakes of the past and the plans for the future if
> he were to vote for this appropriation?
> MR. JAVITS: I do not accept such a statement. I believe that
> there is all the difference in the world, as I tell my most re-
> spected colleague, between backing up what we have involved, or
> even the making of sufficient preparation should we wish to go
> further, and a command decision which would set forces in action
> in a totally new way from the way in which they had been used
> before.
> I do not regard a vote for the appropriation—which I propose
> to support—as being of the same character or quality as a com-
> mand decision to send U.S. combat troops to participate in the
> ground struggle against the Vietcong. 111 *Cong. Rec.* 9454

The debate continued:

>   . . .

> MR. GORE: Mr. President, U.S. soldiers are in South Viet-
> nam under orders. They are there at the command of the Com-
> mander in Chief of the U.S. Armed Forces. They have no choice.
> I expect to support the appropriation. I find it untenable for
> American servicemen to be sent into an area of danger without
> having supplied to them the equipment and the materials by which
> they can execute their orders with maximum safety to themselves
> and the interest of the United States.
> However, lest my vote be interpreted as a 100-percent endorse-

ment of the policy by which American combat troops are in South Vietnam, I wish to say emphatically that it is not. 111 *Cong. Rec.* 9497

. . .

MR. AIKEN: Mr. President, I quote from the President's message yesterday: "This is not a routine appropriation. For each Member of Congress who supports this request is also voting to persist in our effort to halt Communist aggression in South Vietnam." Mr. President, I wish to make it plain that my vote is not intended as an endorsement of the costly mistakes of the past, nor as authority to wage war in the future unless such war has been declared by Congress. . . .

I cannot let the impression go out from this Chamber that in voting for this appropriation I am giving blanket approval to waging undeclared war anywhere or delegating the right to express my thoughts to anyone. 111 *Cong. Rec.* 9499.

Senator CHURCH said:

I understand that there is no limiting language that would reduce the powers the President now holds. But what concerns the senior Senator from Idaho, is that his vote, which he would like to give in support of the money requested because American lives are involved out there, and American troops must be furnished with all the equipment, supplies, ammunition, and protection that we can give them, may be construed as giving advance approval for decisions in the future that I have no possible way of knowing, such as the bombing of Hanoi, or, let us say, the enlargement of American combat forces in South Vietnam by some striking degree.

I do not know what might happen. I would not want my vote to be construed as an endorsement of moves which might entirely change the character or dimension of our involvement in southeast Asia.

As I understand it, the joint resolution is for the purpose of paying bills. . . . 111 *Cong. Rec.* 9500

. . .

In discussing the Defense Appropriation Act of 1966, Senator Morse registered his "continued protest of the war itself" (111 *Cong. Rec.* 21732). Morse contended, "in the absence of a declaration of war, the President in my opinion has no constitutional right to send a single American boy to his death in Southeast Asia." However, Morse went on to declare:

> But I shall vote for it also because of its many other features with which I find myself in enthusiastic support; namely, the long overdue pay increase for the military; the provision that was adopted in regard to the so-called 35–65 formula in connection with the building of ships. *Ibid.*

He also commented:

> American boys in South Vietnam did not go there of their own volition. They went there because they were sent by their Government. I fully realize that as long as they are there, they must have every possible bit of protection that can be given to them, although I deplore the fact that, in my opinion, they are sent there to participate in a war that is unwise, unconstitutional, and illegal, in that the President has no constitutional power to make war in the absence of a declaration of war.
>
> It will be said, "You should not vote money to conduct such a war," and there is much merit in that.
>
> But as a liberal, I never overlook human values. When I vote for a bill that includes that $1,700 million—and I will have a question to ask my good friend from Mississippi momentarily, as to where the $1,700 million came from, and its justification— I am voting still protesting the war, but I am voting to protect the human values of the American boys who are fighting and dying under governmental orders in that war. *Ibid.*

In introducing the Supplemental Appropriation Authorization Bill of 1966 (PL 89-367) Senator Richard Russell, chairman of the Senate Armed Services Committee, declared:

> I stated when I brought the bill to the floor that I did not regard this authorization for weapons, medicine, and facilities— including port facilities—as being either an affirmation or a rejection of our policies in Vietnam and that the bill did not set policy in the slightest degree. 112 *Cong. Rec.* 4370

Furthermore, during the debate on the above legislation, Senator William Fulbright commented:

> . . . Although I think the pending bill has a significance as to our overall policy, it authorizes money to carry on the war, and

is not a policy statement. I am dubious of this legislation because passage of the measure may be viewed as an endorsement of the present policy in Vietnam for the reasons that I have just offered —which policy I do not endorse. 112 *Cong. Rec.* 4382

He continued:

An appropriation is normally not inclined to be considered as a statement of policy. It is normal that legislation, according to our rules, should not be included in an appropriation bill. *Ibid.*

Continuing the debate, Senator Joseph Clark declared:

I wish to make it very clear indeed that my votes, both against the Morse amendment and for the bill, do not indicate an endorsement of the policy which I fear the administration is following. *Ibid.*

Senator George McGovern concluded:

I am voting today to provide the necessary equipment and supplies for our forces in Vietnam. My Senate colleagues and my constituents know that I have opposed our growing military involvement in southeast Asia. I believe that we have no interest there that justifies the heavy loss of life involved in trying to settle a Vietnamese civil conflict with American troops.

But since we have sent 300,000 men to southeast Asia we have no practical alternative now except to provide them with the equipment they need to survive.

I want to make it clear that my vote for this military equipment bill is not an endorsement of our Asia policy. Rather, my vote reflects my conviction that we must protect men we have sent into battle no matter how mistaken the policy may be that sent them to that battlefield. 112 *Cong. Rec.* 4409

In presenting the supplemental defense authorization bill to the House, Congressman Mendel Rivers declared:

Our men are in Vietnam. They need our support and our help. Passage of this bill is that support and that help.

Let the debate as to whether we should be in Vietnam, or how we should conduct the war in Vietnam, be carried on at another time. I will join in such debate. This is not the time for that debate. This is the time for only one thing—and that is to vote our fighting men the weapons they need. 112 *Cong. Rec.* 4441.

During the House debate of March 1, 1966, in which the . . . measure was considered, Congressman Abbitt noted:

. . .

> Our boys, through no choice of their own, are in Vietnam where they are being shot at, many of whom are being wounded, mutilated, and killed. It is inherent upon us to furnish them with all necessary military material that is at our command so that they will not be lacking one whit to protect themselves and to achieve the goals for which they have been sent. We either must furnish every needed article of offense and defense or else it is our duty to pull them out. We must support them wholeheartedly and fully or else bring our boys back home. It is not fair to them and it is not fair to America to do less.
>
> This is not the time to argue whether we should be in Vietnam or whether we should have gone. We are there and our boys are being killed by the Communists daily. It is inherent upon us to put up or get out and I call upon the administration to do everything necessary by way of supplying our men with the needed munitions of war immediately and constantly and I, therefore wholeheartedly support this bill and hope that it will be passed unanimously. 112 *Cong. Rec.* 4431

Congressman Yates further noted:

> What is important now is that our troops be given the weapons to carry on the fight, and we shall do that in this bill. 112 *Cong. Rec.* 4473

And Congressman Dow explained his motivation in voting for the supplemental authorization, with the following statement:

> (A)s one who is not in favor of escalating the conflict in Vietnam, let me say that I will vote for the bill before us. . . .
>
> My affirmative vote for this bill is given with a sad heart. The men at the front should not be allowed to run short of the ammunition and equipment they need to defend themselves. That is the only reason I can see to vote for this authorization.

Congressman Kastenmeier manifested a similar position when he declared:

> Mr. Chairman, the vote today . . . like the war in Vietnam itself, poses a great dilemma for Americans inside and out of Congress. The fact is that our war policies have gotten us into

a situation which cannot be reversed by a vote on a single measure, but which will require a significant change in our approach
to the terms by which we are willing to accept a settlement.
However strong my reservations, objections, or criticisms of the
policies that are engulfing us in a southeast Asia war, I am constrained to view and to vote for this measure as one to provide
material support for our troops in the field.

I do want to emphasize that I oppose our war policy in Vietnam. . . . 112 *Cong. Rec.* 4468

Congressman Fraser similarly observed:

(M)y vote for this supplemental appropriation for the Vietnam conflict is not an endorsement of the policies the United
States has been following in Vietnam.

. . .

My vote today is based on the need to sustain the troops already in Vietnam. 112 *Cong. Rec.* 4468

And Congressman Bingham explained his vote thusly:

Why, then, am I voting for this supplemental authorization
bill? First, for the simple and obvious reason mentioned in the
joint statement, that we must give our forces in Vietnam all the
support they need, so long as they are there. The second reason
is more complicated: I fear that a substantial vote against the
authorization might actually impede our objective of getting
talks started by encouraging Hanoi to continue its apparently
total intransigence. 112 *Cong. Rec.* 4460

Congressman Kupferman followed with the statement that:

. . . I am voting for this appropriation because I cannot leave
our American troops in the lurch without proper protection on a
foreign shore. But it must be pointed out that it was a great
mistake to have put them and us in this position. 112 *Cong.
Rec.* 4460

Congressman Anderson cautioned against "read(ing) too
much into the passage of a military authorization bill" when he
declared:

. . . It could be argued that implicit in the approval of this authorization bill is the approval of current policy. However, I
think that we would be establishing an unwise precedent indeed

if we were to attempt to read too much into the passage of a military authorization bill. By the same token, I think that the 76 Members of this body who have signed a manifesto or declaration that their vote for this measure does not carry with it approval for the escalation of the war or our deeper involvement in southeast Asia will also "carry coals to Newcastle." . . . I support his measure and with it the heroic sacrifices being made by our men in South Vietnam. At the same time I do not want history to record that by this vote I gave this administration my blank check with respect to its future conduct of policy in South Vietnam. 112 *Cong. Rec.* 4462

And Congressman Farbstein explained his position:

Mr. Chairman, in the past, I have expressed reservations about some of the administration's actions in Vietnam. Recently, I joined a number of other Representatives in urging the President, among other things, to de-escalate our military efforts in Vietnam as a further effort to bring the war from the battlefield to the conference table. I still feel no good can come from further escalation and do not wish this vote to be considered otherwise. I desire to create a climate leading to the conference table.

. . .

American boys are committing their lives and honor to this fight in the Far East. These young men must not be deprived of equipment, necessary hospitals, medical treatment, essential supplies, and helicopters needed to help them survive in this jungle war. The Congress, regardless of any reservations and unanswered questions on administration policy, must not fail to grant the funds to supply these brave men. . . .

On the scale, I find I must vote in favor of the appropriation. 112 *Cong. Rec.* 4448

Congressman Rosenthal presented the following assessment:

I am not happy with the minimal role to which Congress is thus consigned. Nor am I convinced that the Congress had been adequately consulted or respectfully attended in the formulation of policies in Vietnam. But I do not accept the proposition that this vote today constitutes a considered and broad sense of Congress.

I do not believe my own vote, simply as a vote, properly represents my viewpoint on this matter, any more than the total vote of Congress adequately represents the total sentiment of Congress. Complicated positions on matters of war and peace are not to be abbreviated by such simple symbolism. So I deny the legitimacy of this vote as a deep expression of individual or collective viewpoint on the full range of policy in Vietnam. I am voting for support and supplies for the American troops already committed to Vietnam. 112 *Cong. Rec.* 4455

Congressman Cohelan presented the following statement in behalf of seventy-eight members of the House of Representatives:

Mr. Chairman, we will vote for this supplemental defense authorization. The support of the American and allied troops who are fighting in South Vietnam requires it.

We agreed with President Johnson's statement that "we will strive to limit conflict, for we wish neither increased destruction nor increased danger." We therefore reject any contention that approval of this legislation will constitute a mandate for unrestrained or indiscriminate enlargement of the military effort, and we strongly support continued efforts to initiate negotiations for a settlement of the conflict.

We, in particular, wish to express our concurrence with the President's statement of last week in which he declared the Vietnamese conflict to be a limited war for limited objectives calling for the exercise of "prudent firmness under careful control." (Signed by 78 Members of the House of Representatives) 112 *Cong. Rec.* 4431

The debate on PL 89-374 (Supplemental Defense Appropriations Act, 1966) came so close in time to the authorization bill (PL 89-367) that little was added to what already had been said. However, Congressman George W. Andrews stated:

Mr. Chairman, as a member of this subcommittee, I support this bill.

There has been a lot of argument about how we got into Vietnam and whether or not we should be there, and so on. In my opinion such arguments are academic. The fact remains that our people are committed in South Vietnam today, our men are being wounded and killed in South Vietnam, our flag is being fired upon in South Vietnam. It behooves Americans to support those men in South Vietnam all the way, and that is all this bill does. It provides the tools of war for our men in the hope—in the prayerful hope—Mr. Chairman, that this war can soon be terminated. 112 *Cong. Rec.* 5819

Congressman Edwards also said:

I will vote for H.R. 13546, the supplemental southeast Asia appropriation measure before this House today. I will do so because I feel it is unwise to decide policy issues through the appropriations process. It is the job of the authorizing committees to debate policy matters. It is the job of the Appropriations Committees to oversee the administration of duly authorized funds. . . .

My vote for this appropriation means two things. It does not alone mean that I do not believe it is proper to express any policy preferences in an appropriations measure. It also means that an appropriations measure should not be used by anyone else to express their policy preferences. My vote today is not an endorsement of our past policy in Vietnam. It is merely a certification of prior House action on authorization measures. 112 *Cong. Rec.* 5820

Rep. George M. Mahon from Texas, Chairman of the House Appropriations Committee, introduced PL 89-687 (Defense Appropriation Bill, 1967) by noting:

Although the war is of deep concern to all members of Congress, there is little dispute over the necessity for providing adequately for our military forces. 112 *Cong. Rec.* 16186

John Flynt of Georgia also said:

It is the responsibility of each of us in the official capacity in which we serve to make certain that the members of the armed services committed in Vietnam receive the unreserved support of the Congress of the United States and of the American people. 112 *Cong. Rec.* 16274

Senator Stephen Young confirmed that the appropriations bill was to support the men in Vietnam:

Congress certainly has a responsibility to the public, and especially to the men who are fighting in South Vietnam—a country, Mr. President, about the size of my State of Ohio,

10,000 miles distant from our shores, of no strategic nor economic importance whatever to the defense of the United States. We have approximately 400,000 men of our Armed Forces, the cream of the crop, the finest soldiers, airmen and sailors in the world, fighting in that far-away country, in the poisonous jungles and swamps of Vietnam, and with our 7th Fleet, close to the Vietnam coast in the Tonkin Gulf and the South China Sea.

. . . The least that we in Congress can do for them is to cut down on non-essential spending in order to provide properly for their welfare and their maintenance without, at the same time, weakening the economy our Nation. (sic) 112 *Cong. Rec.* 19830

PL 90-5 (Armed Forces Supplemental Authorization, 1967) contained a "Statement of Congressional Policy" concerning Vietnam which reads as follows:

Sec. 401. The Congress hereby declares—

(1) its firm intentions to provide all necessary support for members of the Armed Forces of the United States fighting in Vietnam;

(2) its support of efforts being made by the President of the United States and other men of good will throughout the world to prevent an expansion of the war in Vietnam and to bring that conflict to an end through a negotiated settlement which will preserve the honor of the United States, protect the vital interests of this country, and allow the people of South Vietnam to determine the affairs of that nation in their own way; and

(3) its support for the convening of the nations that participated in the Geneva Conferences or any other meeting of nations similarly involved and interested as soon as possible for the purpose of pursuing the general principles of the Geneva accords of 1954 and 1962 and for formulating plans for bringing the conflict to an honorable conclusion.

It appears that not too much can be inferred from this law. It seems to express what much of the legislative history in this affidavit does: it was necessary to supply the soldiers in the field with all necessary equipment; it also expresses the view that it was necessary to seek ways for an honorable peace.

The policy statement was introduced by Senator Mansfield. He commented about its purpose in an exchange with Senator Pastore:

MR. PASTORE: Is the Senator from Rhode Island correct in interpreting the amendment to mean nothing more than the fact that—even though we appropriate this money to support our troops in Vietnam—our objective is peace?

MR. MANSFIELD: Yes.

MR. PASTORE: And we would welcome support from anyone, anywhere——

MR. MANSFIELD: For an honorable peace.

MR. PASTORE: To bring us peace.

MR. MANSFIELD: To bring us an honorable peace.

MR. PASTORE: That is all the amendment means?

MR. MANSFIELD: That is all I had in mind. 113 *Cong. Rec.* 4946

He then spoke further with Senator McClellan:

MR. McCLELLAN: What is the actual purpose of such an amendment? Why is it felt that it is needed?

MR. MANSFIELD: Because, if I may use the words, and if they can be understood in that way, it will furnish a consensus of the feeling of the Senate regardless of one's particular position on the war in Vietnam. *Ibid.*

He also said:

. . . This substitute simply voices the intent of the Congress to give the full measure of support to the needs of the men who risk their lives daily in Vietnam. It expresses to the Americans who are fighting in southeast Asia that Congress will do its part to see that they are well equipped and supplied. I am confident that this expression represents the opinion of the entire Senate. It should not have to be stated. However, even the slightest prospect of misinterpretation or misunderstanding at home and abroad justifies this affirmation of complete and unequivocal support for he men who have been sent to Vietnam in pursuit of the Nation's policies. 113 *Cong. Rec.* 4941

Senator Hartke commented:

. . . I hope that the amendment we have adopted will have the effect of encouraging the President to put every possible emphasis on peace. I think it clearly shows that the Senate has gone on record as wanting the emphasis not on escalation but on peace and on a settlement of the war, on a negotiated basis, using those institutions which are available. 113 *Cong. Rec.* 4949

The Mansfield Amendment was adopted by a vote of 72–19 with the "nay" votes being cast by the Senate "hawks," the most vigorous defenders of the Executive's Vietnam policy (113 *Cong. Rec.* 4948): Senators Russell, Stennis, Talmadge, Thurmond, Tower, Murphy, Eastland, Long, McClellan and others. Senator Cotton complained that the Mansfield Amendment was "a very innocuous and nicely-worded substitute, the sentiments of which anyone finds it difficult to disagree with." But he thought it might be interpreted "as a definite declaration on the part of the Senate that we were adopting a so-called dove policy." 113 *Cong. Rec.* 4944.

As for the appropriations bill itself, there was little debate concerning the need to continue to support the troops. Senator Murphy said:

> Mr. President, it serves little purpose to debate at this point whether we should have become involved initially in Vietnam. We are there. About 450,000 brave American boys are daily placing their lives in jeopardy in defense of freedom. . . . 113 *Cong. Rec.* 4951

In the House the same type of debate occurred. Rep. Yates commented:

> . . . The reason for the amendment offered by the gentleman from Wisconsin [Mr. Reuss], I believe, will be to clarify that point and to say those of us who may vote for the bill do not necessarily endorse every detail of the policy in Vietnam. What we do, all we do, is to support our troops in the field. 113 *Cong. Rec.* 5115

Rep. Mendel Rivers, Chairman of the House Armed Service Committee, said, in supporting the bill:

> I would like to state at the outset that regardless of the debate that is raging on South Vietnam, one thing is crystal clear to me: our troops are in South Vietnam. And they need weapons. This bill is an essential step in providing those weapons. For my part, I do not need to know anything else. 113 *Cong. Rec.* 5117

A discussion between Rep. Bates and Rep. Brown [of California] indicates that the authorization bill was not intended as an endorsement of administration policy:

MR. BROWN: Mr. Chairman, going back to this question of escalation, would it be proper to say that there is nothing contained in this bill which either provides for or prevents the escalation of the war?

MR. BATES: That was the essence of my general statement.

MR. BROWN: Mr. Chairman, if the gentleman will yield further, is it not true that, for example, the greater escalation which I believe any of us could imagine—the dropping of a nuclear device upon Hanoi—would require no additional funds above those which have already been provided to the Department of Defense?

MR. BATES: I feel that it would require a decision, not additional funds. The gentleman is correct.

MR. BROWN: I recognize the fact that it would require a decision.

MR. BATES: The gentleman is correct.

MR. BROWN: So additional legislative authorization by the Congress is not required?

MR. BATES: It would not require that.

MR. BROWN: In other words, the basic decisions as to escalation are not contained in any of the documents before us?

MR. BATES: Escalation, whether it would be represented by decisions or not, is not in this bill, as I tried to indicate to the gentleman from Illinois. 113 *Cong. Rec.* 5121

In commenting on the Mansfield Amendment, Rep. Farbstein noted:

> I think we can very readily state that although we are seeking to support our boys and that we refuse to turn our back on our boys who are fighting in Vietnam, we nevertheless are seeking an early and honorable peace and that it is our prime aim to do so.
>
> This declaration in the preamble will give evidence of our intention to seek peace as early as possible. 113 *Cong. Rec.* 5134

Mrs. Mink followed:

> . . . Mr. Chairman, I will support the supplemental appropriation. I wish to state that this vote should not be interpreted to mean that I support the escalation of the war in Vietnam. I support the supplemental appropriation only because our men in Vietnam who are there at the will of this Government need

these funds for their personal security and safety. Until we can urge our Government to proceed with the necessary moves toward a negotiated settlement, I believe that I have a moral obligation to provide these men with whatever is deemed necessary for their personal safety. *Ibid.*

Mr. Tenzer spoke about the bill:

. . . [I]t is most important that we dispel any notion that a "yes" vote on the appropriation measure is a blank check to escalate the Vietnam conflict or even that it indicates tacit approval of every aspect of our policy in that area.

I am voting in favor of the supplemental appropriation because I believe that full support of the American and allied troops in Vietnam requires this action notwithstanding my concern over recent developments. 113 *Cong. Rec.* 5137

When Mr. Reuss introduced the Mansfield amendment in the House, Mr. Rivers raised a point of order on the ground that the amendment was not germane to the bill:

MR. RIVERS: Mr. Chairman, I rise to a point of order on the ground that the amendment is not germane to the bill. The bill before the House is a supplemental authorization bill. The amendment contains no limitation. It declares a matter of policy which obviously is under the jurisdiction of another committee since it deals with foreign affairs and commitments. We are not privy to the 1954, 1958, or 1962 Geneva agreements, nor are we signatory to the Geneva accords. 113 *Cong. Rec.* 5139

The acting Chairman of the House upheld the point of order:

The Chair is of the opinion that the subject matter of the amendment comes within the jurisdiction of the Committee on Foreign Affairs, and not the Committee on Armed Services which reported the bill now before the Committee.

The Chair refers the Committee to a decision by Chairman Metcalf, of Montana, in the 85th Congress. The bill then under consideration authorized the sale or loan of certain vessels to friendly foreign nations. It had been reported by the Committee on Armed Services. The amendment on which the Chair was called upon to rule provided that no vessels could be made available under the act unless the recipient country agreed to waive criminal jurisdiction over troops of the United States stationed therein—an amendment which clearly called for diplomatic negotiations with the foreign nations involved.

In holding the amendment not germane, the Chair stated that it consisted of an unrelated matter under the jurisdiction of the Committee on Foreign Affairs—Congressional Record, volume 103 part 6, page 7272.

The Chair feels that this precedent is very persuasive in the present situation. Here, as there, the bill before the Committee deals with military authorizations. Here, as there, the amendment touches upon the foreign policy of the United States.

The Chair, applying one of the accepted tests for germaneness, is of the opinion that the amendment is essentially on a "subject other than that under consideration" and is not germane to the bill under consideration. 113 *Cong. Rec.* 5141

The ruling made by Chair supports the point noted above, that policy determinations even on military authorization bills are procedurally inappropriate.

Eventually the Mansfield amendment was acted upon and passed by the House after Senate conferees had insisted on retaining it (113 *Cong. Rec.* 5769). Mr. Bates, the ranking Republican on the Armed Services Committee, said about it:

With respect to the so-called Mansfield amendment, I think we made sufficient adjustment with him here so that everyone, regardless of what their views might be on the committee report, can live with this. It is almost innocuous. It is barely a pious preachment. *Ibid.*

Mr. Reuss said about his amendment:

Until today, Congress had made no declaration of congressional policy on Vietnam. This is one of the most destructive wars in history, yet it is being waged without a congressional declaration of war. I hasten to add that I do not favor a declaration of war. To declare war, once we determine just whom we were declaring war against, would make it that much more difficult to extricate ourselves.

But the inappropriateness of a declaration of war does not mean that the President, in making war pursuant to his role as Commander-in-chief, should be exempt from a Congressional declaration of Congressional policy on the war. The only piece of legislative paper relating to the war has been the Tonkin Gulf Resolution of 1964. The record of that debate is clear that the Congress had no intention of putting its stamp of approval upon military activities of anywhere near the scale such as those now conducted in Vietnam. 113 *Cong. Rec.* 5771

The quoted discussion does not suggest that the amendment is to be interpreted as explicit authorization of the Executive's conduct of the Vietnam war.

In presenting PL 90-22 (Armed Forces Appropriations Authorization, 1968) to the House of Representatives, Congressman Mendel Rivers declared:

This bill is, of course, the fiscal year 1968 authorization for appropriations for weapons procurement and research and development. It is essentially the same as many previous bills for which rules have been requested over the past several years. Some of them have been regular fiscal year programs—as this one is— and some of them have been supplemental authorizations. This bill and all of the others have merely represented more of the same kind of thing. 113 *Cong. Rec.* 11982

Again during the passage of this bill there was virtually no debate over substantive considerations of foreign policy. It is hard to see how such little debate as there was can be said to amount to an explicit authorization of hostilities.

PL 90-110 (Military Construction Authorization Act, 1968) merely referred to the establishment of military installations in southeast Asia. There was no significant debate on American policy.

PL 90-392 (Second Supplemental Appropriations Act, 1968) appropriated moneys for various departments for fiscal year 1968. The debates were chiefly concerned with allocation of priorities:

MR. PASTORE: With respect to the Headstart program the amount sought was $25 million, which was the amount in the urgent supplemental bill, the bill that languished in conference. On that, we finally could reach a figure of only $5 million.

I wish to make it abundantly clear that we did the best we could. We hit a stone wall. If anybody ever hit a stone wall, we did. There is no question about that.

But the Senator from Rhode Island is not completely pleased with this result. He feels refreshed and encouraged because we did get something, but it was my hope that we could have secured more.

MR. CLARK: How much is there in this bill for Vietnam and other military affairs?

MR. PASTORE: Almost $4 billion for Southeast Asia. Our committee decided to cut out $80.3 million for military construction in Vietnam, because we felt that a complete planning had not been instituted. We felt that there were some projects they could not even name, and there was a tremendous carry over of $225 million.

There, again, the House was adamant in restoring the full amount. We hassled over that for a number of hours and finally reached a compromise in cutting it in half. 114 *Cong. Rec.* 19673

The debate on PL 90-500 (Armed Forces Appropriation Authorization, 1969) for procurement of aircraft, missiles, naval vessels, and research and development did not focus on Vietnam. Senator George McGovern commented along the lines of many previous statements:

It is, of course, important that we not interfere with the procurement and research efforts related to the ability of our men in Vietnam to defend themselves. That is an engagement in which we are already involved—although as Senators know I disagree with the policies that have so heavily involved American troops in Vietnamese affairs. 114 *Cong. Rec.* 9940

The following remarks by Senators Gore and Pastore took place during the debates on PL 90-580 (Defense Appropriations Act, 1969):

MR. GORE: I am grateful for the able speech the Senator is making. I join him in opposing the amendment.

With respect to policy, as the able senior Senator from Virginia is aware, I have resisted this country's policy in Vietnam. I have questioned it over a period of years. I believe in so doing I was within the proper function of a U.S. Senator.

But the men who are there are there in consequence of a policy which, though I disapprove it, has nevertheless been the policy of the Government. The soldiers are there, not by their wish, but at the command of their Government, and I do not wish to withhold bombs, ammunition, artillery, weapons, equipment or whatever they need to execute this mission, erroneous as it may have been as a matter of policy. It is a mission assigned to them, and I wish to see them execute it with maximum efficiency and with maximum safety to themselves.

MR. PASTORE: I wish the Senator from Tennessee had been here yesterday to hear the point I tried to make. I, too, have had my qualms about Vietnam, and whether or not we should have been involved there in the first place. But the Senator has put his finger right on the problem. I think it would be a tragic mistake for us to try to make the Senate of the United States a war room, to attempt to decide what kind of strategy we are going to follow.

I think if Senators believe our policy ought to be changed, they should do whatever they can about changing the policy; but as long as our boys are there, we should not do anything which will serve in any way to demoralize our troops. We must promote their safety and do everything we possibly can to assist them while they are there. As the Senator from Tennessee has pointed out, they are not there by their own choice, and most of them would rather be at home. 114 *Cong. Rec.* 18832

Congressman Bingham, commenting in the House on the same act, stated:

.   .   .

I know that there are expenditures contemplated in this legislation that are undesirable and others that are unnecessary. I believe that once again we have witnessed the phenomenon that requests by the military for appropriations are treated far more kindly and with a less critical eye in this House than the requests made by those officials who have charge of our essential domestic programs. Nevertheless, in my judgment, there is so much in this bill that is clearly necessary and desirable that, overall, an affirmative vote is called for.

I might have considered casting a negative vote as a gesture of protest if I believed that such a gesture would be an effective way of pressing for a change of policy with respect to Vietnam, but I do not so believe. It would be a grave mistake for anyone, including the Saigon government, to measure the degree of dissatisfaction with our policy on Vietnam by the number of negative votes on this bill. The dissent on Vietnam is better measured by the 40 percent vote for the minority plank at the Democratic National Convention in Chicago. 114 *Cong. Rec.* 26567

In late 1969 Congress passed limited legislation, PL 91-121 and PL 91-171 (Defense Appropriations Authorization Act, 1970; Defense Appropriation Act, 1970), to deny the President complete control over military affairs in southeast Asia. Section 643 of PL 91-171 specifically provided that

> . . . In line with the expressed intention of the President of the United States, none of the funds appropriated by this Act shall be used to finance the introduction of American ground combat troops into Laos or Thailand.

Senator Fulbright commented on this limitation:

> I was pleased that the Senate . . . approved an amendment prohibiting the introduction of ground combat troops into Laos or Thailand.
>
> . . .
>
> I did not initially support the language offered by the distinguished Senator from Idaho (Mr. Church) because it appeared to imply Senate approval for an open-ended policy of bombing in Laos—an activity authorization which I do not believe any President has sought, nor has any Congress granted.
>
> Since the White House—and therefore the administration—has apparently embraced the Senate amendment on ground combat troops, I now wonder what assurances can be given the American people through the Senate on the question about bombing in Laos.
>
> It was testified the other day, as the Senator knows, that there are very large numbers of bombing strikes mounted from Thailand going on in Laos, and particularly that bombing associated with the Laotian war rather than the Vietnam war, or as they related it in our testimony, the Ho Chi Minh Trail.
>
> Is there any limit on the amount of bombing we will undertake?
>
> What are the prospects for the level of bombing in the coming months?
>
> Why has this administration continued the secrecy surrounding disclosure about the extent of our bombing?
>
> What are the prospects for the administration to make full disclosure to the American people as they now have done to the Senate? 115 *Cong. Rec.* 17185 (December 18, 1969)

. . . Thus an analysis of the legislative history of the military authorization and appropriations bills passed since 1965 does raise the question whether one can conclude that they were intended to be explicit ratifications of or authorizations for the Executive's military policy in Vietnam. Members of Congress indicated they appropriated money only to protect the men sent to southeast Asia by the Executive. Various other reasons—other than approval of the government's policy—were also advanced to support these expenditures.

The District Court Decisions

As the oral argument indicated, both District Court judges agreed that the basic issue of the war's legality was properly the subject of judicial scrutiny. Both judges agreed that the president's-inherent-authority argument was nonsense. However, both judges were deeply troubled by a sense that Congress, in systematically voting the funds to pay for the war, had knowingly given its assent to the war's prosecution.

District Court Decision, Orlando v. Laird

DOOLING, J.:

It is concluded that an injunction *pendente lite* is not warranted. The order is authorized in the constitutional sense. Whether other avenues of relief are open to plaintiff under Army procedures in view of his present conscientious attitude toward Vietnam combat is not properly involved in this action.
. . . In the light of Berk v. Laird, . . . it is seen that the question of the validity of the order to plaintiff is justiciable,

and the immediate issue is whether the matter is specifically decidable by standards of the kind that the judiciary have found manageable. No unusual subject matter is presented. Decisions in the entire area of the taking and arresting of combat action are exclusively political in kind, but determining whether or not a political decision has been taken by the appropriate set of governmental acts inescapably presents a purely judicial question when the existence or non-exisence of a valid political authorization as the source of a particular command is drawn in question by one directly affected by it in his individual liberty as a citizen. The fear that judicial decision—by injunction or habeas corpus—could produce an effect of a scope and nature usually absorbed in political action is unreal. Necessarily based on identification of a defect in authorization, the only consequence can be resumption of conformity to constitutional norms of political conduct to achieve, dilute, deflect or reverse the desired political objectives. Neither the range of political invention nor the content of political decision concerning the deployment and use of combat force is determinable or terminable by judicial decisions that unflinchingly point to and insist upon compliance with the required constitutional components of any political decision to commence, continue and terminate the use of the nation's combat resources in men and materials.

. . . Neither the language of the Constitution nor the debates of the time leave any doubt that the power to declare and wage war was pointedly denied to the presidency. In no real sense was there even an exception for emergency action and certainly not for a self-defined emergency power in the presidency. The debates, so often strangely—to our ears—devoid of respect for and alive with fears of the presidency that the Convention was forming, are clear in the view that (as Wilson put it) the power to make war and peace are legislative (1 Farrand, Records of the Federal Convention of 1787 (Rev.Ed.1937, Repr. 1966) 65, 73). The issue was where to poise it. Mason was concerned that "The purse & the sword ought never to get into the same hands (whether Legislative or Executive.)" 1 Farrand 139–140. The draft presented by the Committee of Detail on August 6, 1787, expresses the power as the power "'To make war'' (2 Farrand 182) and on August 17th that language was amended (2 Farrand 318–319) to read ''To declare war''—Madison and Gerry so moving on the ground of its ''leaving to the Executive the power to repel sudden attacks''; Sharman thought ''make'' the better word for the amenders' purposes—''The Executive shd. be able to repel and not to commence war. 'Make' better than 'declare' the latter narrowing the power too much''; to which Gerry answered that he ''never expected to hear in a republic a motion to empower the Executive alone to declare war''; Elseworth thought the cases of ''making *war*'' and ''making *peace*'' materially different—''It shd. be more easy to get out of war, than into it. War also is a simple and overt declaration peace attended with intricate & secret negociations''; Mason opposed granting the power either to the Executive (as Butler had proposed on the ground that he had ''all the requisite qualities, and will not make war but when the Nation will support it'') ''because not [safely] † to be trusted with it,'' or to the Senate (as Pinkney had proposed) ''because not so constructed as to be entitled to it. He was for clogging rather than facilitating war; but for facilitating peace. He preferred 'declare' to 'make' '''; the motion to substitute ''declare'' for ''make'' was then agreed to. Pinkney's motion to strike the clause entirely, and Butler's motion ''to give the Legislature power of peace, as they were to have that of war,'' by adding ''and peace'' after ''war,'' were both lost (2 Farrand 319).

The language of the Constitution makes the war power a legislative power rather than an executive power, and it makes it a federal power rather than a state power, without in either instance negating the co-existence of a duty to repel attack or actual invasion. Nothing relevant flows from the designation of the president as commander-in-chief of the armed forces except to confirm that his executive power includes the power to ''conduct'' wars declared by legislative act (cf. 2 Farrand 319, footnote), to deny autonomy to the military, and to locate the fountainhead of necessary emergency combat initiatives when the straitness of the exigency denies the Congress the time to act.

† Brackets in original.

The genuine questions presented by the combat activities in Vietnam are whether the activities constitute "war," or are a genus of Governmental activity that cannot be characterized as war, whether, if the latter, they can be authorized by the Executive, and, if they are "war" or otherwise are beyond the authority of the Executive, whether they have been authorized by legislative action. Plaintiff contends that the Vietnam combat activities are "war" and require explicit Congressional sanction that cannot be found in the Tonkin Gulf resolution, 78 Stat. 384, the appropriation acts, the extension and amendment of the Selective Service Act, and other such supportive acts. The defendants argue broadly that there exists a genus of combat activities distinct from war that is only politically definable, that historically the presidency has dealt with these usually exigent situations without Congressional authorization or constraint, and that, so far as the Vietnam combat activities are concerned, they do not constitute "war," they are within the range of recognized presidential powers, and, whatever their precise classification, have been ratified and authorized by repeated Congressional actions which may also be viewed as a cumulative and authoritative political determination that the action of the presidency is not usurpation of legislative authority.

The historic examples of the variety of the occasions on which the presidency has used combat force, or deployed the military as a threat of such force (given to considerable extent in Wormuth, The Vietnam War: The President versus the Constitution, 1968, 21–35, in the United States Attorney's Brief in the *Berk* case in the Court of Appeals, and, summed up by classes in the ACLU Brief, pp. 6–8), and the examples of more or less specific Congressional authorizations of limited combat authority, do not solve the questions presented, but clearly indicate the difficulty and variety of the cases presented, and the absence of compelling judicial precedent. The instances having a magnitude approaching Vietnam (conspicuously the Korean instance) would inevitably have been, as Vietnam is, instances in which the only problem is to elucidate the nature and effect of Congressional responsibility for the waging of the combat activity.

The Constitution does not simply make the power to declare

war a legislative power, it makes the related powers over the military, their provision and their governance equally matters of legislative concern, and extends the legislative power to calling up the militia to repel invasion and even to the granting of letters of marque, a species of authorized predation seemingly of a dimension to concern the Executive rather than to involve the legislative process. The systematic vesting of control over the means and the determination of the occasions of belligerency in the Congress makes inevitable that no combat activity of magnitude in size and duration can continue without affirmative and systematic legislative support. That Vietnam long ago attained that magnitude is history. It is, therefore, needless to stop now to decide whether the aggregate of the Constitutional provisions and the debates in the constitutional convention teach that no combat initiative is lodged in the presidency or in the states nor any authority to take combat action except where defensive exigency requires it and time does not admit of a resort to Congress or to decide whether, beyond peradventure, there can be no presidential power to take combat initiatives where the question whether or not to do so involves a political determination of national policy and is not compelled by military exigency. *Cf.* Indochina: The Constitutional Crisis, reprinted, Congressional Record May 15, 1970, pp. S 7117–S 7123.

The military activities of the United States in Vietnam have been a central national political issue for years; no issue has been more bitterly, if not honestly, debated. The outcome of two presidential elections has reputedly been influenced if not determined by the candidates' positions on the issues; a very considerable number of elections to Senate and to House have reportedly been influenced if not determined by the Vietnam issue. Reports of public opinion samplings on Vietnam issues are regualr news staples. The statistical measures, in lives of men, numbers of wounded, annual cost in money, and in men engaged, are doubtless the most publicized statistics in recent history. The Congress, particularly, has been deeply concerned in the issue, and its implementation of the Vietnam combat activities has been complete and unstinting.

The huge appropriations annually voted to sustain the expanding combat activity cannot be read out of being as extorted by the exigencies created by presidential seizures of combat initiatives. *Cf.* Congress, the President, and the Power to Commit Forces to Combat, 1968, 81 Harv.L.Rev. 1771, 1801. The power of the purse was lodged in the House and the appropriation power was expressly limited when exercised to raise and support armies as part of the conscious constitutional scheme for controlling the Executive's resort to combat activities. Specific appropriation statutes here, as the Government's brief points out, leave no uncertainty about Congressional will and purpose. The repeated amendment of the Selective Service Act with, inevitably, the knowledge that the numbers drafted were determined in large part by the demands of the expansion in the number of men committed to Vietnam combat and, later, by the need to maintain the rotation of men to Vietnam, has been a specific and purposeful provision of men to the continuance of the combat activity. Even in modest points of legislative detail, Congressional concern in the combat activities is perfectly explicit and advertent. For Veterans' Benefits purposes "period of war" has now been defined by the Congress as including "the Vietnam Era" which in turn is defined as the period beginning August 5, 1964, and to end upon still future Presidential proclamation or concurrent resolution of the Congress. 38 U.S.C. § 101(11), (29). Aliens are relieved of paying naturalization fees if they have served in the armed forces between February 28, 1961, and the future date to be designated by Presidential Executive Order as the date of the termination of the Vietnam hostilities.

It is passionately argued that none of the acts of the Congress which have furnished forth the sinew of war in levying taxes, appropriating the nation's treasure and conscripting its manpower in order to continue the Vietnam conflict can amount to authorizing the combat activities because the Constitution contemplates express authorization taken without the coercions exerted by illicit seizures of the initiative by the presidency. But it is idle to suggest that the Congress is so little ingenious or so inappreciative of its powers, including the power of impeachment, that it cannot seize policy and action initiatives at will, and halt courses of action from which it wishes the national power to be withdrawn. Political expediency may have counseled the Congress's choice of the particular forms and modes by which it was united with the presidency in prosecuting the Vietnam combat activities, but the reality of the collaborative action of the executive and the legislative required by the Constitution has been present from the earliest stages.

It is urged that evidence can be produced to demonstrate, in effect, that a steady course of executive usurpation of initiatives that, constitutionally, require the coaction of the Congress and the Executive had rendered the Congress impotent to withhold the grudging and involuntary appropriations and implementing laws relied on as constituting its authorization of combat activities in Southeast Asia. But extended argument has brought out that the reference is to the now-familiar compilations and analyses of the combat occasions of the past coupled with proffered testimony of members of Congress that their supportive votes were coerced by the predicament in which unauthorized executive action had placed the lives of men and the honor of the nation and do not reflect a will to ratify usurped initiatives. That, however, is simply a charge of Congressional pusillanimity. Such evidence, and its extent and validity are not to be supposed, could only disclose the motive and could not disprove the fact of authorization. The Constitution presents the Congress with the opportunity for it, but it cannot compel the making of unpopular decisions by the members of Congress. The long-term trend of the basic initiatives of Government to emanate from the presidency—an outgrowth possibly of the duties imposed by Article II, Section 3—is not confined to the context of foreign affairs and limited warfare, and it may as much reflect the necessities of national government today as the failure of the Congress itself to function effectively in the affirmative formation of national policy.

The place of the controversial Tonkin Gulf Resolution (Public Law 88-408, 78 Stat. 384) in the whole of Congressional action is unclear; its importance no doubt lay in its practical effect on the presidential initiative rather than its constitutional meaning, but it has not the compelling significance of the steady legislative support of the prosecution of the war.

District Court Decision, Berk v. Laird

Judd, J.:

Memorandum and Order Granting Summary Judgment for Defendants

An action for an injunction against sending an enlisted Army man to Vietnam challenges the constitutional basis for the presence of United States armed forces in South Vietnam. The case is before the court on defendants' motion to dismiss on the three grounds of lack of jurisdiction, failure to state a valid claim, and summary judgment for lack of genuine issues of material fact.

General Outline

The following controlling conclusions seem appropriate on the basis of the pleadings, affidavits, memoranda and public documents which the court has studied:

1. From the early days of our republic, there has been a recognized distinction between a ''perfect war'' or total war, initiated by a formal declaration of war, and an ''imperfect war'' or partial war, which involves military action authorized by Congress without a formal declaration of war.

2. There is no doubt that Congress has authorized the President to send members of the armed forces to South Vietnam to engage in hostilities.

3. The question whether Congress should declare total war or rely on some other mode of authorizing military action is a

political question, on which a court should not overrule Congress' determination.

4. The controversies between the parties raise only questions of law, and no disputes of any material fact.

Pre-trial conferences were held in this case, without waiting for the expiration of the defendants' time to answer the complaint. It appeared that the best way to present the merits expeditiously was by motion, at least in the first instance. The defendants submitted extensive legislative material and copious briefs in support of their motions, and the plaintiff countered with affidavits which serve as an offer of proof of this case. In a supporting memorandum, plaintiff set forth a detailed set of proposed standards to show the extent of legislative action requisite to authorize various levels of military activity. . . .

Plaintiff suggests three different categories of military action, requiring different measures of legislative-executive cooperation. The first category includes various types of emergency action, such as repelling an attack on the United States or protecting American citizens from attack, which the President may take without any action by Congress. In the second category are placed other acts of war against organized states, and aid in protecting any other nation from attack; plaintiff says these acts may be authorized or ratified by any explicit Congressional action, but not by appropriations acts, unless such acts "explicitly and by their own terms authorize, sanction and/or direct military action."

The third category is described as "hostilities of the highest magnitude," as measured by numbers of men involved, amounts of equipment, and use of the most powerful weapons. Such actions, plaintiff says, cannot be initiated without *prior* explicit Congressional authority. Even if the military action began in the first or second category, plaintiff says that the action may not be escalated to the highest level without prior explicit action by Congress. Plaintiff says that the third category of military action can be authorized only by:

> Prior explicit Congressional approval either through a declaration of general war or limited war or treaty, law or resolution explicitly authorizing the use of military force. * * *

Plaintiff asserts that neither the Gulf of Tonkin Resolution nor the appropriation acts and other legislative acts cited by the government constitute *prior explicit* authorization for the use of military force.

In number of men involved (accepting for this purpose the 3,000,000 figure used by plaintiff), numbers of killed (42,000) and wounded (280,000), amounts of equipment (half our entire air force), and amounts of money expended (over $100 billion), the Vietnam conflict ranks as a major war. There may be a question whether it involves ''the highest magnitude'' of military action, since it has not been extended to a land invasion of North Vietnam, or a blockade of the North Vietnam coast, among other potential forms of escalation. Nevertheless, the case will be considered on the basis of its belonging in the third category listed by plaintiff, without thereby accepting his requirement of *prior explicit* Congressional authority.

1. THE EARLY DISTINCTION BETWEEN TOTAL WAR AND PARTIAL WAR.

Although France under King Louis XVI had supported America's revolutionary efforts against England, the relations between the young nation that emerged here and the newer French Republic soon became unfriendly. The Fifth Congress, in 1798, authorized the President to issue instructions to United States armed vessels to seize any armed vessel that had committed depredations on vessels belonging to the United States, or that was hovering on the coasts for such purpose. 5th Cong. Sess. II, c.48, 1 Stat. 561. * * * Other acts of the same Congress suspended commercial intercourse between the United States and France (c.53, 1 Stat. 565) and authorized U.S. merchant vessels to defend themselves against French vessels (C.60, 1 Stat. 572). The last-mentioned statute (in Section 2) provided for an award of salvage, of one-eighth to one-half the value of the vessel and cargo, in case of the recapture of any United States vessel.

The 1798 statutes were treated by the Supreme Court as authorizing a state of partial war between the United States and France. *The Eliza (Bas v. Tingy)*, 4 U.S. (Dall.) 37 (1800). The case arose on a claim for salvage for retaking an American ship which had been taken by the French. It was necessary to find that the ship had been taken by an "enemy" to justify a salvage award. Justice Washington acknowledged that France was nowhere described as an "enemy," but held that there was "war of the imperfect kind." (p. 41). He distinguished between a "solemn" or "perfect" war, declared as such, and a limited or "imperfect" war. (p. 40). In the first case all members of one nation are at war with all members of the other nation; in the second case, those who are authorized to commit hostilities act "under special authority." (*ibid.*) Justice Chase pointed out that the popular "prepossessions" in favor of France led Congress not to want to declare a "solemn" war. Although Congress had not used the word "war," all the Justices agreed that there was a situation of war (Justice Moore, p. 39), albeit "a limited, partial war" (Justice Chase, p. 43), or an "imperfect war" (Justice Paterson, p. 45). See to the same effect *The Amelia* (*Talbot* v. *Seeman*, 5 U.S. [Cranch] 1 [1801]), in which Chief Justice Marshall said that "congress may authorize general hostilities * * * or partial hostilities" (p. 28).

Other early authorizations of limited hostilities were statutes authorizing the seizure of vessels of Tripoli (2 Stat. 129, Feb. 6, 1802) and Algiers (3 Stat. 230, March 3, 1815). Those statutes referred to the commencement of "predatory warfare against the United States" by the regency of Tripoli, and the Dey of Algiers, and authorized the President "to cause to be done all such other acts of precaution or hostility as the state of war will justify." Only Tripoli ever declared war on the United States, and the Acts of Congress were not regarded as declarations of "solemn" war.

An appendix to plaintiff's memorandum of law lists 159 instances of use of United States Armed Forces abroad from 1798 to 1945, of which only six involved formal declarations of war by either side. Sen. Comm. on For.Rel. and on Armed Services, Hearings on the Situation in Cuba, 87th Congr.2d Sess., Sept. 17, 1962, pp. 82–87.

The concept of an imperfect war was again discussed in *Montoya* v. *United States*, 180 U.S. 201 (1901). There the court held that certain depredations by Indians were not within a Congressional act providing indemnity for property taken by

Indians, because the particular taking was an act of war. Indian wars were put in the class of "imperfect" wars as described in *Bas* v. *Tingy*. See 180 U.S. at 267.

More recently, Congress by Joint Resolution determined that President Wilson was "justified in the employment of armed forces to enforce his demand for unequivocal amends for certain affronts and indignities committed against the United States" by Mexico. 38 Stat. 770, April 22, 1914. The resolution disclaimed "any purpose to make war upon Mexico."

In the years since World War II, Congress has authorized the President, by a series of Resolutions, to use the armed forces as he might deem necessary to protect Formosa and the Pescadores against armed attack (Pub.L. 84-4, 69 Stat.7, Jan. 29, 1955), to assist any nation in the Middle East requesting assistance against armed communist aggression (Pub.L. 85-7, 71 Stat.5, Mar. 9, 1957), to prevent "the Marxist-Leninist regime in Cuba" from extending its aggressive or subversive activities to any part of this hemisphere (Pub.L. 87-733, 76 Stat.697, Oct. 3, 1962), and to prevent any violation by the Soviet Union of the right of access to Berlin (House Conc.Res. 570, 87th Cong., 26 Stat. 1429, passsed by Senate Oct. 10, 1962). The Senate Foreign Relations Committee stated that "the exact line of authority between the President and the Congress" had been "in doubt for the past 160 years." Sen. Rep. 175, Mar. 14, 1951, partially reprinted in *Background Information Relating to Peace and Security in Southeast Asia and Other Areas*, Sen. Comm. on For. Rel., Jan. 1970, p. 35.

The resolutions just listed, fortunately, did not give rise to the extent of military activity which has taken place in Vietnam, but they are instances of Congressional authorization of partial war, and are pertinent background for the Gulf of Tonkin Resolution described in the next section of this opinion.

2. CONGRESS HAS AUTHORIZED HOSTILITIES IN VIETNAM.

Plaintiff does not assert that Congress must say, "We declare war," but he argues that the Constitution requires a prior explicit authorization to use troops abroad in actions of the highest magnitude, and that there was no prior explicit authori-

zation for the Vietnam hostilities. It is therefore necessary to
review the various executive and legislative steps from 1964.

The Gulf of Tonkin Resolution (Pub.L. 88-408, 78 Stat. 384,
Aug. 10, 1964) was passsed within a week after the second
alleged attack on United States naval vessels by North Vietnam.
* * * After reciting that the Communist regime in North Vietnam was engaged in a systematic campaign of aggression against
its neighbors, whom the United States was assisting to protect
their freedom, it set forth that:

> the Congress approves and supports the determination of the
> President, as Commander in Chief, to take all necessary measures
> to repel any armed attack against the forces of the United States
> *and to prevent further aggression.* (Emphasis added [by Judge
> Judd]).

It is true that the President said in recommending action by
Congress, that the United States "seeks no wider war" (110
Cong.Rec. 18132), but the Resolution gave him authority to
prevent aggression against Southeast Asia peoples who were
protecting their freedom. This court cannot say that the pressent
conflict is "wider" than was authorized by the Joint Resolution
and the subsequent acts of Congress. Plaintiff points out that the
State Department said in 1970 in a letter to Senator Fulbright
that *"this* administration has not relied on or referred to the
Tonkin Gulf Resolution of August 10, 1964, as support for its
Vietnam policy." He omits the next sentence of the same letter
that "Repeal at this time, however, may well create the wrong
impression abroad about U.S. policy." Sen.Rep. No. 91-872,
May 15, 1970, p. 23. (Emphasis added [by Judge Judd]). Moreover, this same State Department letter said of the Formosa,
Mid-East, Cuba and Tonkin Gulf resolutions, that they were "a
highly visible means of executive-legislative consultation * * *
indicating congressional approval for the possible employment of
U.S. military forces." Sen. Rep. No. 91-872, p. 20.

Five months after the Tonkin Gulf Resolution, the President
told Congress in his 1965 State of the Union message that we
were in Viet-Nam because a friendly nation asked for help
against Communist aggression, and that our security was tied to
the peace of Asia, continuing:

> Twice in one generation we have had to fight against aggression in the Far East. To ignore aggression now would only increase the danger of a much larger war. *Public Papers of President Lyndon B. Johnson, 1965*, Item 2, p. 3.

Although the Defense Department was operating under the 1964 appropriations bill, the President asked and obtained a special appropriation of $700,000,000 for "military activties in southeast Asia." Pub.L. 89-18, 79 Stat. 109, May 7, 1965. This was a single-item appropriation, which read:

> The following is appropriated, out of any money in the Treasury not otherwise appropriated, for the period ending June 30, 1965, namely:
>
> Department of Defense Emergency Fund, Southeast Asia
>
> For transfer by the Secretary of Defense, upon determination by the President that such action is necessary in connection with military activities in southeast Asia, to any appropriation available to the Department of Defense for military functions, to be merged with and to be available for the same purposes and for the same time period as the appropriations to which transferred
>
> $700,000,0000, to remain available until expended: * * *

The vote was 408 to 7 in the House (111 Cong. Rec. 9540) and 88 to 3 in the Senate (111 Cong. Rec. 9772).

This is the sort of single-purpose appropriations act concerning which it has been said:

> Although it may be admitted that an appropriations bill could be introduced under circumstances which leave room for no interpretation other than "a vote for the bill is a vote for the war," it is hard to see why, even in such cases, resort to implied rather than express authorization is necessary. Note, *Congress, The President, and the Power to Commit Forces to Combat,* 81 Harv.L.Rev. 1771, 1801 (1968).

The comment admits the purpose of the enactment, but merely suggests that Congress might use a different form of words for the same purpose.

Plaintiff quotes a Congressman who said that the President had sufficient funds without this appropriation, and that the bill was merely "an engineering of consent" to his military policies.

He quotes others as saying that their votes for the appropriation did not constitute approval of an undeclared war. Whatever the comments of individual Congressmen, the act nevertheless gave Congressional approval to military expeditures in Southeast Asia. That some members of Congress talked like doves before voting with the hawks is an inadequate basis for a charge that the President was violating the Constitution in doing what Congress by its words had told him he might do.

Plaintiff asserts that the President was always ahead of Congress in sending troops, and that Congress was always presented with a *fait accompli* which it was compelled to ratify. The course of events described above is more consistent with Congress and the President moving in concert.

Congressional support continued after 1967. Subsequent authorization and appropriations bills specifically mentioned Vietnam. Pub.L. 90-110, § 501, 81 Stat. 279, 301, Oct. 21, 1967; Pub.L. 90-392, 82 Stat. 307, 311, July 9, 1968; Pub.L. 90-500, § 401, 82 Stat. 849, 850-51, Sept. 20, 1968; Pub.L. 90-580, § 537, 82 Stat. 1120, 1136, Oct. 17, 1968; Pub.L. 91-121, §§ 101, 401, 83 Stat. 204, Nov. 19, 1969; Pub.L. 91-171, § 638, 83 Stat. 469, Dec. 29, 1969. The State of the Union Messages and budget messages continued to describe the status of the war in Vietnam. Jan. 17, 1968, in Jan. 22, 1968 *Weekly Compilation of Presidential Documents,* pp. 70-71; Jan. 29, 1968, in Feb. 5, 1968 *Weekly Compilation,* etc., p. 156; Jan. 14, 1969, in Feb. 5, 1969 *U.S. Code Congr. and Admin. News,* p. 12; Jan. 15, 1970, *ibid.,* pp. 14, 25; Jan. 22, 1970, in Feb. 20, 1970 *U.S. Code Congr. and Admin. News,* pp. 7–8; Feb. 2, 1970, *ibid.,* pp. 15, 27.

Authorized expenditures for Vietnam increased from $21.9 billion in 1967 to $25.8 billion in 1968 and $28.8 billion in 1969, declining to $25.4 billion in 1970.

In 1969, Congress added a policy statement to the Defense Appropriations Act, 1970, which was very different from the 1967 Mansfield amendment. The new statement was:

> Sec. 643. In line with the expressed intention of the President of the United States, none of the funds appropriated by this Act shall be used to finance the introduction of American ground combat troops into Laos or Thailand. Pub.L. 91-171, 83 Stat. 469.

Since the submission of this case, copies have become available of an amendment made by Congress to the War Claims Act of 1948, revising the definition of "prisoner of war" to include members of the U.S. Armed Forces held as prisoner of war "during the Vietnam conflict by any force hostile to the United States." Pub.L. 91-289, 84 Stat. 323, June 24, 1970, amending 50 U.S.C. App. § 2005. By the same act, provision was made for compensation to any civilian American citizen captured by hostile forces during "the Vietnam conflict." Pub.L. 91-289, *supra*, §3. As with respect to the statute including "the Vietnam era" within the definition of "period of war" for purposes of veterans' benefits, the 1970 amendments may have been motivated in part by humanitarian compassion for those captured by hostile forces. Nevertheless, the statutes may appropriately be regarded as express recognition by Congress that the United States is engaged in a state of partial war in Vietnam.

CONGRESS MAY SPEAK THROUGH APPROPRIATIONS ACTS

The Supreme Court has held that powers can be conferred on the President by appropriations acts. The creation of a new agency by Executive Order was held to have been ratified when Congress appropriated funds for the agency. *Fleming* v. *Mohawk Wrecking & Lumber Co.*, 331 U.S. 111, 67 S.Ct. 1129 (1947), stating:

> And the appropriation by Congress of funds for the use of such agencies stands as confirmation and ratification of the actions of the Chief Executive. 331 U.S. at 116, 67 S.Ct. at 1132.

See also *Brooks* v. *Dewar, 313 U.S. 354, 61 S.Ct. 979 (1941)*. There was a dictum to the same effect in *Ex parte Endo*, 323 U.S. 283, 303 n.24, 65 S.Ct. 208, 219 (1944), so long as the appropriations "plainly show a purpose to bestow the precise authority which is claimed."

Of course, there are instances where appropriations do not confer authority or ratify action—as where there is an appropriation to support an agency, without proof that Congress knew what the agency was doing. *Greene* v. *McElroy*, 360 U.S. 474,

506, 79 S.Ct. 1400, 1418 (1959). The court there held that an appropriation to the Department of Defense for its security program did not constitute ratification of a procedure which denied the right an individual to confront the witnesses against him. The conflict in Vietnam was not something hidden in department regulation; it was a matter of wide discussion in the press and in Congress before the appropriations were made.

An appropriations act is like any other act of Congress. It must be introduced by a member of Congress, and obtain a majority vote in both House and Senate. The Constitution is not concerned with boundaries between the jurisdiction of appropriations sub-committees and substantive committees. Rules limiting amendment, even if enforced, are not of constitutional significance. In fact, appropriations are entitled to special weight because the Congress customarily acts twice, once to authorize the expenditure and again to appropriate money.

While this court ruled above that Congress had met plaintiff's standard of *prior* authorization for high-level military activity, the usual rule permits ratification of any act that could have been authorized. A.L.I., *Restatement of Agency*, 2d (1958) —§§ 84, 92.

Plaintiff contends that any authorizations for Vietnam hostilities are not sufficiently explicit. This argument puts too narrow a limit on Congress' manner of expressing its will. The entire course of legislation shows that Congress knew what it was doing, and that it intended to have American troops fight in Vietnam.

The disclaimers by individual Congressmen of any approval of the Vietnam conflict were dealt with by Judge Dooling, who said:

> Such evidence * * * could only disclose the motive and could not disprove the fact of authorization. *Orlando* v. *Laird,* 3 SSLR at 3146.

3. HOW CONGRESS SHOULD EXPRESS ITSELF IS A POLITICAL QUESTION.

Having found that Congress authorized the sending of American troops to Vietnam, the court would be entering the realm of politics in saying that the authorization should have been couched in different language.

In connection with the French Naval War, it was noted above that the Supreme Court referred to political sentiment in the United States as not supporting a declaration of war against France, but still held that Congress had created a state of limited war. *The Eliza, supra,* 4 U.S. 37.

In connection with the Vietnam conflict, Congress may also have had reasons for acting in a manner short of an express declaration of war. A declaration of war might have consequences far beyond North Vietnam, and might trigger unknown responses from Communist China and the Soviet Union. Congress may also have considered the well known fact that many of our friends in the free world look askance at our Vietnam adventure. To change the professed character of the conflict from a defense of South Vietnam against aggression to a declared war against North Vietnam might affect our relations with friendly powers abroad, and with non-aligned nations.

That Congress may use a variety of methods in authorizing military activities is illustrated by the Supreme Court's statement in *The Prize Cases,* 67 U.S. (2 Black) 635, 670 (1862) that

> If it were necessary to the technical existence of a war, that it should have a legislative sanction, we find it in almost every act passed at the extraordinary session of the Legislature in 1861, which was wholly employed in enacting laws to enable the Government to prosecute the war with vigor and efficiency.

Other Issues

Plaintiff's reliance on Section 5 of the New York Civil Rights Law gives him no support in resisting a constitutionally valid order to report for duty in the armed forces of the United States. The section, set forth in full in the Court of Appeals opinion (p. 3381, n.1), expressly recognizes that any restrictions on the military service of New York citizens must be subject to the Supremacy Clause of the United States Constitution. Art. VI.

This court will not deal with the question whether South

Vietnam or the United States violated the provisions of the Geneva Agreements concerning general elections in Vietnam. That question does not affect the authority given to the President by Congress.

Interpretation of the SEATO Treaty or other international agreements cited by the parties is also unnecessary to the decision of the question of United States "municipal law," whether Congress has authorized American troops to fight in Vietnam.

Conclusion

The Congress repeatedly and unmistakably authorized the use of armed forces of the United States to fight in Vietnam. Whether this was a prudent course of action or a tragic diversion of men and money, is immaterial. The Vietnam conflict cannot be blamed on usurpation by either the Presidents who have held office from 1964 to date. Having reached that decision, the court's function is ended.

It is ORDERED that defendants' motion for summary judgment be granted, and that the Clerk enter judgment dismissing the complaint without costs.

The Impact of the District Courts' Opinions

Although disappointed by the failure of the District Court to rule the war unconstitutional, plaintiffs were encouraged by the court's reaffirmation of judicial review of presidential war power and their total rejection of the president's-inherent-power position. In effect, Judges Dooling and Judd elaborated a requirement of substantial collaboration between the president and Congress as a precondition to the waging of a major war.

Such a standard was quite acceptable.

Plaintiffs could not accept, however, the assumption in both District Court opinions that the substantial collaboration required of Congress by the Constitution could be implied from the passage of appropriations acts generally supportive of the war effort. They believed that Congress's decision to authorize a war had to be explicitly stated. They believed that the legislative history surrounding the Vietnam appropriations bills indicated that it was highly doubtful that Congress had intended them as an expression of approval of the Vietnam war. Moreover, they believed that, regardless of intent, appropriations bills, as a matter of law, simply could not provide the independent, unfettered congressional authorization required to sanction a major war.

The issue of whether congressional authorization of a major war could be implied from appropriations acts or whether it must be concluded independently in explicit terms became the primary legal battleground on which the war cases proceeded to the appellate courts.

PART FOUR

The Appellate Process

By the time Judge Judd issued his decision in *Berk* on September 16, 1970, the burden of litigation in both *Berk* and *Orlando* had been willingly shouldered by the New York Civil Liberties Union.

The *Berk* and *Orlando* cases were consolidated for argument before the United States Court of Appeals for the Second Circuit— the same court which had opened the door in the first *Berk* appeal. Elaborate appellate briefs were prepared by the parties.

The *Berk* brief presented a comprehensive historical attack on the notion that Congress could exercise its war powers by implication and argued that, in fact, Congress, by enacting appropriations bills, had never intended to authorize the war in Vietnam.

The *Orlando* brief presented legal and jurisprudential arguments against the acceptance of any rule of law which permitted congressional assent to war to be implied from appropriations. *Orlando* argued that the factual issue of whether congressmen intended to authorize the war when they voted for appropriations was largely irrelevant, since congressional authorization of a war could not, as a matter of law, be implied from such collateral acts.

The government's brief restated its contention that the court lacked the power to review the legality of the Vietnam war. The government also argued that Congress, by systematically providing support for the war effort, and by passing the Gulf of Tonkin Resolution, had fulfilled its obligation under the war-powers clause of the constitution.

The Consolidated Reply Brief, submitted by Berk and Orlando, dealt primarily with the legal implications of congressional repeal of the Gulf of Tonkin Resolution during the pendency of the appeal.

Extracts from Appellant's Brief, Berk v. Laird, Second Circuit Court of Appeals †

Argument

Point I

> *The lower court erred in holding that appellant's orders were constitutional and that explicit congressional authorization was not constitutionally required to wage a war of the dimensions of Vietnam.*

It is appellant's position that a major war such as Vietnam must be sanctioned and authorized by Congress in an explicit legislative act, and that such authorization cannot be inferred by the passage of appropriations acts to pay for the military forces of the nation. The relevant division of power between Congress and President urged by appellant in this regard is the familiar one, frequently found in the Constitution, namely that

† All bracketed material between this heading and p. 168 was bracketed in the original brief. Cross references to material reproduced in this book have been changed to reflect the paging of this book.

the Congress must explicitly declare a policy and the President must execute the policy set by Congress. The language of the Constitution, the constitutional debates, the early writings of the founding fathers and nearly two hundred years of American history all support the basic proposition that the war power was lodged in Congress alone and that it was to be exercised by Congress in an explicit and definitive manner. There is no support anywhere in our history for the proposition that the constitutional requirement of Congressional authorization can be satisfied from inferences to be drawn from legislative action in the appropriations field.[1]

A. THE CONSTITUTION.

Article I, Section 8, of the Constitution provides:

> "The Congress shall have Power * * *

> To declare War, grant Letters of Marque and Reprisal, and make Rules concerning Captures on Land and Water."

This section vests the entire power to commit the United States to military hostilities to the Congress. War is, of course, the greatest and most complete form of military hostilities; Letters of Marque and Reprisal and Captures involve more specific and limited forms of military activity. Congress was thus given the exclusive power over every form of military activity that might arise.

---

[1] This court in its decision of June 19, 1970 remanded the case with the direction that appellant resolve the "question of when specified joint legislative action is sufficient to authorize various levels of military activity." 429 F.2d at 305 (32a). Such a standard was presented to the district court with extensive supportive material. (See Appendix A to the decision below and Appendix A herein). Appellant has not attempted to reintroduce that material on this appeal in view of Judge Judd's finding that "the Vietnam conflict ranks as a major war" (163a) and this court's prior finding that Executive action alone would be insufficient to carry on such a war. We do not understand the appellees to argue that the Executive has the power to wage the Vietnam war alone. Thus all agree that some mutual participation by Congress is necessary to authorize a major war. According to the constitutional standards set forth by appellant, such a war requires explicit Congressional authorization, as explained herein.

The meaning and purpose of this language is further clarified by examination of the debates of the framers and other contemporary writings. Soon after the Philadelphia Convention opened, the delegates debated the type of powers to be given to the Executive. James Wilson, later one of the first Supreme Court Justices, compared the prerogatives of the British Monarch with those which the American chief executive should possess: "[the English] Prerogatives were not a proper guide in defining the executive powers. Some of these * * * were of a legislative nature. Among others that of war and peace". 1 *Farrand, Records of the Federal Convention*, 65–66 (1911) (hereafter "Farrand").

In one of the early drafts of the Constitution prepared by the Committee of Detail, Congress alone was given the power "to make war." 2 Farrand 182. When the Convention debated this proposal on August 17, 1787, Charles Pinckney of South Carolina suggested that the power be further restricted to the Senate:

> Mr. Pinkney opposed the vesting this power in Legislature. Its proceedings were too slow. It wd. meet but once a year. The Hs. of Reps. would be too numerous for such deliberations. The Senate would be the best depositary, being more acquainted with foreign affairs, and most capable of proper resolutions. 2 Farrand at 318.

Pierce Butler felt the President alone should have that power:

> Mr. Butler. The objections agst the Legislature lie in a great degree agst the Senate. He was for vesting the power in the President, who will have all the requisite qualities, and will not make war but when the Nation will support it. *Ibid.*

But this recommendation was rebuked:

> Mr. Gerry never expected to hear in a republic a motion to empower the Executive alone to declare war. *Ibid.*

James Madison moved that the word "declare" be substituted for "make" which would "leave to the Executive the power to repel sudden attacks." *Ibid.* Roger Sherman agreed that the "Executive should be able to repel and not to com-

mence war.'' *Ibid.* Oliver Ellsworth and George Mason also
spoke to this point:

> Mr. Ellsworth. There is a material difference between the
> cases of making war, and making peace. It shd. be more easy to
> get out of war, than into it. War also is a simple and overt
> declaration, peace attended with intricate & secret negotiations.
>
> Mr. Mason was agst giving the power of war to the Execu-
> tive, because not [safely] to be trusted with it; or to the Senate,
> not so constructed as to be entitled to it. He was for clogging
> rather than facilitating war; but for facilitating peace. He pre-
> ferred "declare" to "make." 2 Farrand 319.

The Convention then passed Madison's amendment.

The Federalist Papers took the same view of the war powers
as those mentioned above. See *Federalist* No. 69 (Cooke ed.
1961):

> The President is to be Commander in Chief of the Army and
> Navy of the United States. In this respect his authority would
> be nominally the same as that of the King of Great Britain, but
> in substance much inferior to it. It would amount to nothing
> more than the supreme command and direction of the military
> and naval forces, as first General and Admiral of the con-
> federacy; while that of the British King extends to the declaring
> of war and to the raising and regulating of fleets and armies; all
> which by the Constitution under consideration would appertain
> to the Legislature. (at 465)

Some years later Alexander Hamilton further explained the
meaning of the war power clauses:

> The Congress shall have the power to declare war; the plain
> meaning of which is, that it is the peculiar and inclusive duty of
> Congress, when the nation is at peace, to change that state into
> a state of war; whether from calculations of policy, or from
> provocations or injuries received; in other words, it belongs to
> Congress only to go to war. But when a foreign nation declares
> or openly and avowedly makes war upon the United States, they
> are then by the very fact already at war, and any declaration on
> the part of Congress is nugatory; it is at least unnecessary. Mor-
> ris, ed. *Alexander Hamilton and the Founding of the Nation,* 256
> (1957).

If, as Hamilton wrote, it is the "peculiar and inclusive" duty of Congress to change the state of peace "into a state of war," that duty cannot be discharged by the President initiating a major war and then asking Congress to pay for the military bills some time after the war has been raging.

The constitutional division of powers as expressed by the framers allows the President as Commander-in-Chief the power to act on his own initiative only to defend against attacks, since Congress might be slow to act, and otherwise to permit him to conduct hostilities after they had been declared by Congress. In this way the presidential power to commit troops to battle was very strictly limited, in part, to avoid many of the evils of the monarchies of Europe. In granting the power to initiate war solely to Congress, it was the framers' declared intention that a decision of such gravity should only be made by the people's representatives.

B. SUBSEQUENT INTERPRETATION.

The language of the Constitution as originally set forth by the framers does not come before this court for interpretation as a matter of first impression. Nearly two hundred years of our history have given life and more definite scope to the boundary lines encompassed in the language of the Constitution.

The meaning of the war clause and its specific application to concrete situations have been faced numerous times in our history. It has become recognized that the Executive has the power to initiate certain limited forms of military activities, along with the more general power to repel direct attacks on the United States that was understood by the framers to be inherent in the word "declare". Included in the limited emergency instances are numerous cases where the President used military force to protect American citizens or property located in foreign countries, or to commit reprisals against politically unorganized bandits or pirates.[2]

---

[2] As noted in the proposed standard, the Executive has the authority to initiate hostilities without Congressional sanction in four separate instances: (1) to repel sudden attack; (2) to protect American citizens or property abroad;

Beyond these very limited powers, it has been recognized, declared and accepted by President, Congress and Court alike that the Executive has no power to initiate or prosecute hostilities without having been first authorized to do so by Congress. Set out in Appendix B to this brief are the statements of Presidents Jefferson, Madison, Jackson, Polk, Buchanan, Lincoln, Grant, Arthur, Taft and Roosevelt, all of which confirm the recent National Commitments Report of the Senate Foreign Relations Committee to the effect that:

> the founders of our country intended decisions to initiate either general or limited hostilities against foreign countries to be made by the Congress, not by the executive. Far from altering the intent of the framers, as is sometimes alleged, the practice of American Presidents for over a century after independence showed scrupulous respect for the authority of the Congress except in a few instances. The only uses of military power that can be said to have legitimately accrued to the executive in the course of the nation's history have been for certain specific purposes such as suppressing piracy and the slave trade, "hot pursuit" of fugitives, and, as we have noted, response to sudden attack. Only

(3) to pursue politically unorganized pirates or bandits; (4) to protect American interests when immediate action or secret planning is necessary. This standard has been accepted by the State Department; see testimony of Under Secretary of State Nicholas Katzenbach before the Senate Foreign Relations Committee: "I think it [the commitment of troops without the consent of Congress] can be done certainly when they are attacked themselves directly. I think it can be done for the purpose of protection of American citizens, American shipping, that kind of obligation of which there is abundant historical precedent, and I think he can do it in an emergency if circumstances require rapid action. . . ." United States Committments to Foreign Powers, *Hearings before Committee on Foreign Relations,* U.S. Senate, 90th Cong. 1st Sess. on S. Res. 151 (1967), p. 99. Of the 162 instances in which American troops were sent into hostilities abroad, 99 involved temporary expeditions to protect American citizens, 19 involved an attack on politically unorganized pirates or bandits, 10 involved an excursion into contingent American territory (Florida, Mexico or Oregon) to protect American borders; in six cases Naval forces were used to open trade routes and in five others American troops made a peaceful intrusion under an existing treaty. In the ten most serious cases before 1950, Congressional authorization was secured by way of a declaration of war or explicit Congressional legislation. See Instances of the Use of United States Armed Forces Abroad, *Hearings before the Committee on Foreign Relations* and *Committee on Armed Services on the Situation in Cuba,* U.S. Senate, 87th Cong. 2d Sess. (1962) pp. 84–88.

in the present century have Presidents used the Armed Forces of the United States against foreign governments entirely on their own authority, and only since 1950 have Presidents regarded themselves as having authority to commit the Armed Forces to full-scale and sustained warfare. *Senate Report No. 91–129* to accompany *S. Res. 85*. 91st Cong., 1st Sess. April 16, 1969, p. 31.

The power of Congress to declare war has also been given more certain meaning by the course of events. The power, as it has evolved, has not been restricted to an inflexible and mechanistic requirement that the talismanic words "We declare war" be uttered. As it has become understood and applied, the declaration power is a flexible instrument to be used by Congress to give precise authorization to the President and to set guidelines as to the purpose and scope of military hostilities to be conducted by the President.

Congress has declared war five times: to begin the War of 1812 (2 Stat. 755), the Mexican War of 1846 (9 Stat. 9) the Spanish American War of 1898 (30 Stat. 738), World War I (40 Stat. 1) and World War II (55 Stat. 795). It also gave the President unlimited powers to meet the emergencies of the Civil War (12 Stat. 326). In numerous other cases Congress has authorized the Executive to involve the nation in military hostilities of a secondary nature, involving a less than maximum commitment of the nation's military resources. Even in these secondary military commitments, falling far below the level of commitment reached in the Vietnamese conflict, explicit Congressional approval was sought and forthcoming.

For example the naval war with France, waged from 1798–1801, was authorized by explicit Congressional resolution. 1 Stat. 561; [3] 1 Stat. 572, extended 2 Stat. 39 (April 22, 1800); 1 Stat. 574; 1 Stat. 578; 1 Stat. 743; see discussion in *Bas* v. *Tingey*, 4 Dall. 37 (1800); *Talbot* v. *Seeman*, 1 Cranch 1 (1801).

The naval war against Tripoli (1802) was authorized by explicit Congressional resolution. 2 Stat. 129.

---

[3] It should be noted that such resolutions clearly authorized the use of force and that there was no problem of interpreting questionable and ambiguous

The naval war against Algiers (1815) was authorized by explicit Congressional resolution. 3 Stat. 230 (March 3, 1815).

In 1839 Congress specifically authorized the President "to resist any attempt on the part of Great Britain to enforce, by arms, her claim to exclusive jurisdiction over that part of Maine which is in dispute . . . and for that purpose to employ the naval and military force of the United States" 5 Stat. 355. By joint resolution of June 2, 1858, President James Buchanan was authorized by Congress to use such force as "may be necessary and advisable" to settle differences with Paraguay, 11 Stat. 370. The President was also empowered to initiate hostilities against Venezuela in 1890 after three American steamships had been seized, 26 Stat. 674. Following the capture of eight American sailors by the Mexican Army in 1914, Congress permitted President Wilson to employ the "armed forces to enforce his demands for unequivocal amends for affronts and indignities committed against the United States," 38 Stat. 770.

All of these declarations, laws and resolutions show Congress, acting under its constitutional powers, working swiftly in collaboration with the Executive to meet threats or difficulties

---

Congressional language in other areas. Thus the resolution of May 28, 1798 authorizing the naval war with France read:

> CHAP. XLVIII.—*An Act more effectually to protect the Commerce and Coasts of the United States.*
>
> WHEREAS armed vessels sailing under authority or pretence of authority from the Republic of France, have committed depredations on the commerce of the United States, and have recently captured the vessels and property of citizens thereof, on and near the coasts, in violation of the law of nations, and treaties between the United States and the French nation. Therefore:
>
> *Be it enacted by the Senate and House of Representatives of the United States of America in Congress assembled,* That it shall be lawful for the President of the United States, and he is hereby authorized to instruct and direct the commanders of the armed vessels belonging to the United States to seize, take and bring into any port of the United States, to be proceeded against according to the laws of nations, any such armed vessel which shall have committed or which shall be found hovering on the coasts of the United States, for the purpose of committing depredations on the vessels belonging to citizens thereof; and also to retake any ship or vessel, of any citizen or citizens of the United States which may have been captured by any such armed vessel. 1 Stat. 561

abroad. None of the supposed problems concerning legislative co-operation with the Executive occurred—there were no endless deliberations or weakening vacillations or compromises, nor were there two governmental voices speaking to the world on behalf of the United States. The constitutional collaboration planned by the framers worked as they foresaw.

Furthermore, Congress has continued to insist on the most explicit kind of authorization before hostilities can be commenced. The Senate Foreign Relations Committee recommended in its recent National Commitments Report:

> The committee therefore recommends that, in considering future resolutions involving the use or possible use of the Armed Forces, Congress—
> (1) debate the proposed resolution at sufficient length to establish a legislative record showing the intent of Congress;
> (2) use the words *authorize* or *empower* or such other language as will leave no doubt that Congress alone has the right to authorize the initiation of war and that, in granting the President authority to use the Armed Forces, Congress is granting him power that he would not otherwise have;
> (3) state in the resolution as explicitly as possible under the circumstances the kind of military action that is being authorized and the place and purpose of its use; and
> (4) put a time limit on the resolution, thereby assuring Congress the opportunity to review its decision and extend or terminate the President's authority to use military force. *Senate Report No. 91–129, op. cit.* p. 33.

This position was confirmed last year in the National Commitments Resolution, S. Res. 85, 91st Cong., 1st Sess. passed by a vote of 70 to 16 on June 25, 1969 (115 *Cong. Rec.* 17245):

> Resolved, That (1) a national commitment for the purpose of this resolution means the use of the armed forces of the United States on foreign territory, or a promise to assist a foreign country, government, or people by the use of the armed forces or financial resources of the United States either immediately or upon the happening of certain events, and (2) it is the sense of the Senate that a national commitment by the United States results only from affirmative action taken by the executive and legis-

lative branches of the United States Government by means of a treaty, statute, or concurrent resolution of both Houses of Congress specifically providing for such commitment.

From the earliest days of our history, the federal courts fixed the boundaries of the Executive's military authority in accordance with the above standard. In *The Flying Fish* (*Little* v. *Barreme*), 6 U.S. (2 Cranch) 170 (1804), Congress had forbidden intercourse with France and instructed the President to use military forces to seize American vessels bound to French ports. The President issued an order to navel commanders that was broader in scope and the Flying Fish was seized while bound to a neutral port. The Flying Fish, which was found to be a Danish vessel, was awarded damages against the naval captain for the unlawful detention. The defenses of the captain that he was acting within the scope of his instructions from the President, and that he had probable cause to detain the vessel because the log had been thrown overboard, were held to be insufficient. There was no suggestion in Chief Justice Marshall's opinion that the Executive had inherent war powers himself which allowed him to exceed the limits explicitly established by Congress.

In *Ex parte Milligan,* 71 U.S. (4 Wall.) 2, 139 (1866), the Supreme Court held that the President did not have the power to establish military tribunals to try civilians without the authorization of Congress. It stated "But neither can the President, in war more than in peace, intrude upon the proper authority of Congress, nor Congress upon the proper authority of the President."

Squarely in point is *Youngstown Sheet & Tube Co.* v. *Sawyer,* 343 U.S. 579 (1952), where the Supreme Court enjoined the Secretary of Commerce from seizing and operating a number of the nation's steel mills. The President sought to sustain his power to act in that instance squarely on the war power, asserting that steel was essential to the war effort then being conducted in Korea. The government also argued that an adverse decision would hurt the war effort and cause chaos, the very arguments made here. Nonetheless, the Court decided that under the Constitution the question of whether the steel mills should be seized was committed to Congress. The Supreme Court granted the injunction, based on its view that the Executive had exceeded its constitutional powers. If the steel mills of this country are entitled to enjoin an unlawful seizure of their property based on a purported authority arising out of the war power, surely the nation's ordinary citizens ordered to a war theater are equally entitled to an injunction to protect themselves against arbitrary and unauthorized actions by the President based on a purported war power.

C. RECENT DECISIONS.

This view of the scope of the Executive's war power is confirmed by all the recent decisions on the Vietnam War. This court's decision of June 19, as well as Judge Judd's opinion below, Judge Dooling's opinion in *Orlando,* and Judge Sweigert's opinion in *Mottola* † are all in accord that executive action alone is insufficient to initiate and carry on the war in Vietnam. The contention that the Executive can act on his own cannot seriously be raised in this case.

Thus, this court said: "If the executive branch engaged the nation in prolonged foreign military activities without any significant congressional authorization, a court might be able to determine that this extreme step violated a discoverable standard calling for some mutual participation by Congress in accordance with Article I, section 8." 429 F.2d at 305 (31a).

Judge Dooling wrote in *Orlando:*

> Neither the language of the Constitution nor the debates of the time leave any doubt that the power to declare and wage war was pointedly denied to the presidency. In no real sense was there even an exception for emergency action and certainly not for a self-defined emergency power in the presidency. The debates, so often strangely—to our ears—devoid of respect for and alive with fears of the presidency that the Convention was forming,

† a new case challenging the constitutionality of the war was started by a University of California law student, Gary Mottola. The federal judge hearing the case refused to dismiss the action on political-question grounds and held that Mottola, an army reservist, had standing to bring the lawsuit. See 318 F. Supp. 538 (N.D. Calif. 1970).

are clear in the view that (as Wilson put it) the power to make war and peace are legislative. 3 SSLR at 3145.

The Court in *Mottola* commented:

> The question remains, however, whether the President may otherwise initiate or continue a war operation, such as the Vietnam operation has now become, without requesting as soon as reasonably possible, and receiving, a congressional authorization, either general or limited, but in any event phrased to indicate a congressional intent to consent, pursuant to its prerogative under Article I, Section 8(11), to the initiation or continuance of the war.
>
> Most commentators and some courts concede that the Vietnam operation has now obviously gone far beyond mere emergency repulsion of any 1964 Tonkin Gulf attack upon our armed forces and that it is obviously a "war" within the meaning of Article I, Section 8(11); that it has come to involve not only defensive, but also offensive military operations of great magnitude, and that it has continued over a period more than sufficiently long to permit and to require exercise by the Congress of its power and responsibility under Article I, Section 8(11). 3 SSLR at 3312–13.

In sum, it is well recognized that the Executive may act alone to defend United States property, territory or citizens in an emergency situation where the necessity to use force is clear and urgent and the extent of the use is limited. However, the President cannot engage the country in major combat without the authorization of Congress. Such a major war is the Vietnam War, as the lower court found. The question on appeal, therefore, is whether there has been proper Congressional authorization. We submit there has not.

We do not suggest, nor need this Court decide, that a formal Congressional declaration of war is required for every military action. Nor is this Court called upon to delineate precisely what legislative action is required to authorize every conceivable military move by the government, whether it be the use of bombers in Laos or Cambodia, the dispatch of military advisors to Latin America, or the shipment of radar equipment to Israel.[4] We deal

---

[4] Appellant's standard recognizes that emergency situations may arise when swift Executive action is necessary and the Executive may believe that there

only with the current military activity in Vietnam, which the lower court found as a fact constitutes a major war:

> In number of men involved (accepting for this purpose the 3,000,000 figure used by plaintiff), numbers of [Americans] killed (42,000) and wounded (280,000), amounts of equipment (half our entire air force), and amounts of money expended (over $100 billion), the Vietnam conflict ranks as a major war. (162a–163a)

At no time has the basis of our military involvement in Vietnam been based on one of the emergency powers of the President—nor, in view of the length and scope of the war, could it

simply is no time to secure Congressional authorization. In such cases, as the Harvard Law Review note on Presidential war power comments, "where he believes that Congress would agree with his judgment that the interest at stake is worth defending at the risk of war, the President should be able to take action while *simultaneously* seeking Congressional authorization." "Congress, the President, and the Power to Commit Troops to Combat," 81 *Harv. L. Rev.* 1771, 1797 (1968). Furthermore, in conflicts which gradually escalate, a useful dividing line can be found, as noted by a leading international law expert, Professor John Norton Moore:

> As a dividing line for presidential authority in the use of the military abroad, one test might be to require congressional authorization in all cases where regular combat units are committed to sustained hostilities. This test would be likely to include most situations resulting in substantial casualties and substantial commitment of resources. Under this test, the Mexican War, the Korean War and the Vietnam War would all require congressional authorization. The test has the virtue of responsiveness to precisely those situations historically creating the greatest concern over presidential authority but like all tests is somewhat frayed at the edges. In conflicts which gradually escalate, the dividing line for requiring congressional authorization might be initial commitment to combat of regular United States combat units as such. As to the suddenness of Korea and conflicts like Korea, I would argue that the president should have the authority to meet the attack as necessary but should immediately seek congressional authorization. In retrospect the decision not to obtain Congressional authorization in the Korean War, in which the United States sustained more than 140,000 casualties seems a poor precedent. John Norton Moore, "The National Executive and the Use of the Armed Forces Abroad," in 2 Falk ed, *The Vietnam War and International Law,* 814 (1969).

Any escalation from a lower order of conflict to a major war requires the same type of explicit Congressional authorization as a major war would have required in the first instance. Otherwise the requirement of Congressional participation would be completely undercut by a series of moves each raising the level of conflict by several degrees until it reaches a maximum stage.

conceivably be. Therefore, the Executive must point to some specific congressional authorization pursuant to the Constitution for the current military activities. Appellees and the lower court appear to have accepted this basic principle. We turn therefore to the purported Congressional authorization on which they rely.

Point II

The lower court erred in holding that the Gulf of Tonkin Resolution authorizes the Vietnam war and thereby authorizes the orders to appellant.

The court below relied on the Gulf of Tonkin Resolution (P.L. 88-408, 78 Stat. 384, Aug. 10, 1964) as authorizing the Vietnam War:

> * * * the Resolution gave him [the President] authority to prevent aggression against Southeast Asia peoples who were protecting their freedom. This court cannot say that the present conflict is "wider" than was authorized by the Joint Resolution and the subsequent acts of Congress. (182a)

That conclusion is curious because the Executive itself has expressly conceded since 1967 that *it does not rely* on the Gulf of Tonkin Resolution for authority to carry on military operations in Southeast Asia. That concession, we submit, removes the issue from this case.

On August 18, 1967, more than three years ago, President Johnson disclaimed reliance on the Tonkin Resolution when he said:

> We did not think the resolution was necessary to do what we did and what we are doing. But we thought * * * if we were going to ask them to stay the whole route, and if we expected them to be there on the landing, we ought to ask them to be there on the takeoff. *Hearings on S. Res. 151 Before the Senate Comm. on Foreign Relations,* 90th Cong., 1st Sess. 126 (1967).

As recently as March 12, 1970, the State Department took the same position in an official communication to the Senate Foreign

Relations Committee which was considering repeal of the Tonkin Resolution.

> [T]his administration has not relied on or referred to the Tonkin Gulf resolution of August 10, 1964, as support for its Vietnam policy. * * * [T]he administration does not consider the continued existence of th[is] resolution * * * as evidence of congressional authorization for or acquiescence in any new military efforts or as substitute for the policy of appropriate and timely congressional consultation to which the administration is firmly committed. *Letter from H. G. Torbert, Jr., Acting Assistant Secretary of State for Congressional Relations to Senator J. William Fulbright.* Quoted in Senate Report No. 91-872, 91st Cong., 2d Sess. 20, 23 (1970).

The Senate did in fact repeal the Tonkin Resolution on June 24, 1970 by the overwhelming vote of 81 to 10, (116 *Cong. Rec.* S 9670, daily ed. June 24, 1970). It is important to note that the amendment to repeal the Resolution was introduced by a spokesman for the current Administration, Senator Robert Dole and was not opposed by the Administration. Senator Dole, speaking on behalf of the Administration, made it clear that the Executive does not rely on the Tonkin Resolution, as the following exchange demonstrates:

> MR. EAGLETON: As the author of the Dole amendment, which would repeal the Gulf of Tonkin resolution, does the Senator, as the principal author of the amendment, view the Gulf of Tonkin resolution as authority for 400,000 troops being in South Vietnam today?
>
> MR. DOLE: No, and President Nixon has not relied on it. *Ibid.* S. 9598, (daily ed. June 23, 1970).

Senator Dole also said:

> The point, I might say, is that this administration has not relied upon the Gulf of Tonkin resolution and does not now rely upon the Gulf of Tonkin resolution. I assume the Senator from Missouri favors repeal of the Gulf of Tonkin resolution, as does the Senator from Kansas. There is no opposition to its repeal from the administration. They are not relying on the Gulf of Tonkin resolution. They have not relied on the Gulf of Tonkin resolution. *Ibid.* S. 9591.

Clearly the Executive, having supported the repeal of the Tonkin Resolution, could not consider such action tantamount to Congressional repeal of authorization of the war. How then can the original passage be urged as authorization for the war?

The fact that the State Department officially informed Congress that the Tonkin Resolution was not legal authority for its actions in Southeast Asia should bar appellees from taking a contrary position in this litigation. It is one thing for spokesmen of the Executive Department to claim in a political speech that the Gulf of Tonkin Resolution is not authority for continued actions in Vietnam. It is quite another for the Administration to represent to Congress in an official comment on proposed legislation that the Resolution is not being relied upon. Such an official representation might well lead Congress to forego legislative action which it would otherwise take. In the face of this official position, the appellees should not be heard to urge a contrary position.

Nor could such a contrary position be sustained. For Congress, in passing the resolution, did not intend to give the Executive the authority to launch and wage a war in Southeast Asia.

The resolution has a very narrow purpose. It was enacted in response to a particular set of circumstances in the Gulf of Tonkin. On August 5, 1964, the President asked Congress for "a resolution expressing the unity and determination of the United States in supporting and in protecting peace in southeast Asia." The Executive reported that on August 2 and August 4, 1964, two United States naval vessels operating in international waters in the Gulf of Tonkin were attacked by North Vietnamese patrol boats, and that on August 4, 1964, in response to these incidents he had ordered retaliatory air attacks on the North Vietnamese torpedo-boat bases and their oil-storage depots. 110 *Cong. Rec.* 18132 (1964). As the State Department itself has pointed out, Congress passed the Resolution in response to that specific situation. It understood that it only approved the Executive's limited response to that specific situation; and it did not authorize massive military activity in Southeast Asia:

Each of the resolutions specified in section 1 [Formosa resolution, Middle East resolution, Cuba resolution and Gulf of Tonkin resolution] was passed in respnse to a crisis situation in the affected area. Thus * * * the Tonkin Gulf resolution responded to an assault upon our naval forces in international waters * * *

The crisis circumstances giving rise to these resolutions have long since passed. As indicated by the specific analyses below, the administration is not depending on any of these resolutions as legal or constitutional authority for its present conduct of foreign relations or its contingency plans. *Letter of H. G. Torbert,* Acting Assistant Secretary of State quoted in Senate Report No. 91-872, *op. cit.,* p. 20.

The Gulf of Tonkin Resolution (209a) is substantially less precise than resolutions that Congress used in other situations. The Formosa Resolution (P.L. 84-4, 69 Stat. 7, January 29, 1955), for example, specifically authorized the use of armed forces to defend Formosa and the Pescadores:

Resolved by the Senate and House of Representatives of the United States of America in Congress assembled, That the President of the United States be and he hereby is authorized to employ the Armed Forces of the United States as he deems necessary for the specific purpose of securing and protecting Formosa and the Pescadores against armed attack, this authority to include the securing and protection of such related positions and territories of that area now in friendly hands and the taking of such other measures as he judges to be required or appropriate in assuring the defense of Formosa and the Pescadores.

The Formosa Resolution expressly authorizes use of the Armed Forces of the United States; and the Tonkin Resolution does not. The Formosa Resolution sets a specific goal for the use of the Armed Forces: it specifies the area to be defended and other action to be taken (securing and protecting related positions). The Tonkin Resolution does not.

Although the last clause gives the President a certain amount of discretion in protecting Formosa, it has never been claimed that the Formosa Resolution constitutes authority to send 500,-000 American soldiers to fight on mainland Asia against Red China. Yet precisely such a claim is now being made with respect to a wholly ambiguous resolution that did not authorize any specific action.

That the Gulf of Tonkin Resolution was not intended to authorize anything more than a response to the specific situation that precipitated it and that it was not intended to authorize a major war is clear from its legislative history.

In his message to Congress on August 5, 1964 requesting the Resolution, the President did not ask Congress to authorize greater levels of military activity [5] for or to change the nature of the military operations in the Indochina area. On the contrary, he said:

> As I have repeatedly made clear, the United States intends no rashness and seeks no wider war. 110 *Cong. Rec.* 18132.

Just as the President did not request it, statements made on the floor of Congress indicate that Congress did not intend to authorize any change in the nature of the military operations in Vietnam.

During the debates on the Tonkin Resolution, Senator Brewster observing that he "would look with great dismay on * * * the landing of large [American] land armies on the continent of Asia," asked Senator Fulbright whether there was anything in the resolution which would approve, authorize or recommend the landing of large American armies in Vietnam or China. *Id.* at 18403. Senator Fulbright replied, "There is nothing in the Resolution, as I read it, that contemplates it. I agree with the Senator that that is the last thing we would want to do." *Id.* Senator Morton shared Senator Brewster's concern that the United States might send large American armies to southeast Asia. *Id.* at 18404. Senator Fulbright again agreed that the purpose of the Tonkin Resolution was to prevent this from happening. *Id.* Senator Nelson then asked whether Congress, by enacting the Tonkin Resolution, would be agreeing in advance that

[5] At the time of the Executive's request, the level of military forces was between 18,000 to 20,000 troops. 116 *Cong. Rec.* S. 9591 (daily ed. June 23, 1970) (Remarks of Senator Dole). By the end of 1964, the military forces in Vietnam had not greatly increased and are reported to have totaled 23,300. U.S. Bureau of the Census, *Statistical Abstract of the United States: 1968* 258 (89th ed. 1968).

the President could land as many divisions as he deemed necessary and could then engage in direct military assault on North Vietnam. *Id.* at 18406. In response, Senator Fulbright indicated that this was not the sense of the Resolution and that he thought it would be very unwise under any circumstances to put a large land army on the Asian continent. Senator Nelson also made the following statement:

> I do not think * * * that Congress should leave the impression that it consents to a radical change in our mission or objective in South Vietnam * * * I would be most concerned if the Congress should say that we intend by joint resolution to authorize a complete change in the mission which we have had in South Vietnam for the past 10 years and which we have repeatedly stated was not a commitment to engage in a direct land confrontation with our Army as a substitute for the South Vietnam Army or as a substantially reinforced U.S. Army to be joined with the South Vietnam Army in a war against North Vietnam and possibly China. *Id.* at 18407.

Senator Russell was also of the opinion that the sole purpose of the Resolution was to approve the retaliatory action that the President ordered in defense of the United States ships in the Gulf of Tonkin. *Id.* at 18411.

On the House side, Representative Morgan, Chairman of the House Committee on Foreign Affairs, stated unequivocally, "This *is definitely not an advance declaration of war.* The committee has been assured by the Secretary of State that the constitutional prerogative of the Congress in this respect will continue to be scrupulously observed." *Id.* at 18539 (emphasis added). On this same point, Congressman Adair said that Congress did not want the approval of the Tonkin Resolution to indicate that Congress was giving approval in advance for the President to take such actions as he might see fit to take in the future. *Id.* at 18543. Moreover, Congressman Fascell explicitly stated:

> This resolution is not a declaration of war. The language of the resolution makes that clear as does the legislative history. Therefore this resolution in no way impinges on the prerogative

of the Congress to declare war. Furthermore, no one here today has advocated a declaration of war. * * *

Mr. Speaker, the pending resolution does, however, ratify and support the military action recently ordered and taken by President Johnson to respond to the unprovoked Communist armed attack against the U.S. Navy while in international waters. *Id.* at 18549.

It is uncontrovertible that it was not the intention of Congress in passing the Tonkin Resolution to authorize a major war in Indochina. Rather Congress intended to express nothing more than its approval of the President's response to the specific situation that gave rise to it and the unity and purpose that President Johnson requested.

The language of the resolution carries out this intent and nothing more. Section 1 of the resolution states that "the Congress approves and supports the determination of the President, as Commander in Chief, to take all necessary measures to repel any armed attack against the forces of the United States and to prevent further aggression." Manifestly, the resolution *does not* grant him authority "to prevent aggression against Southeast Asia peoples who were protecting their freedom," (182a) as the lower court stated. Rather it "approves and supports" the Executive's exercise of his constitutional authority as Commander-in-Chief in response to the specific situation that gave rise to the resolution. It merely approves his "determination." It does not authorize him to engage in a major war.

This interpretation is clearly revealed in the floor debates at the time of its passage. Senator Fulbright, Chairman of the Senate Foreign Relations Committee, which jointly reported the resolution, stated:

We are not giving to the President any powers he has under the Constitution as Commander-in-Chief. We are in effect approving of his use of the powers that he has. 110 *Cong. Rec.* 18409 (1964).

The debate continued:

MR. COOPER: I understand that, too. In the first section we are confirming the powers.

MR. FULBRIGHT: We are approving them. I do not know that we give him anything that he does not already have.

* * *

MR. COOPER: We support and approve his judgment.

MR. RUSSELL: Approve and support.

MR. FULBRIGHT: Approve and support the use he has made of his powers.

The court in *Mottola* has interpreted the Resolution in the same way:

> It will be noted, * * * that the first part of the Resolution, an expression of approval and support for the President's determination "to repel attack against the forces of the United States," falls far short of a declaration of war, or even of implied authorization for the kind of all out, full scale war subsequently launched by the President in Vietnam. 3 SSLR at 3314

Section 2 of the resolution states, in part:

> Consonant with the Constitution of the United States * * * and in accordance with its obligations under the Southeast Asia Collective Defense Treaty, the United States is, therefore, prepared, as the President determines, to take all necessary steps, including the use of armed force, to assist any member or protocol state of the Southeast Asia Collective Defense Treaty requesting assistance in defense of its freedom.

This section is no more than the statement of "unity and determination" that the President requested. The Congress did not declare to authorize war; it instead affirmed that "[c]onsonant with the Constitution * * * the United States is * * * *prepared* * * * to take all necessary steps." *Tonkin Resolution* § 2 (emphasis added †).

It does not authorize the President to take steps, it merely asserts in a warning that the United States Government as a whole is "prepared" to take steps. Moreover, it expressly states that such steps will be taken only "consonant with the Constitution," i.e. that they will only be taken upon Congressional authorization pursuant to Article I, Section 8.

† In original brief.

Point III

The district court erred in holding that military spending acts could be construed as ratification or authorization of the Vietnam war and thereby authorized the orders to appellant.

The Constitutional text, debates and the subsequent interpretation described in Point I show that explicit Congressional authorization is necessary to initiate and wage a major war. Nevertheless the court below and Judge Dooling in *Orlando* found that Congress had in fact authorized the Vietnam War merely by passing military appropriation bills.

These rulings were unprecedented. No court has ever found that an appropriations bill could be a substitute for explicit exercise of any enumerated power in Article I, Section 8, much less the power to declare war. Moreover, it cannot be shown that Congress intended the appropriations bills to constitute an authorization for the war. In addition, as demonstrated below, an appropriations act can never be constitutionally adequate to authorize a major war.

A. THE ACTS DO NOT AS A MATTER OF FACT AUTHORIZE THE WAR.

Since 1964 when the United States' involvement in Vietnam increased from more than adviser level, there have been eighteen laws passed by Congress relating to military expenditures for our armed forces: eight authorization bills and ten appropriations bills (Wallace affidavit, 57a). Of these eighteen bills passed, five contain no reference to Vietnam. The other acts merely authorize or appropriate money to be spent for our forces in Vietnam.

1. THE TEXT OF THE APPROPRIATIONS ACTS:

The various appropriations acts passed do not by their terms explicitly authorize or empower the Executive to carry on hostilities in Vietnam. The first such act (P.L. 89-18, 79 Stat. 109, May 7, 1965) stated in its entirety:

> The following is appropriated, out of any money in the Treasury not otherwise appropriated, for the period ending June 30, 1965, namely:
>
> Department of Defense Emergency Fund, Southeast Asia
>
> For transfer by the Secretary of Defense, upon determination by the President that such action is necessary in connection with military activities in southeast Asia, to any appropriation available to the Department of Defense for military functions, to be merged with and to be available for the same purposes and for the same time period as the appropriations to which transferred $700,000,000, to remain available until expended: * * *.

The next such law (P.L. 89-214, 79 Stat. 863, Sept. 29, 1965) repeated the same language, but appropriated $1.7 billion.

The third law (P.L. 89-367, 80 Stat. 36, March 15, 1966) read:

> Sec. 401. (a) Funds authorized for appropriation for the use of the Armed Forces of the United States under this or any other Act are authorized to be made available for their stated purposes in connection with support of Vietnamese and other free world forces in Vietnam, and related costs, during the fiscal years 1966 and 1967, on such terms and conditions as the Secretary of Defense may determine.

Later laws carried forward the same type of language.

In no way can such bills be construed as authorizing the war in Vietnam. They do not empower, authorize, or sanction combat. They simply appropriate a certain sum of money "in connection with military activities in Southeast Asia," or "in support of Vietnamese and other free world forces in Vietnam." As the Supreme Court held in *Ex Parte Endo,* 323 U.S. 283, 303, n. 24, an appropriations statute must '*plainly show* a purpose to bestow the *precise* authority which is claimed," (emphasis added) if additional legal significance is claimed for it. Certainly such precise authority is lacking in the statutes cited.

2. LEGISLATIVE HISTORY

Nor is there anything in the legislative history of these bills that will fill the crucial void.[6] In fact the legislative history is precisely to the contrary. Viewed most generously in favor of appellees' position, the legislative history of the appropriations bills cannot show any manifestation of Congressional intent to ratify or authorize the war.

At the very outset of the Congressional debates on Vietnam authorization and appropriations bill, key Congressional figures made clear that they were *not* to be considered as determining policy in any way or as authorizing any military moves by the Executive. Thus Senator Richard Russell, Chairman of the Senate Armed Forces Committee which was responsible for framing all defense authorization bills, said on February 16, 1966 when he introduced the first supplemental authorization bill that focused on Vietnam appropriations:

> I do not wish to make a disingenuous argument, but I think it important that the Senate and the Nation clearly recognize this bill for what it is: an authorization of defense appropriations. It could not properly be considered as determining foreign policy, as ratifying decisions made in the past, or as endorsing new commitments.
>
> That ours is a Government of three equal and coordinate branches and that there are checks and balances in this system are concepts we all learn in elementary civics. Under the Constitution, the President is the Commander in Chief of the Armed Forces. By approving or disapproving a bill of this type, Congress can neither enlarge nor diminish the President's power to command these forces; it merely can influence how many members of the Armed Forces the President has to command, and determine the nature of the equipment with which they will be provided, and how they will be cared for and protected. 112 *Cong. Rec.* 3135.

---

[6] Since the appropriations bills do not by their own terms authorize hostilities, resort to legislative history is appropriate. *United States* v. *Louisiana,* 363 U.S. 1, 16 (1960). *United States* v. *Public Utilities Commission,* 345 U.S. 295, 315 (1953).

Senator Russell acknowledged that Congress did have an important voice in foreign relations, but that voice should not be expressed in military money bills:

> Of course, I would not suggest that Congress does not have a role in the formulation of foreign policy. Under the division of legislative labor that Congress has prescribed for itself, the Senate Committee on Foreign Relations and the House Committee on Foreign Affairs are the instrumentalities specializing in foreign relations. Accordingly, I think it is important to emphasize that it would be inappropriate for this authorization to be used as a poll of congressional opinion on whether our foreign policy is sound. In my opinion, such action would tend to oust the jurisdiction of the committees charged with primary responsibility for such consideration. Instead, I prefer to think of this authorization as facilitating the arming and equipping of persons in the Armed Forces with the most effective weapons to assure their survival when they are carrying out the orders of their Commander in Chief. *Ibid.*

As noted in the debates described in detail in the Appendix (52a-83a) this view was constantly expressed by Congressional leaders both supporting and opposing the government's war policy.

The debates show quite clearly that Congress never considered its vote on the appropriations bills as sanctioning or authorizing the war in any way. The chief reason for the consistent appropriations toward the war has been that Congress has found itself confronted by a *fait accompli.* With American troops having been committed to action, most Congressmen undoubtedly felt that they could not as a matter of common humanity undercut the fighting men by withholding appropriations.

During the debate on the national commitments resolution, Senator Joseph Tydings said:

> It might be suggested that Congress has the opportunity to make the resource-allocation choice when it passes on defense appropriations. It is true that, in many areas, national priorities are established through the appropriations process. But once our military might has been committed to action, we cannot undercut our fighting men. The issue on a single defense appropriation

bill becomes couched in terms of whether we can afford to give our boys less than maximum protection. Congress never has the opportunity to decide if we can afford to have them risking their lives at all—in other words, whether our priorities permit allocating a significant portion of our manpower and economic resources to certain military objectives. 115 *Cong. Rec.* 17243–44. (June 25, 1969)

Senator Pastore once said:

> MR. PASTORE: Mr. President, I shall vote for this bill. I believe that all of us feel, right down deep in our hearts, that however we feel about Vietnam, we are there now, and cannot take our feeling out on those boys by not supporting this bill. 113 *Cong. Rec.* 23501 (August 22, 1967)

But the Senate "doves" were not the only ones to take this position. Senator John Stennis, for example, during the National Commitments debate said:

> I feel very strongly that the resolution, if adopted, will be the first step whereby Congress, and especially the Senate, can reestablish its coequal role in foreign relations. The resolution asks only that the legislative branch be consulted during the decision-making process with respect to national commitments. It is not enough that we be informed on an after-the-fact basis and then handed the responsibility to provide the men, money and material resources to fulfill commitments already made by the executive branch. The adoption of the resolution, in my judgment, will contribute substantially to the restoration of the constitutional balance between the executive and legislative departments. 115 *Cong. Rec.* 17241. (June 25, 1969).

Senator Sam Ervin of North Carolina said:

> If the President takes action and puts our troops into battle overseas in an offensive war, and our boys are being shot at and killed, Congress is put into a position where it must furnish them with weapons to defend themselves on foreign soil. "U.S. Commitments to Foreign Powers," *Hearings before the Committee on Foreign Relations, U.S. Senate,* 90th Cong. 1st Sess. on S. Res. 151 (1967), p. 220.

Many legislators who found themselves voting for the defense appropriations bills expressed concern about the procedural propriety of raising questions of policy and authorization during the debate over an authorization and appropriation bill.[7]

For example, Senator Young of North Dakota commented during debate on the Supplemental Defense Appropriation Bill of 1967 (P.L. 90-8):

> MR. YOUNG: If the Senate adopts the policy of determining war policy on an appropriation bill, would it not be a precarious situation, sometime in the future, when we might be engaged in another war, soldiers would be reluctant to enlist because they would not know whether they would be supported financially with adequate equipment and supplies which they would need to fight a war? 113 *Cong. Rec.* 7198 (March 20, 1967)

This position was clearly articulated by Congressman Donald Edwards during the debate over the Supplemental Defense Appropriations Act of 1966 (P.L. 89-374). During that debate, Edwards declared:

> Mr. Chairman, I believe my position is clear on our commitment in southeast Asia. I have been opposed to our military policy in Vietnam. I am strongly opposed to escalation of the war, and I am distressed by the deterioration of our foreign and domestic policies which has been brought on by our Vietnam operations.
>
> I will vote for H.R. 13546, the supplemental southeast Asia appropriations measure before this House today. I will do so because I feel it is unwise to decide policy issues through the appropriations process. It is the job of the authorizing committees to oversee the administration of duly authorized funds. * * *

---

[7] As explained in the Wallace Affidavit (see pp. 85–109) an appropriation bill ordinarily is not considered by Congress until the program or activity to be funded has been previously authorized by specific legislation. Thus spending by the government consists of a two-step process: the passing of an authorization bill and then an appropriation bill. The substantive legislative committee which has authority over the subject matter involved originates an authorization bill. Both the House and the Senate have produced an elaborate body of rules and precedents to govern the relationship between the appropriations committees and the substantive committees in order to prevent the appropriations committees of either House from engaging in substantive legislation through appropriation bills.

My vote for this appropriation means two things. It does not alone mean that I do not believe it is proper to express any policy preferences in an appropriations measure. It also means that an appropriations measure should not be used by anyone else to express their policy preferences. My vote today is not an endorsement of our past policy in Vietnam. It is merely a certification of prior House action on authorization measures. 112 *Cong. Rec.* 5820 (March 15, 1966)

Moreover, it is not clear that even authorization bills constitute an exercise of Congress' powers under Article I, Section 8 with respect to the declaration of war. Generally defense authorization bills cover the number and kind of missiles, planes and naval vessels which the Department of Defense is authorized to procure and the total amount of money it is authorized to spend on such items. They rarely express any policy determinations such as how or where the weapons are to be used. In fact, Senators or Congressmen often object to the use of military authorization bills for this purpose. For example, Senator Richard Russell, then Chairman of the Senate Armed Services Committee, said during the debate on the Armed Forces Supplemental Appropriation Authorization of 1967 (P.L. 90-5) :

MR. RUSSELL. It was a very undesirable approach to the whole subject. I do not favor statements of policy on authorizing legislation or appropriations. As a general rule, it is a very bad practice.

I have no particular quarrel with the language of this substitute, but I have very grave doubts about the propriety of attaching it to an authorization bill. It ought to be considered separately. 113 *Cong. Rec.* 4938 (March 1, 1967)

Senator Tower of Texas commented during the same debate :

What we have done in the Senate today points up the inadvisability of debating policy when we are passing on the matter of providing the money to provide our American fighting men with the hardware and the resources they need to fight a war. 113 *Cong. Rec.* 4949 (March 1, 1967)

In the proceedings below, Professor Don Wallace, Jr. of the Georgetown University Law Center submitted a thirty-two page affidavit analyzing the eighteen laws passed by Congress relating to military expenditures from 1965 to 1970 (see p. 85). The affidavit quotes extensively from the debates from each and every authorization or appropriations bill passed. The court's direction is respectfully directed to that portion of the Appendix.

The survey of the legislative history made by Professor Wallace showed that it is impossible to conclude that the enactment of the Vietnam authorization and appropriations bills manifested an intent by Congress to authorize the war.

It must be understood that the compendium made by Professor Wallace is not proffered so that this court might engage in a "head count" or "judicial roll call". Rather, appellant maintains a two-fold purpose in rendering to the court statements of legislators. First, such statements unequivocally refute the contention of the court below that "the course of events described above [showing Congressional action in the appropriations field] is more consistent with Congress and the President moving in concert." (192a) In its revealing pages, the legislative history of the nation's involvement in the war in Southeast Asia demonstrates that the "collaborative action" between the President and Congress of which Judge Dooling also spoke in *Orlando,* and upon which the appellees rely, was nonexistent. Secondly the compendium indicates the variety of reasons which prompted Congress to vote for the authorization and appropriations bills. It demonstrates that, in fact, it is the appellees who are engaged in a "head count" when they attempt to conclude that the appropriations bills manifested a clear intent to authorize or ratify war. It is appellees, not appellant, who are trying to squeeze a far-fetched inference out of bills whose texts do not support their contention. They, not we, ask the court to infer authorization based not on the language of the bills but on what they argue was in the minds of various Congressmen while voting for these bills.

3. EXECUTIVE-LEGISLATIVE ''COOPERATION'':

When read against the actual facts of the war, the legislative history contradicts the lower court's statement that Congress and the President ''mov[ed] in concert'' in the course of hostilities.

The first commitment of American combat troops (other than ''advisers'' who had been in Vietnam since the 1950's) took place in March, 1965 when a force of Marines were sent to Danang. (See Raskin Affidavit, 93a.) Additional forces continued to be sent through the spring and by May there were 34,000 American troops in Vietnam. (*Ibid.*) No Congressional action sanctioned this change in the nature of our mission.

When President Johnson asked for $700 million in additional funds on May 4, 1965, he did not ask Congress to authorize any additional escalation in Vietnam. He merely mentioned that 35,000 troops were in Vietnam and stated:

> The additional funds I am requesting are needed to continue to provide our forces with the best and most modern supplies and equipment. They are needed to keep an abundant inventory of ammunition and other expendables. They are needed to build facilities to house and protect our men and supplies. The entire $700 million is for this fiscal year. 111 *Cong. Rec.* 9283.

By June, 1965 the President had sent 75,000 men to Vietnam and announced that he was immediately ordering up to 125,000 troops to that country. (Raskin Affidavit, 93a.) Up to that point the only Congressional action on Vietnam was the appropriation of $700 million through June 30, 1965, ostensibly to support the 34,000 men sent through May, 1965.

In September, 1965, the Defense Department appropriation bill for fiscal year 1966 was passed by Congress. The bill included a special expenditure of $1.700 billion for Vietnam. However, it is clear that this sum in no way sanctioned or covered the cost of additional escalation in Vietnam. As Representative Glenard P. Lipscomb (the ranking Republican on the Defense Subcommittee on Appropriations) explained:

In spite of all this, Secretary McNamara's statement dated August 4, 1965 which covered his request for the additional $1.7 billion made it clear that such funds would not cover costs for additional military personnel and the added costs for operations and maintenance. What he proposed instead is that the additional costs be financed during the interim under section 512 of the fiscal year defense appropriations bill. Section 512a provides emergency authority to spend money in advance rather than on the prescribed quarterly basis. 111 *Cong. Rec.* 24255 (September 17, 1965).

By the spring of 1966, there were 250,000 troops in Vietnam, all ordered by the Executive (Raskin Affidavit, 93a). The only Congressional action to support this escalation was the emergency bill of May, 1965 and the general appropriations bill of September, 1965 (with the $1.7 billion outlined above) which the Defense Department itself stated would not cover costs for additional military personnel.

At that point (early 1966) the President asked for an additional $12.3 billion (and $4.8 billion in additional authorization) to meet the costs of the continued escalation. Various Congressmen then complained about the manner in which the Executive had been keeping Congress in the dark about its plans for war. Representative George E. Brown of California said:

> Last year when the President asked this Congress for $700 million in supplemental defense appropriations, many of my colleagues made similar statements as they voted for that modest sum. At the very moment we were voting, operations were being conducted that required many times that amount of additional funding. Plans were then in existence, and were announced within a few weeks, to triple our military manpower in Vietnam and to expand our military construction program in Vietnam many times over. In addition, those plans, since carried out, have been doubled and may be doubled again before the year is out. Not once has Congress been asked to vote on these decisions prior to their being taken. 112 *Cong. Rec.* 4465 (March 1, 1966).

This complaint is amply borne out by the facts of the Defense Appropriations bills. The following chart shows the way in which the funds for the Vietnam War were voted by Congress.

Vietnam Appropriations (in millions of dollars)

Fiscal Year	Regular Defense Dept. Appropriations	Amount out of Regular Appropriations Specifically Earmarked for Vietnam	Supplemental Appropriations Earmarked for Vietnam	Total Funds Specifically Earmarked for Vietnam	Amount Actually Spent in Vietnam
1965	—	—	700	700	1,500
1966	46,800	1,700	12,720	14,420	18,600
1967	58,300	—	12,300	12,300	19,400
1968	69,900	—	3,750	3,750	26,500
1969	71,900	—	—	—	28,800
1970	69,640	—	—	—	25,400

Sources: 115 *Cong. Rec.* H. 11874 (daily ed. December 8, 1969); 114 *Cong. Rec.* 28938; 113 *Cong. Rec.* 15605; 113 *Cong. Rec.* 19121; 112 *Cong. Rec.* 6391; 111 *Cong. Rec.* 9283.

From 1966 to 1968, the Defense Department would not ask for sufficient appropriations to meet all its contemplated costs in Vietnam through the entire fiscal year. Indeed it would not even earmark funds from the regular appropriations bills for Vietnam after 1965. Instead it would come back to Congress toward the end of the fiscal year (and in one case, after it was over) for additional funds only for the last few months of that period. This was done in May, 1965 in P.L. 89-18; in March, 1966 in P.L. 89-374; in April, 1967 in P.L. 90-8; and in July, 1968 (after the fiscal period had ended) in P.L. 90-392. In short, the Executive did not look for cooperative action with Congress to fund the war in Vietnam. It constantly did whatever it wanted to do, and then came back to Congress at the last possible moment to have it pay the bills for the action taken. Certainly this belies the notion that Congress and the President acted ''in concert'' in any significant sense.

4. ANCILLARY CONGRESSIONAL ACTION:

The court below and Judge Dooling in the *Orlando* case found other Congressional action which recognized the state of war in Vietnam. The District Court mentioned (191a) the extension of the Military Selective Service Act in 1967 (P.L. 90-40, 81 Stat. 100, June 30, 1967). It also cited (193a) an amendment of the War Claims Act of 1948 revising the definition of "prisoner of war" to include soldiers captured by the Viet Cong. (P.L. 91-289, 84 Stat. 323, June 24, 1970). Judge Dooling cited the fact that for veterans benefits purposes "period of war" was to include "the Vietnam Era," 38 U.S.C. Sect. 101 (11) (29). Aliens were also to be relieved of paying naturalization fees if they served in the armed forces during the Vietnam period. 3 SSLR at 3146.

However, the most that can be said for these laws is that they *recognized* that a war was being waged in Vietnam and that certain adjustments had to be made for those who found themselves fighting in that war. In no sense can such humanitarian actions be taken as an authorization of that war. If Congress voted certain benefits to flood victims after a river had overflowed, its action could not be taken as an authorization, sanctioning or approval of that disaster.

Furthermore, the extension of the Selective Service law could not be interpreted to sanction any use of the conscripted army that the Executive chooses to make. We have had a draft law in effect in this country since 1940, and no one has ever pretended that the existence of such a law gave the President carte blanche powers over the use of troops during that period.

THE ACTS DO NOT AS A MATTER OF LAW AUTHORIZE THE WAR.

As a matter of Constitutional law, Congress does not comply with Article I, Section 8, by passing vague appropriations bills, extensions of the Selective Service Act, or the like. The Constitution simply does not permit Congress to take the country to war by implication arising from such bills.

· · ·

CONGRESSIONAL AUTHORIZATION OF A MAJOR WAR CANNOT BE IMPLIED FROM THE PASSAGE OF MILITARY APPROPRIATION BILLS.

Both Judge Judd in *Berk* and Judge Dooling in *Orlando* ruled that the constitutionally-required Congressional authorization for the waging of a major war in Indochina could be implied from "the acts of Congress which have furnished forth the sinews of war." 3 SSLR at 3146.

· · ·

It is appellant's contention that the appropriations-as-authorization argument makes a mockery of explicit Constitutional language of Article I, Section 8, Clause 11. It reduces the quantum of political power which the framers decided was necessary to initiate war and destroys a major constitutional check upon unbridled Executive authority in the awesome realm of war and peace. And it undermines the Constitutional requirement of explicit legislative action in an area where such action is vitally important to a full and open discussion of the reasons why this nation should go to war.

· · ·

UNDERMINING OF CONGRESSIONAL WAR POWER.

Judge Dooling wrote in his opinion in *Orlando:*

> * * * it is idle to suggest that the Congress is so little ingenious or so inappreciative of its powers, including the power of impeachment, that it cannot seize policy and action initiatives at will, and halt courses of action from which it wishes the national power to be withdrawn. 3 SSLR at 3146.

Under the theory of Judge Dooling and the court below, it was up to Congress to stop the war after the President had started it, either by impeachment, use of the purse power, or in some other way. By not exercising that considerable power, the courts concluded, Congress must be taken to have authorized the war.

Whatever the powers of Congress might be, the framers did not intend that Congress would have to take the positive step of exercising them in order to *stop* a Presidential war. They explicitly committed the initial war power to Congress, requiring the concurrence of a majority of legislators in both houses before war could begin. Any rule which undermines that power or subjects it to extraneous pressures, whether practical or political, runs directly counter to the wishes of the Constitution's framers.

In order to see how seriously such a rule undermines the Congressional war power and reduces the quantum of political power necessary to begin a war, it is necessary to examine Judge Dooling's examples.

Theoretically, Congress can impeach a President who steps beyond his constitutional limits and begins a war of which Congress disapproves. But aside from the fact that this is a most heavy-handed and extreme way to meet the problem, removal of the President requires a two-thirds vote of the Senate. Thus thirty-four Senators would have the power to keep the nation on a war course (by refusing to vote for impeachment) in defiance of the will of sixty-six others. The crucial, initial decision to begin hostilities would have been made by the Executive, who was expressly denied that power in the Constitution, and maintained by a lesser number of legislators than the Constitution requires.

But Judge Dooling says, Congress can seize other "policy and action initiatives at will and halt courses of action from which it wishes the national power to be withdrawn." Even if such affirmative action were possible,[9] the onus is put upon the antiwar party to marshal and organize a majority of legislators in both houses to stop the President's action. But under the constitutional scheme envisaged by the founding fathers, those who wished to change the state of peace into a state of war had the

---

[9] Any substantive action that Congress took to stop a Presidential war, such as reducing the size of the army or repealing previous appropriations, would be subject to a Presidential veto and would therefore require a two-thirds vote.

onus of marshaling a legislative majority. This plan is destroyed by permitting the President to start a war and requiring the Congress to stop it.

Under the normal constitutional legislative process, those who wish to pass a new law have the burden of obtaining a majority in each house to vote in favor of the new law. Securing such a majority can be a difficult burden indeed, since, in addition to any other problems, there are always many legislators who reasonably desire to be very slow and careful and deliberate when it comes to changing the existing situation. Under Judge Dooling's plan the normal, inertial burden of passing new legislation is shifted to the peace party in direct violation of the framers' wishes.

It is very clear that the framers wished to make it difficult to have the nation enter into a war. Oliver Ellsworth commented during the Philadelphia Constitutional Convention that he thought the cases of "making war" and "making peace" materially different.

> It shd. be more easy to get out of war, than into it. War also is a simple and overt declaration, peace attended with intricate and secret negotiations. 2 Farrand, *Records of the Federal Convention of 1787*, 319.

George Mason also commented: "He was for clogging rather than for facilitating war, but for facilitating peace." *Ibid.* If the anti-war party must secure a majority in the manner indicated above, then this aim of the framers is completely vitiated. For the President on his own initiative can then start a war and hope to block Congressional countermoves at some time in the future. Such an approach would facilitate war far beyond the aim of the Constitution-makers.

Furthermore, this approach leads to a dangerous and practically irreversible expansion of the powers of the President. The terrible danger to the constitutional balance of powers of letting the President place the Congress in such a position is emphasized by Justice Jackson's words regarding the aggrandizement of Presidential power in *Youngstown Sheet & Tube Co.* v. *Sawyer*, 343 U.S. 579, at 653-654 (concurring opinion) (1952):

* * * it is relevant to note the gap that exists between the President's paper powers and his real powers. The Constitution does not disclose the measure of the actual controls wielded by modern presidential office. That instrument must be understood as an Eighteenth-Century sketch of a government hoped for, not as a blueprint of the Government that is. Vast accretions of federal power, eroded from that reserved by the States, have magnified the scope of presidential activity. Subtle shifts take place in the centers of real power that do not show on the face of the Constitution. * * * I cannot be brought to believe that this country will suffer if the Court refuses further to aggrandize the presidential office, already so potent and so relatively immune from judicial review, at the expense of Congress.

There is no constitutionally permissible reason to permit the Executive to impose upon those who oppose the war the burden of securing a legislative majority in favor of stopping his *fait accompli*. On the contrary, there is every constitutional and practical reasons to make him bear the burden of convincing a legislative majority that the country should be at war in the first instance.

At some point after the war has been raging, the President must come back to Congress for additional appropriations. If Congress has taken no action to block the President after he has begun the war and furthermore passes the appropriations he says he requires to continue it, should such appropriations be considered sufficient authorization of the war under the Constitution? It is clear that the answer is no.

In the first place the nation may be placed in a long twilight period before it knows whether the war that is being waged is legal or not. Since the President can use pre-existing defense appropriations for up to two years (see Article I, Section 8, Clause 12), neither the courts nor the citizens can guess what Congress will do about the next appropriations bill. Any rule of law that creates that much uncertainty in the vital area of war and peace for a period up to two years is questionable to say the least. The only sensible Constitutional rule that can void that dilemma is one that would require an explicit act by Congress before any war can be legally initiated.

Secondly, even if the appropriations bills are subsequently passed by Congress, it may do so for many reasons other than an intent to authorize the war. Funds must be appropriated for the defense establishment as a whole. It may be impossible to sever appropriations for an unwanted war from a general appropriation bill for national defense. A lump authorization or appropriation bill may provide for development of new weapons or an increase in soldiers' pay or construction of needed ships or docks or planes. How is a court to decide that the enactment of a general defense appropriation bill manifests an intent to authorize any military activity that the nation is then engaged in?

Thirdly, the practical pressures on Congress to "support our boys" in the field may become irresistible after the war has been raging for some period of time. This idea was expressed by numerous Senators and Congressmen in the past five years. (See discussion above at pp. 153–158 . . .) Can any legislator vote to cut off appropriations necessary to prevent men from dying in battle? Imposing such a burden on the legislature again facilitates the commencement of a Presidential war, directly contrary to the expressed wishes of the founders.

Indeed, imposing such a requirement on Congress makes it far easier for the President to initiate a large war rather than a small one. The greater the step taken by the President, the more troops he commits to combat, the stronger is the pressure on Congress to vote for their continued support. The legislature might be willing to cut off funds for a small expeditionary force, knowing that the President can easily extricate them. But it would find it impossible to do so when hundreds of thousands of troops are committed to battle.

Furthermore, history attests to the fact that Congress' power to cut off appropriations to end a war is illusory. Appellant knows of no instance in American history where Congress has cut off funds to stop a military, or military related, *fait accompli* perpetrated by the Executive. See generally, Wilmerding, *The Spending Power*, 9–18 (1943); Corwin, *The President: Office and Powers*, 229, 339 n. 58 (4th Ed. 1964); Lieutenant Colonel Hollander, "The President and Congress—Operational Control of the Armed Forces," 27 *Milit. Law Rev.* 49, 60–63 (1965);

T. Roosevelt, *An Autobiography*, 552–553 (1929 ed.). History thus provides no encouragement to those who would argue that the appropriations power is a realistic check on the President. Once the military die has been cast by the Executive, Congress must pay the bill or risk the wholesale slaughter of innocent Americans.

The "paying of the bill" for an Executive *fait accompli* cannot therefore, in any meaningful manner, provide the independent, unfettered, clear-cut Congressional exercise of the war power which the founding fathers so carefully erected as a critical safeguard against Executive military involvement.

Conclusion

For the foregoing reasons, it is respectfully prayed that the judgment of the District Court be reversed and that a judgment be issued declaring that appellees are without authority to order appellant to Vietnam and/or ordering his return from Vietnam to the United States.

Respectfully submitted,

LEON FRIEDMAN, ESQ.
BURT NEUBORNE, ESQ.
NEW YORK CIVIL LIBERTIES UNION
  84 Fifth Avenue
    New York, New York 10010

THEODORE C. SORENSEN, ESQ.
  345 Park Avenue
    New York, New York 10022

NORMAN DORSEN, ESQ.
N. Y. U. SCHOOL OF LAW
  40 Washington Square South
    New York, New York 10012

KAY ELLEN HAYES, ESQ.
1 Chase Manhattan Plaza
New York, New York 10005
Attorneys for Plaintiff-Appellant *

Of Counsel:

MARC LUXEMBERG, ESQ.

. . .

Appendix

Presidential Statements Acknowledging Need for Explicit Congressional Exercise of the War Power

During Jefferson's first administration, Tripoli attacked American vessels in the Mediterranean. After an American schooner, *The Enterprise,* had crippled an enemy cruiser, Jefferson reported to Congress:

> Unauthorized by the Constitution, without the sanction of Congress, to go beyond the line of defense, the vessel, being disabled from committing further hostilities, was liberated with its crew. The Legislature will doubtless consider whether, by authorizing measures of offense also, they will place our force on an equal footing with that of its adversaries. *I communicate all material information on this subject, that in the exercise of this important function confided by the Constitution to the Legislature exclusively* their judgment may form itself on a knowledge and consideration of every circumstance of weight. 1 *State of the Union Messages of the Presidents* 59 (Israel ed. 1966) (emphasis added [in original brief]).

Jefferson also asked for Congressional authority in settling the dispute with Spain on the Florida border:

* Attorneys for the plaintiff gratefully acknowledge the assistance of Messrs. Arthur Eisenberg and Edwin J. Oppenheimer, Jr., staff members of the New York Civil Liberties Union and candidates for admission to the bar, for their invaluable assistance in the preparation of this brief. Attorneys for plaintiff also acknowledge the research of Mr. Martin Guggenheim, student, New York University School of Law.

That which they have chosen to pursue will appear from the documents now communicated. They authorize the inference that it is their intention to advance on our possessions until they shall be repressed by an opposing force. *Considering that Congress alone is constitutionally invested with the power of changing our condition from peace to war, I have thought it my duty to await their authority for using force in any degree which could be avoided.* I have barely instructed the officers stationed in the neighborhood of the aggressions to protect our citizens from violence, to patrol within the borders actually delivered to us, and not to go out of them but when necessary to repel an inroad or to rescue a citizen, or his property; and the Spanish officers remaining at New Orleans are to depart without further delay. . . .

But the course to be pursued will require the command of means which it belongs to Congress exclusively to yield or to deny. To them I communicate every fact material for their information and the documents necessary to enable them to judge for themselves. To their wisdom, then, I look for the course I am to pursue, and will pursue with sincere zeal that which they shall approve. 1 *Messages and Papers of the Presidents,* 389-90 (Richardson Ed. 1908) (emphasis added [in original brief]).

When English vessels increased their raids on American commerce immediately before the war of 1812, President James Madison specifically asked Congress for guidance. In his message on June 1, 1812, he said:

Whether the United States shall continue passive under these progressive usurpations and these accumulating wrongs, or, opposing force to force in defense of their national rights, shall commit a just cause into the hands of the Almighty Disposer of events, avoiding all connections which might entangle it in the contests or views of other powers, and preserving a constant readiness to concur in an honorable re-establishment of peace and friendship, is a *solemn question which the Constitution wisely confides to the legislative department of the Government.* Quoted in Putney, "Executive Assumption of the War Making Power," 7 *National University Law Review,* 1, 9 (May, 1927) (emphasis added [in original brief])

President Andrew Jackson similarly asked Congress for authority to protect American shipping in South American waters. In his third annual message Jackson said:

In the course of the present year one of our vessels, engaged
in the pursuit of a trade which we have always enjoyed without
molestation, has been captured by a band acting, as they pre-
tend, under the authority of the Government of Buenos Ayres. I
have therefore given orders for the dispatch of an armed vessel
to join our squadron in those seas and aid in affording all lawful protection to our trade which shall be necessary, and shall
without delay send a minister to inquire into the nature of the
circumstances and also of the claim, if any, that is set up by
that Government to those islands. In the meantime, I submit
the case to the consideration of Congress, to the end that they
may clothe the Executive with such authority and means as they
may deem necessary for providing a force adequate to the complete protection of our fellow-citizens fishing and trading in
these seas. 1 *State of the Union Messages,* 352

In the same message, Jackson commented about troubles with
Spain:

* * * I have therefore dispatched a special messenger with instructions to our minister to bring the case once more to his (i.e.
the King of Spain) consideration, to the end that if (which I
cannot bring myself to believe) the same decision (that cannot
but be deemed an unfriendly denial of justice) should be per-
sisted in, the matter may before your adjournment be laid before you, the constitutional judges of what is proper to be done
when negotiations for redress of injury fails. *Ibid.* 349

In 1848 President James K. Polk referred the problem of
Yucatan to Congress:

I have considered it proper to communicate the information
contained in the accompanying correspondence, and I submit it
to the wisdom of Congress to adopt such measures as in their
judgment may be expedient to prevent Yucatan from becoming
a colony of any European power, which in no event could be
permitted by the United States * * * 4 *Messages of the Presidents,* 583

Ten years later President James Buchanan reiterated this view
of the war power:

Under our treaty with New Granada of the 12th December,
1846, we are bound to guarantee the neutrality of the Isthmus

of Panama, through which the Panama Railroad passes, "as well as the rights of sovereignty and property which New Granada has and possesses over the said territory." This obligation is founded upon equivalents granted by the treaty to the Government and people of the United States. Under these circumstances I recommend to Congress the passage of an act authorizing the President, in case of necessity, to employ the land and naval forces of the United States to carry into effect this guaranty of neutrality and protection. 1 *State of the Union Messages,* 953

In his annual message of December 6, 1858, the same President said:

The executive government of this country in its intercourse with foreign nations is limited to the employment of diplomacy alone. When this fails it can proceed no further. It cannot legitimately resort to force without the direct authority of Congress, except in resisting and repelling hostile attacks. *Ibid.,* 988

Buchanan had occasion in his third annual message to repeat these views:

It will not be denied that the general "power to declare war" is without limitation and embraces within itself not only what writers on the law of nations term a public or perfect war, but also an imperfect war, and, in short, every species of hostility, however confined or limited. Without the authority of Congress the President cannot fire a hostile gun in any case except to repel the attacks of an enemy. *Ibid.,* 1018

Abraham Lincoln took a similar view of the Presidential war powers. Writing at the time of the Mexican War, Lincoln said:

* * * Allow the President to invade a neigboring nation whenever he shall deem it necessary to repel an invasion, and you allow him to do so whenever he may choose to say he deems it necessary for such a purpose, and you allow him to make war at his pleasure. Study to see if you can fix any limit to his power in this respect, after having given him so much power as you propose. * * *

The provision of the Constitution giving the war-making power to Congress was dictated, as I understand it, by the following reasons: Kings had always been involving and improverishing their people in wars, pretending generally, if not always, that the good of the people was the object. This our convention understood to be the most oppressive of all kingly oppressions, and they resolved to so frame the Constitution that no one man should hold the power of bringing oppression upon us. But your views destroys the whole matter, and places our President where kings have always stood. 2 *Writings of Abraham Lincoln,* 52 (Lapstez ed. 1905)

President Ulysses Grant recognized that he would have to come to Congress for authority to act abroad. In commenting on the situation in Cuba in 1875, he said:

Persuaded, however, that a proper regard for the interests of the United States and of its citizens entitles it to relief from the strain to which it has been subjected by the difficulties of the questions and the wrongs and losses which arise from the contest in Cuba, and that the interests of humanity itself demand the cessation of the strife before the whole island shall be laid waste and larger sacrifices of life be made, I shall feel it my duty should my hopes of a satisfactory adjustment and of the early restoration of peace and the removal of future causes of complaint be, unhappily, disappointed, to make a further communication to Congress at some period not far remote, and during the present session, recommending what may then seem to me to be necessary. 2 *State of the Union Messages,* 1302.

Chester Arthur also called for Congressional authority to wage even limited war:

A recent agreement with Mexico provides for the crossing of the frontier by the armed forces of either country in pursuit of hostile Indians. In my message of last year I called attention to the prevalent lawlessness upon the borders and to the necessity of legislation for its suppression. I again invite the attention of Congress to the subject. 2 *State of the Union Messages,* 1455.

President William Howard Taft refused to move into Mexico in 1911 despite the danger to American interests in that country:

It seems my duty as Commander in Chief to place troops in sufficient number where, if Congress shall direct that they enter

Mexico to save American lives and property, an effective movement may be promptly made. * * *

The assumption by the press that I contemplate intervention on Mexican soil to protect American lives or property is of course gratuitous, because I seriously doubt whether I have such authority under any circumstances, and if I had I would not exercise it without express congressional approval. 3 *State of the Union Messages,* 2447–48.

More recently when Germany overran France in May and June 1940, Premier Paul Reynaud of France wired President Roosevelt for material assistance on June 10, 1940. President Roosevelt responded on June 15, 1940 that material and supplies would be sent in ever-increasing quanties and kinds. He continued:

I know that you will understand that these statements carry with them no implication of military commitments. *Only the Congress can make such commitments. The Public Papers and Addresses of Franklin D. Roosevelt,* 1940, 267 (emphasis added [in original brief]).

Extracts from Appellant's Brief, Orlando v. Laird, Second Circuit Court of Appeals [†]

. . .

The Executive May Not Wage a Major War Without Constitutionally Sufficient Congressional Authorization.

The Executive has argued that there exists a genus of military activity which it may prosecute in a unilateral fashion without

[†] Footnotes adopting parallel points advanced in *Berk* v. *Laird* have been omitted.

Congressional authorization. Brief of the Solicitor General of the United States in *Massachusetts* v. *Laird,* No. 42 Original Oct. Term, 1970, motion for leave complaint denied, 39 USLW 3196 (November 9, 1970), pp. 18–24. Whether or not there exists a residuum of constitutional authority which would permit the Executive to wage "limited" wars without seeking the authorization of Congress, . . . it is absolutely clear that the waging of a war of the magnitude of Vietnam requires Congressional authorization pursuant to Article I, Section 8, clause 11 of the Constitution. . . .

> Congressional Authorization of a Major War, Required Pursuant to Article I, Section 8, Clause 11 of the Constitution, Cannot Be Implied From the Passage of Military Appropriation Bills or From the Enactment of Collateral Laws Supportive of the "War Effort."

The court below ruled that the constitutionally required Congressional authorization for the waging of a major war in Vietnam could be implied from "the acts of the Congress which have furnished forth the sinew of war." *Orlando* v. *Laird.*

Appellant believes that a substantial issue of fact exists as to whether the votes of members of Congress on collateral bills supportive of the war effort can be deemed as a matter of fact to manifest assent to the general war policy. . . .

However, even if the court below was correct in implying "unstinting" Congressional support of the war from the passage of appropriation bills and the extension of the Selective Service Act, the Constitution requires that Congressional authorization of a major war be manifested by an explicit, formal act of Congress, rather than by implication from collateral acts.

Thus, a pure issue of law is raised on this appeal as to whether the constitutionally required Congressional authorization for the prosecution of a major war must be couched in a formal, explicit act of Congress, . . . or whether such alleged Congressional authorization may be implied from collateral Congressional activity supportive of the war effort, such as the passage of appropriation bills and the extension of the draft.

1. THE DOCTRINE OF "IMPLIED EXERCISE" OF THE CONGRESSIONAL "WAR POWER" FINDS NO SUPPORT IN PRECEDENTS RECOGNIZING THAT CONGRESS MAY CONFIRM AN EXECUTIVE CONSTRUCTION OF A PRE-EXISTING CONGRESSIONAL STATUTE BY APPROPRIATING FUNDS CONSISTENTLY WITH SUCH CONSTRUCTION.

The decision of the court below turns upon the assumption that Congress, by appropriating funds to support the war in Vietnam, has manifested an intention to authorize the war and that such "ratification by appropriation" constitutes a satisfactory constitutional substitute for a formal, explicit manifestation of Congress' will with respect to the war.

In support of the "ratification by appropriation" argument, appellees have relied upon a series of cases for the proposition that Congress may constitutionally authorize an Executive's action merely by knowingly appropriating funds to pay for it. *Ludecke* v. *Watkins,* 335 U.S. 160 (1948); *Fleming* v. *Mohawk Wrecking and Lumber Co.,* 331 U.S. 111 (1947); *Brooks* v. *Dewar,* 313 U.S. 354 (1941). However, an analysis of the cases advanced by the appellees reveals that no case has ever recognized "appropriation" as a substitute for formal substantive Congressional action. In each case cited by Appellees, the appropriation of funds by Congress was seen by the courts, not as a substitute for an underlying formal Congressional act, but merely as confirmation of an Executive construction of a pre-existing Congressional substantive grant of authority.

Thus, in *Ludecke* v. *Watkins,* 335 U.S. 160 (1948), the issue before the Supreme Court was whether the Alien Enemy Act, passed by Congress in 1798, authorized the summary deportation of alien enemies after the cessation of actual hostilities. The Executive branch had construed the statute as authorizing such deportations. Mr. Justice Frankfurter, in a footnote to his opinion for a five-man majority, noted that Congress had confirmed the Executive's construction of the Alien Enemy Act by appropriating funds for the detention of alien enemies even after hostilities had ended. No suggestion was advanced, however, that the appropriations in question could have authorized the deportations in the absence of the Alien Enemy Act.

In *Fleming* v. *Mohawk Wrecking and Lumber Co.*, 331 U.S. 111 (1947), the issue before the Supreme Court was whether the First War Powers Act, passed by Congress in 1941, authorized the consolidation of existing Executive departments into consolidated agencies. The Executive branch had construed the statute as authorizing such consolidations. Mr. Justice Douglas, writing for the Court, noted that Congress had confirmed the Executive's construction of the First War Powers Act by appropriating funds for such consolidated agencies. No suggestion was advanced, however, that the appropriations in question could have authorized the consolidations in the absence of the First War Powers Act.

In *Brooks* v. *Dewar*, 313 U.S. 354 (1941), the issue before the Supreme Court was whether the Public Grazing Act, passed by Congress in 1934, authorized the imposition of fees for temporary grazing permits. The Executive branch had construed the statute as authorizing the imposition of such fees. Mr. Justice Murphy, writing for the Court, noted that Congress had confirmed the Executive's construction of the Public Grazing Act by receiving and disbursing the fees from such temporary permits. No suggestion was advanced, however, that the appropriations in question could have authorized the imposition of fees in the absence of the Public Grazing Act.

Finally, in *Isbrandsten-Moller Co.* v. *U.S.*, 300 U.S. 139 (1937), the issue before the Supreme Court was whether the Reorganization Act, passed by Congress in 1933, authorized the abolition of the Shipping Board and the transfer of its powers to the Secretary of Commerce. The Executive branch had construed the statute as permitting such a transfer of functions. The Court found that Congress had explicitly confirmed the Executive's construction of the 1933 Reorganization Act by the passage of the Merchant Marine Act of 1936 and by the appropriation of funds for the expanded office of the Secretary of Commerce. No suggestion was advanced, however, that the appropriations in question could have authorized the consolidation in the absence of the 1933 Act.

An analysis of the four cases described above reveals that in each instance the issue before the Court was the proper construction of a vaguely worded pre-existing Congressional authorization. In each case, Congressional appropriations were utilized as a clue to the meaning of the underlying substantive Congressional enactment. In none of the cases, however, was there any suggestion that Congressional appropriations, standing alone, could supply constitutional justification for the Executive actions in question. If one subtracts the pre-existing Congressional authorization from *Ludecke* (Alien Enemy Act); *Fleming* (First War Powers Act); *Brooks* (Public Grazing Act); and *Isbrandsten* (Reorganization Act of 1933), it becomes readily apparent that the Congressional appropriations, standing alone, could not have served as a constitutional basis for the Executive action involved in each case.

In fact, when Congressional appropriations, standing alone, have been asserted as a justification for Executive action, the Supreme Court has refused to recognize the constitutional sufficiency of the authorization. *Greene* v. *McElroy*, 360 U.S. 474 (1959).

In *Greene*, the loyalty security procedures at issue had been created pursuant to a joint agreement between the three branches of the military with the cooperation of the Department of Defense. No underlying Congressional act existed which could, even arguably, have formed the basis for such procedures.

Chief Justice Warren, writing for the Court, rejected the Executive's contention that mere Congressional appropriations of money to fund the program at issue constituted sufficient legislative sanction for the program.

In *D.C. Federation of Civic Associations* v. *Airis,* 391 F2d 478 (D.C. Cir. 1968), the court specifically recognized that appropriations are not a valid substitute for formal Congressional action when it stated:

> Another characteristic of these cases accepting the ratification by appropriation argument is that there was pre-existing statu-

tory language which arguably authorized the disputed administrative action. 391 F2d at 481 n. 20.

Thus, while the act of appropriating funds may be helpful in ascertaining Congress' construction of a vaguely worded pre-existing statute, it may never be utilized as a substitute for the existence of the formal Congressional statute itself.

Even if, despite the lack of judicial precedent for the proposition, Congress may, by appropriations alone, grant some form of legislative authorization to the Executive, such a casual exercise of the legislative function should never be permitted in connection with critically important determinations of constitutional dimensions.

In *Greene* v. *McElroy, supra,* the Supreme Court firmly rejected the notion that Governmental action of constitutional dimensions could be taken by any means short of formal, explicit approval by the appropriate political branch. In ruling that explicitness must characterize Governmental actions of constitutional dimensions, Chief Justice Warren stated:

> Decisions of constitutional magnitude must be made explicitly not only to assure that individuals are not deprived of cherished rights under procedures not actually authorized * * * but also because explicit action, especially in areas of doubtful constitutionality, requires careful and purposeful consideration by those responsible for enacting and implementing our laws: Without explicit action by lawmakers, decisions of great constitutional import and effect would be relegated by default to administrators who, under our system of government, are not endowed with authority to decide them. 360 U.S. at 507. See also, *Ex Parte Endo,* 323 U.S. 283 (1944) at 303 n. 24.

Finally, even if one may legislate by appropriation in areas of constitutional dimension in spite of *Greene, supra,* no such casual approach to the legislative function should be permitted to impliedly exercise any of the legislative responsibilities specifically enumerated in Article I, Section 8 of the Constitution. As to those central legislative responsibilities, no relaxation of formal explicitness should ever be permitted.

Therefore, appellees' attempt to utilize the Vietnam war appropriations as a substitute for an explicit, formal Congressional declaration of policy concerning the war, is totally without judicial support. One simply cannot use appropriations to bootstrap the Executive into a position unsupported by *any* underlying substantive legislative authority.

2. THE DOCTRINE OF "IMPLIED EXERCISE" OF THE CONGRESSIONAL "WAR POWER" CONSTITUTES A RADICAL DEPARTURE FROM THE TRADITIONAL VIEW THAT FORMAL, EXPLICIT ACTION BY THE APPROPRIATE POLITICAL BRANCH IS NECESSARY TO DETERMINE THE EXISTENCE OR NON-EXISTENCE OF "WAR POWERS."

It is, of course, an accepted canon of constitutional law that the government is endowed with certain extraordinary powers in time of war which it could not otherwise constitutionally exercise. *Korematsu* v. *United States,* 323 U.S. 214 (1944) ; *Ex Parte Endo,* 323 U.S. 283 (1944). The conflict between Executive action taken pursuant to asserted "war power" and constitutional guarantees has resulted in numerous judicial clashes.

Our courts, when confronted with cases raising constitutional questions under the "war power" doctrine, have traditionally engaged in a three-step analytical process.

First, the court must answer the threshold question of whether the "war power" is potentially available to the government in the particular case at bar as a device to extend its theoretical power.

Second, the court must determine whether, even if the "war power" is theoretically available to the government as a basis for its challenged act, the government has elected to make full use of its extended authority.

Finally, the court, if it finds that the government has elected to avail itself of the full scope of its "war power," must determine whether the challenged governmental act is repugnant to the constitution, even under a "war power" analysis.

In making the critical, threshold determination of whether "war power" is available to the government as a device to extend its otherwise limited power, our Courts have universally demanded an explicit, formal act by the appropriate political branch. E.g. *Ludecke* v. *Watkins,* 335 U.S. 160 (1948); *United States ex rel. Knauff* v. *Shaughnessy,* 338 U.S. 537 (1950); *The Protector,* 12 Wall. 700 (1871); *Hamilton* v. *Kentucky Distillers Co.,* 251 U.S. 146 (1919).

On numerous occasions, our courts have rejected the notion, accepted by the District Court below, that Congressional intention in connection with the invocation of "war powers" may be implied from a series of collateral Congressional acts.

In *National Savings and Trust Co.* v. *Brownell,* 222 F2d 395 (D.C. Cir) *cert. den.,* 349 U.S. 955 (1955), the Court was faced with the Executive's attempt to seize trust assets under the Alien Property Act in 1948. The trustees opposed the seizures on the ground that an intention could be inferred from the actions of the government to relinquish the "war power" and that, without the "war power" as a basis for its action, the seizures violated the 5th Amendment.

The Court, speaking through Judge Prettyman, rejected the trustees' "implied exercise" argument in favor of the requirement of an explicit, formal Congressional declaration. Judge Prettyman stated:

> By the Constitution power "to declare" war was vested in the Congress. From that language and upon constitutional principle it would seem that a state of war, constitutionally speaking and as between nations, is a matter of congressional declaration and not a matter of determination from facts and circumstances. 222 F2d at 397. See also *United States* v. *Shaughnessy,* 177 F2d 436 (2nd Cir. 1949).

Thus, in each instance when the issue has arisen, our Courts have demanded that the theoretical availability or non-availability of "war power" as a justification for governmental action be demonstrated by a formal, explicit Congressional act.

In *Ludecke* v. *Watkins,* 335 U.S. 160 (1948), Mr. Justice Frankfurter, speaking for the Court, ruled that the existence or non-existence of the Congressional war power was wholly dependent upon the "express," formal act of the appropriate political branch of government and could not be inferred from collateral acts of Congress, including the appropriation of millions of dollars for German relief pursuant to the European Recovery Plan (Marshall Plan).

In *United States ex rel. Knauff* v. *Shaughnessy*, 338 U.S. 537 (1950), Chief Justice Minton ruled that the power to summarily deport German aliens without a hearing under the "war power" continued to exist up to the express, formal, joint resolution of Congress proclaiming the war with Germany at an end on October 19, 1951 (65 Stat. 451, 50 USCA App. note preceding Section 1). See also *Kahn* v. *Anderson*, 255 U.S. 1 (1921); *McElrath* v. *United States*, 102 U.S. 426 (1880); *United States* v. *Anderson*, 9 Wall. 56 (1869).

In fact, until recently, our Courts, in dealing with the second analytical issue of whether Congress intended to exercise its theoretical "war power" to the fullest extent, refused to rely upon anything short of an express, formal Congressional act. E.g. *Ludecke* v. *Watkins, supra; United States ex rel. Knauff* v. *Shaughnessy, supra.*

However, such a rigid approach (which often created great personal hardship) was relaxed in *Lee* v. *Madigan*, 358 U.S. 228 (1959), when the Supreme Court ruled that Congress, although it could theoretically have provided otherwise under its "war power," intended to suspend civilian trials in capital cases involving military personnel only during actual hostilities. See also, *United States* v. *Sobell*, 314 F2d 314 (2nd Cir. 1963).

It must be noted, however, that both *Lee* v. *Madigan* and *Sobell* continue to recognize that the theoretical availability of the "war power" remains conditioned solely upon an explicit, formal act of Congress. Thus, the District Court below, in accepting the contention that Congress has authorized the use of the "war power" by the Executive by "implication", has ignored one hundred years of contrary judicial determinations.

3. THE DOCTRINE OF "IMPLIED EXERCISE" OF THE CONGRESSIONAL "WAR POWER" WOULD RENDER THE LANGUAGE OF ARTICLE I, SECTION 8, CLAUSE 11 MERE SURPLUSAGE.

Article I, Section 8, clause 11 of the Constitution unequivocally imposes upon Congress the responsibility "to declare War." The independent status of the "war power" as a specifically enumerated legislative responsibility reflects the concern of the Founding Fathers that it be exercised independently from the exercise of the other enumerated legislative powers.

However, if the act of voting military appropriations under the "purse power" of Article 1, Section 8, clauses 1 and 12 automatically triggers the "war power" of clause 11 by implication, what was the purpose of an independent enumeration of the "war power" in the first instance?

It can hardly be assumed that the Founding Fathers intended no tangible extension of Congressional authority by virtue of the independent enumeration of the power "to declare War." However, if Congress impliedly exercises its "war power" whenever it exercises its collateral constitutional responsibilities under the "purse power", have we not effected a virtual emasculation of clause 11, since every military operation, as a matter of necessity, will be either approved or disapproved by Congress under the "purse power" of clauses 1 and 12.

4. THE DOCTRINE OF "IMPLIED EXERCISE" OF THE CONGRESSIONAL "WAR POWER" WOULD DILUTE, AND PERHAPS DESTROY, THE RESPONSIBILITY OF CONGRESS TO BE THE ULTIMATE ARBITER OF WAR AND PEACE.

It was, obviously, uppermost in the minds of the Founding Fathers to erect a Legislative safeguard against the threat of improvident military operations initiated by the Executive. In order to erect such a safeguard, they explicitly committed the "war power" to Congress.

Any rule of constitutional law which renders the unfettered Congressional exercise of the "war power" subject to extraneous pressures, whether practical or political, runs directly counter to the wishes of the Constitution's framers. Yet, the inevitable impact of permitting collateral Congressional action, taken pursuant to the "purse power", to impliedly discharge the Congressional responsibility under the "war power" clause, would have precisely the effect of imposing enormous practical and political pressures upon Congress' discharge of that singularly critical responsibility.

(A) EXTRANEOUS CONSIDERATIONS, UNRELATED TO THE SUP-
PORT OF NON-SUPPORT OF THE WAR IN QUESTION, MOTIVATE
A LEGISLATOR TO SUPPORT COLLATERAL CONGRESSIONAL EN-
ACTMENTS WHICH "FURNISH FORTH THE SINEW OF WAR."

It is a fact that once the Executive has committed the nation
to a major military undertaking, extraneous considerations
render it extremely unlikely that any legislator, regardless of
his views on the war itself, will refuse to grant unstinting material support for the war effort. Once the Executive has placed
large numbers of American troops in a combat situation, is
Congress to deny them bullets, advanced weapons, logistical support, air cover, medical care, housing, veteran's benefits, life
insurance, dependent's allowance, hazard pay or the innumerable other expensive emoluments of war? Are they to be denied
speedy replacements because Congress refuses to extend the
draft? The answer to such questions for the vast majority of
legislators, regardless of their views on the war itself, is in the
negative. Once the military die has been cast by the Executive,
Congress must pay the bill or risk the wholesale slaughter of
innocent Americans. See generally, Brief of Appellant in *Berk* v.
Laird at pp. [153-168].

The "paying of the bill" for an Executive *fait accompli* cannot, in any meaningful manner, provide the independent, unfettered, clear cut Congressional exercise of the "war power"
which the Founding Fathers so carefully erected as a critical
safeguard against Executive military involvement.

(B) A DOCTRINE OF "IMPLIED EXERCISE" OF THE "WAR
POWER" WOULD DRASTICALLY ALTER THE SEPARATION OF
POWERS BETWEEN THE EXECUTIVE AND THE LEGISLATURE.

In the absence of the necessity to take emergency Executive
action to repel a surprise attack, the Constitution's grant of the
"war power" to Congress establishes the Legislature as the
body saddled with the responsibility to make the primary decisions in the realm of war and peace. However, a doctrine which

relegates Congress to ratifying by implication a series of Executive initiated military operations would wreak havoc upon the original constitutional scheme. It would vest the critical initiative in the area of war and peace in the Executive, and demote the Legislature to the secondary level of a ''rubber stamp'' impliedly ratifying Executive initiatives by paying for them.[1] If that is to be the future role of Congress in the area of war and peace, the 20th Century has simply erased Article I, Section 8, clause 11 of the Constitution.

5. THE DOCTRINE OF ''IMPLIED EXERCISE'' OF THE CONGRESSIONAL ''WAR POWER'' RENDERS IT VIRTUALLY IMPOSSIBLE FOR THE ELECTORATE TO PASS JUDGMENT UPON THE PERFORMANCE OF THEIR REPRESENTATIVES.

The Founding Fathers erected a two-step mechanism to guard against improvident military adventures.

First, they provided for an unfettered Congressional determination as to the wisdom of a particular war. They were not content, however, to grant, even to Congress, plenary authority in the area of war and peace.

Therefore, they provided an additional check by insuring that the electorate would possess a speedy and effective method of reviewing any Congressional determination that a given war was advisable.

Article I, Section 8, clause 12 provides that no military appropriation may extend for more than two years. Since the entire House of Representatives and one-third of the Senate must stand for re-election every two years, an effective electoral check upon any Congressional determination that a given war was advisable can never, under any circumstances, be farther away than the next Congressional election.

Thus, any rule of constitutional law which would permit Congress to exercise its ''war power'' by implication in a manner not capable of ready public understanding as to the respective

---

[1] As appellant has noted at p. 183 *supra,* no real choice exists as to whether to pay for an existing war. No legislator would abandon troops in field—no matter who put them there.

position of each individual legislator on the war itself, would frustrate the Constitutional scheme, since the electorate would be deprived of its right to pass judgment upon each legislator's position on the war.

It is, of course, absolutely impossible to discern from the voting patterns of individual legislators on appropriations bills or draft extensions their individual positions on the Vietnam war. The most vociferous critics of the war, moved by the extraneous factors discussed *supra,* at p. 52, have consistently voted to "pay the bill." How then, under a doctrine of "implied exercise" of the "war power," is a constituent to know his Congressman's position on the war? [2]

Would we not, therefore, by recognizing "implied exercise" of the war power, not only vitiate the command of the Founding Fathers that Congress exercise primary responsibility in the area of war and peace, but also drastically weaken effective electoral check upon the exercise of the Congressional "war power"?

6. THE DOCTRINE OF "IMPLIED EXERCISE" OF THE CONGRESSIONAL "WAR POWER" FLIES IN THE FACE OF ACTUAL CONGRESSIONAL PRACTICE IN CONNECTION WITH EVERY MAJOR COMMITMENT OF AMERICAN MILITARY RESOURCES ABROAD THROUGH THE SECOND WORLD WAR.

In our nation's history, the Executive has committed American troops to major combat on eight occasions: a) The War of 1812; b) The Mexican War of 1846–1848; c) The Civil War; d) the Spanish-American War; e) The First World War; f) The Second World War; g) The Korean War, and h) The Vietnamese War.

Prior to the Korean conflict, every major commitment of American men to a combat situation was duly authorized by formal, explicit, Congressional action.

---

[2] Permitting "implied exercise" of the "war power" would be analogous to providing that a vote on the advisability of the war may be taken in closed session with the numerical result publicly announced, but individual votes kept secret. The result in both cases is to rob the electorate of any meaningful ability to pass judgment upon their respective representatives.

In fact, prior to Korea, even second echelon military operations involving the possibility of significant bloodshed received formal, explicit, Congressional sanction. Thus, the French Naval War of 1798–1801, the Naval War with Tripoli (1802); the Naval War with Algiers (1815); and the punitive expedition into Mexico (1914), each were authorized by an explicit, formal act of Congress. Prior to Korea, no Executive had led this nation into prolonged and bloody armed struggle in the absence of an explicit, formal Congressional authorization. If we are to dispense with the requirement of such formal, explicit Congressional authorization, are we not simply inviting a recurrence of the national tragedy that is the "war" in Vietnam?[3]

7. THE DOCTRINE OF "IMPLIED EXERCISE" OF THE CONGRESSIONAL "WAR POWER" SACRIFICES THE JURISPRUDENTIAL VALUES OF "FORMALISM" IN AN AREA WHICH DESPERATELY REQUIRES THEM.

No issue in recent years has caused a greater rift in American society than the war in Vietnam. Of course, the prolonged use of military force must, under any circumstances, create serious tensions within a society. Those tensions, however, are monumentally exacerbated when the government wages war without regard to the accepted political formalities which a significant segment of the society regards as a prerequisite to the war's lawful prosecution. By failing to impress an explicit, formal imprimatur of legality upon the war, we have virtually assured that millions of Americans will view the struggle in Vietnam, not as the lawful expression of the nation's will, but rather as an unlawful exercise in naked power.

Morris R. Cohen recognized the critical role which legal formality plays in impressing potentially divisive governmental action with a sense of legitimacy when he wrote:

[3] The historical practice of explicit, formal Congressional authorization of the commitment of American troops to prolonged combat is discussed at greater length in the Brief *Amicus Curiae* of the New York Civil Liberties Union submitted to the court below and in the Brief of Appellant in *Berk* v. *Laird,* pp. 136–137.

Ceremonies are the channels that the stream of social life creates by its ceaseless flow through the sands of human circumstance. Psychologically, they are habits; socially they are customary ways of doing things; and ethically, they have what Jellinek has called the normative power of the actual, that is, they control what we do by creating a standard of respectability or a pattern to which we feel bound to conform. The daily obedience to the act of the government, which is the basis of all political and legal institutions, is thus largely a matter of conformity to established ritual or form of behavior. Cohen, *The Basis of Contract*, 46 Harv. L. Rev. 553, 582 (1933).

Senator Ervin commented upon the tragic consequences of failing to adhere to constitutional formalities in connection with the war in Vietnam during the National Commitments debate:

The consequences of this failure to observe the Constitution are all too evident. True, no Supreme Court decision has adjudged the war in Vietnam as unconstitutional on the grounds that Congress adopted no formal declaration of war and because the Senate gave no effective advice and consent. Instead, the declaration of unconstitutionality has come from the judgment of the people. We see the decree everywhere. For the first time in our memory, an incumbent President was forced from office. Young men whose fathers and brothers vounteered to serve their country now desert to Canada and Scandinavia rather than bear arms in the country's cause. Thousands march on Washington and picket the White House, the Capitol, and the Pentagon. Now we have riots and violence on our university campuses. ROTC programs are being forced out of schools, and there is dissension and antiwar activity even among those in uniform.

Perhaps not all the anarchy we see today has been caused by the Vietnamese war and the way in which we became involved. No one can say. But no one can say that the war was not the cause, or at least the catalyst. And I cannot shake the feeling that ultimately the reason so many are now disrespectful and unresponsive to authority is because authority was disrespectful and unresponsive to the Constitution in the making of our policy in Vietnam. 115 Cong. Rec. 17217.

As Senator Ervin has noted, the constitutional imperative of formalistic explicitness in the exercise of the Congressional war power is far more than a quaint historical anachronism. Such a requirement of formality, procedural though it may be, shields values of infinite substantive importance, for, as Mr. Justice Frankfurter has observed, "the history of liberty has largely been the history of procedural safeguards." *McNabb* v. *United States,* 318 U.S. 332, 347 (1943).

In the context of decisions of the first magnitude involving war and peace, formalism stands "as a stamp of the finally resolved legal will." It performs the following valuable jurisprudential functions:

(a) formalism provides unequivocal evidence that Congress intended its act to have an accepted legal significance;

(b) formalism provides a psychic check, aiding Congress to consider fully the accepted legal consequences of its act; and

(c) formalism provides public notification that Congress has performed an act of predictable legal significance.

In fashioning a constitutional doctrine which invites Congress to satisfy its responsibilities under Article I, Section 8, clause 11 of the Constitution in a formless, "implied" manner, we deprive ourselves of the benefit of formalistic values in a context which literally cries out for them.

The dichotomy between "formalism" and "implication" is not confined to the awful realm of war and peace. It is a dualism that is present in every branch of the law. In fact, much of our law is explicable in terms of the tension existing between these polar concepts.

Yet, whenever decisions of the first magnitude have been at stake, we have sacrificed the convenience of implication in order to enjoy the certainty of formalism. Whether it be embodied in the Statute of Wills or in the Statute of Frauds or in the Parol Evidence Rule or in the Doctrine of Consideration our law has universally recognized the salutary effect of a formalistic check upon decisions of great importance. In the area of war and peace, where the very existence of man as a species may hang in the balance, can we tolerate the Congressional abdication of that formalistic check?

.   .   .

Conclusion

This Court should declare that the Executive may not continue to prosecute a major war in Vietnam without the formal and explicit authorization of Congress. In order to avoid any unnecessary friction between the branches of government, appellant respectfully suggests that any such determination contain a self-executing stay pending review by the Supreme Court and that any judicial declaration concerning the lack of Executive authority to prosecute the war in Vietnam contain a self-executing stay for a period sufficient to permit Congress to convene and to grant formal and explicit authorization to the Executive to continue the war, should Congress wish to do so.

Respectfully submitted,

BURT NEUBORNE
LEON FRIEDMAN
NEW YORK CIVIL LIBERTIES UNION
    84 Fifth Avenue
        New York, New York 10011

KUNSTLER KUNSTLER & HYMAN
    511 Fifth Avenue
        New York, New York 10017

Attorneys for Appellant *

NORMAN DORSEN
KAY ELLEN HAYES
    Of Counsel

* Counsel herein wish to thank Edwin J. Oppenheimer, Arthur Eisenberg and Nancy Jacoby for valuable research assistance in the preparation of this brief.

Extracts from U.S. Attorney Brief, Berk v. Laird, Orlando v. Laird, Second Circuit Court of Appeals †

Argument

Point I

> *The claim for relief is clearly disclosed to involve a non-justiciable political question, and, therefore, the action was properly dismissed.*

This Court's opinion in the prior expedited appeal quite properly recognized that on the incomplete record then before it,

> "neither the district court nor this court has been adequately informed, and we cannot, in good conscience, now say that the appellant has shown probability of success on the merits if this stage is reached, although once again we do not foreclose the appellant from seeking to establish his claims." (429 F.2d at 306.)

The Court noted, however, the existence of the "Joint Resolution To Promote The Maintenance of International Peace and Security in Southeast Asia", commonly referred to as the Gulf of Tonkin Resolution, various appropriations and other acts in support of the military involvement in Vietnam, and pointed out that the "political question" doctrine would apply here un-

† Brackets within these extracts are in original brief. Cross references to material reproduced in this book have been changed to reflect the paging of this book.

less appellant could "suggest a set of manageable standards and escape the likelihood that his particular claim about this war at this time is a political question" (429 F.2d at 305).

After extensive briefing and argument of the basic legal and constitutional issues and facts relevant thereto, the District Court, on remand, found that the "manageable standards" suggested by appellant were contrary to legal and historical precedent and that, in any event, Congressional authorization for the conduct of the Vietnam war satisfied both the standards suggested by appellant as well as the standards which the District Court found to be applicable.

While the District Court's conclusions are, as shall be demonstrated, correct, the appellant's claim is now more fully disclosed to involve a non-justiciable political question. For that reason, appellees respectfully reassert their view that the appropriate remedy for any alleged departure from Constitutional or statutory limitations on the power of the President to engage the armed forces of the United States in military action must lie with the Congress and not the Judiciary and that jurisdiction of this action should have been declined.

The argument on this point is set forth in the brief filed by the Solicitor General of the United States in *Massachusetts* v. *Laird*, 400 U.S. 886 (1970) (see p. 214) which appellees adopt herein. The relevant portions of the Solicitor General's brief, upon which the appellees will rely, are appended to this brief.

Point II

> *Military action in Vietnam was explicitly authorized by the Congress in the "Joint Resolution To Promote the Maintenance of International Peace and Security in Southeast Asia".*

1. THE LANGUAGE OF THE JOINT RESOLUTION

Appellant advances the argument here, as he did in the District Court, that military action of the scale of the Vietnam conflict must be *explicitly* authorized *in advance* by the Congress. Although this argument is unencumbered by legal or historical precedent and is contrary to the decisions of the Supreme Court, the fact is that military action in Vietnam *was explicitly* authorized *in advance* by Congress. This approval came in the Joint Resolution To Promote The Maintenance of Internal Peace and Security in Southeast Asia (P. L. 88-408, Aug. 10, 1964).

The Joint Resolution, after taking note of the deliberate and repeated attacks on United States naval vessels by naval units of North Vietnam, went on to declare:

> Whereas these attacks are part of a deliberate and systematic campaign of aggression that the Communist regime in North Vietnam has been waging against its neighbors and the nations joined with them in the collective defense of their freedom; and
>
> Whereas the United States is assisting the peoples of southeast Asia to protect their freedom and has no territorial, military or political ambitions in that area, but desires only that these peoples should be left in peace to work out their own destinies in their own way: Now, therefore, be it
>
> *Resolved by the Senate and House of Representatives of the United States of America in Congress assembled, That:*
>
> The Congress approves and supports the determination of the President, as Commander in Chief, to take all necessary measures to repel any armed attack against the forces of the United States and to prevent further aggression.
>
> Sec. 2. The United States regards as vital to its national interest and to world peace the maintenance of international peace and security in Southeast Asia. Consonant with the Constitution of the United States and the Charter of the United Nations and in accordance with its obligations under the Southeast Asia Collective Defense Treaty, the United States is, therefore, prepared, as the President determines, to take all necessary steps, including the use of armed force, to assist any member or protocol state of the Southeast Asia Collective Defense Treaty requesting assistance in defense of its freedom.
>
> Sec. 3. This resolution shall expire when the President shall determine that the peace and security of the area is reasonably assured by international conditions created by action of the United Nations or otherwise, except that it may be terminated earlier by concurrent resolution of the Congress.

The Joint Resolution To Promote The Maintenance of International Peace and Security in Southeast Asia [hereinafter referred to as the Joint Resolution], as the District Court found, gave the President of the United States authority "to prevent aggression against Southeast Asia peoples who were protecting their freedom." (317 F. Supp. at 723.)

2. THE LEGISLATIVE HISTORY OF THE JOINT RESOLUTION

Appellant has attempted to avoid the effect of the *explicit* language of the Joint Resolution by quoting statements made by various members of the Congress both at the time of its enactment and in subsequent years. But, where the words of the Joint Resolution are so unambiguous and unequivocal, the language is controlling and there is no need to have recourse to these Congressional remarks. As Mr. Justice Jackson observed in his concurring opinion in *Schwegmann Brothers, et al.* v. *Calvert Distillers Corp.*, 341 U.S. 384, 395–96 (1951):

> Resort to legislative history is only justified where the face of the Act is inescapably ambiguous, and then I think we should not go beyond Committee reports, which presumably are well considered and carefully prepared. I cannot deny that I have sometimes offended against that rule. But to select casual statements from floor debates, not always distinguished for candor or accuracy, as a basis for making up our minds what law Congress intended to enact is to substitute ourselves for the Congress in one of its important functions * * * It is the business of Congress to sum up its own debates in its legislation. Moreover, it is only the words of the bill that have presidential approval, where that approval is given. It is not to be supposed that, in signing a bill, the President endorses the whole Congressional Record. For us to undertake to reconstruct an enactment from legislative history is merely to involve the Court in political controversies which are quite proper in the enactment of a bill but should have no place in its interpretation.

Justice Jackson concluded (*id.* at 397):

> By and large, I think our function was well stated by Mr. Justice Holmes: "We do not inquire what the legislature meant;

we ask only what the statute means." Holmes, Collected Legal Papers, 207.

Senator Ervin—to whose views appellant devotes a full two pages of his brief—aptly applied this dictum when, in later discussions over the Joint Resolution, he observed:

> I think the quotations you have called to the attention of the committee bear very strongly on what caused the various members of the Senate or the various members of the House to vote for the resolution. But I think the intent, that is what the resolution authorized, has to be determined from the resolution itself. And taking every word and all four corners I think it authorized the President to use armed forces there. *U.S. Commitments to Foreign Powers,* Hearings before the Committee on Foreign Relations, United States Senate, 90th Cong., 1st Session, Hearings on S. 151, p. 209.

Still, because appellant's discussion has by omission so distorted that legislative history, some response is called for here. An accurate reading of the contemporaneous debates reveals that the Congress was fully informed at the time that the Joint Resolution authorized major military steps including, if necessary, the commitment of large numbers of ground forces to combat activity in Southeast Asia. While it was hoped by all members of the Congress that major military involvement would not be required, the sponsors of the Joint Resolution candidly admitted that the Joint Resolution authorized large scale military activities in Southeast Asia.

The following colloquy between Senator Fulbright, Chairman of the Senate Foreign Relations Committee from which the Joint Resolution emerged, and Senator Cooper is particularly illuminating (110 Cong. Rec. 18409 [1964]):

> MR. COOPER [John Sherlman Cooper] * * * The Senator will remember that the SEATO Treaty, in article IV, provides that in the event an armed attack is made upon a party to the Southeast Asia Collective Defense Treaty, or upon one of the protocol states such as South Vietnam, the parties to the treaty, one of whom is the United States would then take such action as might be appropriate, after resorting to their constitutional

processes. I assume that would mean, in the case of the United States, that Congress would be asked to grant the authority to act.

Does the Senator consider that in enacting this resolution we are satisfying that requirement of article IV of the Southeast Asia Collective Defense Treaty? In other words, are we now giving the President advance authority to take whatever action he may deem necessary respecting South Vietnam and its defense, or with respect to the defense of any other country included in the treaty?

MR. FULBRIGHT: I think that is correct.

MR. COOPER: Then, looking ahead, if the President decided that it was necessary to use such force as could lead into war, we will give that authority by this resolution?

MR. FULBRIGHT: That is the way I would interpret it. If a situation later developed in which we thought the approval should be withdrawn it could be withdrawn by concurrent resolution.

A similar construction of the language of the Joint Resolution was voiced by Senator Morse, its leading Senate opponent. Senator Morse argued that the portion of the Joint Resolution authorizing the President "to take all necessary measures to * * * prevent further aggression" by North Vietnam "authorize[d] the President of the United States, without a declaration of war, to commit acts of war." (110 Cong. Rec. 18426–27 [1964]).

In subsequent debates Senator Cooper, looking back upon the discussion, noted that he thought that "when we passed the resolution that we were approving great powers for the President and I believe there is merit to his assertion that he is acting under that authority." *U.S. Commitments to Foreign Powers, supra,* p. 40.

Senator Cooper further observed that the Congress "had to anticipate that situations may occur the way they did and even to the dispatch of large forces of troops and the bombing of the north. I think you had to anticipate those things. * * * [W]e can discuss this now and urge changes in policy * * * but I have found great difficulty in challenging the use of the authority when we gave the President this resolution." Senator Ervin expressed full agreement with Senator Cooper: "That is a conclusion I come to after taking into consideration all of the words of the resolution * * * . I think that it gave the President that authority." *U.S. Commitments to Foreign Powers, supra*, p. 213.

Senator Gore likewise agreed that the Joint Resolution "is as broad an authorization for the use of armed forces for a purpose as any declaration of war * * * could be in terms of our internal Constitutional process." *U.S. Commitment to Foreign Powers, supra*, p. 89.

The Senate Foreign Relations Committee itself recognized that the Joint Resolution, "[c]ouched in broad terms", gave the President the power to dispatch troops to Vietnam. *National Commitments*, Sen. Report #797, Committee on Foreign Relations, 90th Congress, 1st Session, p. 70.

The language of the Joint Resolution To Promote The Maintenance of International Peace and Security In Southeast Asia, the contemporaneous interpretation placed on that language by its leading sponsor and its leading critic, as well as the views of some of the present leading critics of the Vietnam War, leave no room for doubt that Congress intended to and did in fact expressly authorize the President's use of the Armed Forces of the United States in Southeast Asia, including Vietnam.

3. THE EXECUTIVE'S RELIANCE ON THE JOINT RESOLUTION

(1)

Appellant asserts that "the Executive itself has expressly conceded since 1967 that it does not rely on the [Joint] Resolution for authority to carry on military operations in Southeast Asia" (App. Br. p. 29). Even were the assertion accurate, the fact that a President personally viewed the powers of his office as sufficient to justify his actions is hardly relevant. Surely, if a formal declaration of war had been passed, the President would not be estopped from relying upon it merely because he personally believed it to be unnecessary.

In any case, the assertion is misleading. The sole authority for the assertion is a statement by President Johnson at a press conference indicating that, in his personal opinion, he had the power to do what he did, but that if he were going to ask Congress "to stay the whole route" he wanted their approval at the outset. This statement, even when taken out of context, indicates that the President looked upon the Joint Resolution as authorizing his action. And later on he made his position plain when he observed:

> I believe that every Congressman and most of the Senators knew what that resolution said. That resolution authorized the President—and expressed the Congress's willingness to go along with the President—to do whatever was necessary to deter aggression. We are, as I say, trying to provide a maximum deterrent with a minimum loss. We think we are well within the rights of what the Congress said in its resolution. The remedy is there if we have acted unwisely or improperly. . . . But I don't believe we are acting beyond our Constitutional responsibility.*

On the very same day, August 17, 1967, the Under secretary of State, Nicholas Katzenbach, told the Senate Foreign Relations Committee:

> That resolution authorized the President of the United States, by an overwhelming vote, with only two dissents in both Houses of Congress, two together, to use the force of the United States in that situation. The combination of the two [SEATO and the Joint Resolution], it seems to me, fully fulfill the obligation of the Executive in a situation of this kind to participate with the Congress to give the Congress a full and effective voice, the functional equivalent of the constitutional obligation expressed in the provision of the Constitution with respect to declaring war.
>
> * * *
>
> Mr. Chairman, whether a resolution of that kind is or is not, does or does not perform the functions similar to a declaration of war must indeed depend upon what the language of that resolution is and what it says. Now the language of that resolution, Mr. Chairman, is, as the professor complained † but as Congress knew well, a very broad language.
>
> *U.S. Commitments to Foreign Powers, supra,* pp. 82 and 84.

---

* The Transcript of President Johnson's press conference appears in *U.S. Commitments to Foreign Powers, supra,* pp. 125–126.
† The reference is to Professor Bartlett, a prior witness before the Committee.

The views expressed by Mr. Katzenbach had been consistently taken by President Johnson and the members of his Administration from the moment the legality of his actions was questioned until the end of his Presidency.

On March 4, 1966, Leonard C. Meeker, Legal Advisor of the Department of State, told the Senate Foreign Relations Committee in a formal memorandum reprinted in the Congressional Record (112 Cong. Rec. 11202 [1966]) :

> The President of the United States has full authority to commit United States forces in the collective defense of South Vietnam. This authority stems from the constitutional powers of the President. However, it is not necessary to rely on the Constitution alone as the source of the President's authority, since the SEATO treaty—advised and consented to by the Senate and forming part of the law of the land—sets forth a United States commitment to defend South Viet-Nam against armed attack, and since the Congress—in the joint resolution of August 10, 1964, and in authorization and appropriations acts for support of the U.S. military effort in Viet-Nam—has given its approval and support to the President's actions. United States actions in Viet-Nam, taken by the President and approved by the Congress, do not require any declaration of war, as shown by a long line of precedents for the use of United States armed forces abroad in the absence of any congressional declaration of war.

On January 10, 1967, in his State of the Union Message, the President told Congress that we were in Vietnam because of the SEATO Treaty, because of a 1962 agreement which the Communists were violating, and because the people of South Vietnam have a right to remain non-Communist, if they choose. He added:

> *"We are there because the Congress has pledged by solemn vote to take all necessary measures to prevent further aggression."* Weekly Compilation of Presidential Documents, Jan. 16, 1967, p. 36 (Emphasis added).

On March 11, 1968 the Secretary of State, Dean Rusk, again cited the Joint Resolution as authority for the President's action. Hearings Before Committee On Foreign Relations, United States

Senate, 90th Cong., 2d Session, Hearings on S. 309, pp. 137–138.

Thus, while President Johnson felt he could constitutionally have acted without the Joint Resolution, there is no question that he viewed it as Congressional assent to his use of the Armed Forces of the United States in Vietnam, and he and members of his administration so informed the Congress.

(2)

Again, without conceding any legal relevance if the facts were otherwise, it should be pointed out that President Nixon has never suggested that the Joint Resolution did not authorize the massive commitment of American troops in South Vietnam. The Department of State, in a letter of H. J. Torbert, Jr., dated March 12, 1970, upon which appellant relies, advised the Senate Foreign Relations Committee that the Joint Resolution, along with other similarly worded resolutions, involving Formosa, the Middle East and Cuba, were "a highly visible means of executive-legislative consultation * * * *indicating congressional approval for the possible employment of United States military forces.*" (Emphasis added.) *Termination of Southeast Asia Resolution,* Sen. Report No. 91–872, 91st Cong., 2d Session, p. 20; see also: Rehnquist, *The Constitutional Issues—Administration Position,* 45 N.Y.U. Law Rev. 628, 637–38.

President Nixon found no occasion to rely specifically upon the Joint Resolution for the continued employment of our armed forces since his policy in Vietnam is to disengage troops of the United States from combat. In furtherance of this policy over a quarter of a million troops, including most ground combat forces, will have been withdrawn from Vietnam by May, 1971. (Weekly Compilation of Presidential Documents, Jan. 11, 1971, p. 38). On that date American troop strength will approach a five-year low of 284,000. (Weekly Compilation of Presidential Documents, *supra.*)

It is plain that in terminating United States troop participation, the President need not rely upon a resolution which authorized that very war.

4. THE REPEAL OF THE JOINT RESOLUTION

In the closing days of the 91st Congress the Joint Resolution was repealed (Foreign Military Sales Act of 1971, § 12, P.L. 91-672). The repeal does not retroactively invalidate actions which were taken during the period the Joint Resolution existed; nor does the repeal require the Executive to terminate immediately American involvement. In fact, the Congress has expressly refused to order the withdrawal of American forces from Vietnam by any specified date (See 116 Cong. Rec. [Daily Issue]) Sept. 1, 1970, S. 14859, defeating a proposal requiring withdrawal by December 31, 1971.* More significantly, in the Department of Defense Appropriations Act of 1971 Congress has specifically approved the continued employment of the Armed Forces of the United States in Vietnam (Department of Defense Appropriations Act of 1971, § 838, P.L. 91-668). These actions clearly satisfy any requirement of "significant Congressional authorization" for the President's policy of deliberate disengagement.

Moreover, almost six years of war have created innumerable facts involving not only the war itself, but this country's entire foreign policy. These facts must be considered by the Executive in deciding upon the pace and manner of his withdrawal policy. Consistent with Congressional legislation, the President, by virtue of his powers and responsibilities as Chief Executive and as Commander-in-Chief may disengage this country from its involvement in the Vietnam war in a manner he deems consistent with these constitutional responsibilities. *Johnson* v. *Eisentrager,* 339 U.S. 763, 789 (1950); *Chicago & Southern Air Lines* v. *Waterman S.S. Corp.,* 333 U.S. 103, 111 (1947); *United States* v. *Curtiss-Wright Export Corp.,* 299 U.S. 304, 319 (1936); *Ex parte Milligan,* 71 U.S. (4 Wall.) 2, 139 (1866); *Prize Cases,* 67 U.S. (2 Black) 635, 670 (1862); *Fleming* v. *Page,* 50 U.S. (9 How.) 603, 615 (1850), see also *Youngstown Sheet & Tube Co.*

* The text of proposal may be found in 116 Cong. Rec. (Daily Issue) Aug. 26, 1970, S. 14283.

v. *Sawyer,* 343 U.S. 579, 645 (1952) (Jackson, J., concurring opinion).

It is clear that the orders issued to appellant were and remain valid.

Point III

> *Congressional appropriations of funds expressly designated for the support of the military in Vietnam constitute both a prior authorization and a ratification of the commitment of United States armed forces to Vietnam.*

1. LEGISLATION RELATING TO VIETNAM

United States military participation in Vietnam would not have been possible without continuing Congressional assent and authorization. And that assent and authorization manifested itself in many ways over the course of the war.

For almost six years the Congress, exercising its powers under Art. 1, § 8 of the Constitution, has appropriated billions of dollars annually for the support of the war. The entire history of these appropriations as well as other forms of Executive consultation, including various Presidential messages to the Congress —is detailed in the District Court's opinion (317 F. Supp. at 723–25).* The Congress has, in the words of Judge Dooling in

---

* These funds were not simply provided from general appropriations; Congress explicitly and frequently legislated with particular reference to Vietnam, *E.g.,* an "emergency" supplemental appropriation act of May 7, 1965, appropriated $700,000,000 for use "upon determination by the President that such action is necessary in connection with military activities in southeast Asia," P.L. 89-18, 79 Stat. 109. See also P.L. 89-213, 79 Stat. 863, appropriating 1966 funds for the Department of Defense, with specific reference to Vietnam in a $1,700,000,000 emergency fund in Title V. P.L. 89-367, 80 Stat. 36, authorizing Armed Forces expenditures for FY 1966, stated in Title IV: "Funds * * * under this or any other Act are authorized to be made available for their stated purposes in connection with support of Vietnamese and other free world forces in Vietnam, * * *." A supplemental 1966 appropriation act, P.L. 89-374, 80 Stat. 79, contained similar language in Sec. 102(a). See also Sec. 640(a) of the 1967 appropriation act for the Department of Defense, P.L. 89-687, 80 Stat. 980.

P.L. 90-5, 81 Stat. 5, authorizing Armed Forces expenditures for 1967, contained a statement of policy in Sec. 401, declaring Congress' "firm intentions to

the companion *Orlando* case, "furnished forth the sinew of War" (*Orlando* v. *Laird,* 317 F. Supp. 1013, 1019 [1970]). Its support "of the Vietnam combat activities has been complete and unstinting" (*id.* at 1018).

In every year since 1965 either the authorization or appropriations acts * or both specifically "authorized [or appropriated] money to be spent for our forces in Vietnam" (Wallace Aff. 52A at pp. 57A–58A). In one of those authorization acts, the Armed Forces Supplemental Authorization Act of 1967, § 401 (P.L. 90-5), Congress expressly declared "its firm intention to provide all necessary support for members of the Armed Forces of the United States fighting in Vietnam". By their explicit words these laws both recognized and approved the use of the Armed Forces of the United States in combat.

In addition to the appropriation of funds to sustain the commitment of American forces, Congress in 1967 suspended the permanent limitations on the active duty strength of the armed forces. Military Selective Service Act of 1967, P.L. 90-40. This

provide all necessary support for members of the Armed Forces of the United States fighting in Vietnam", and supporting the "efforts being made by the President of the United States * * * to prevent an expansion of the war in Vietnam and to bring that conflict to an end through a negotiated settlement which will preserve the honor of the United States, protect the vital interests of this country, and allow the people of South Vietnam to determine the affairs of that nation in their own way." P.L. 90-22, 81 Stat. 52, authorizing Armed Forces procurement for 1968, specified in Sec. 301 that funds authorized for the use of the Armed Forces "under this or any other Act are authorized to be made available for their stated purposes to support * * * Vietnamese and other Free World Forces in Vietnam." The 1968 Department of Defense appropriation act, P.L. 90-96, 81 Stat. 231, in Sec. 639(a) (1) contains similar language. P.L. 90-392, 82 Stat. 307, contained in Chapter II an additional supplemental appropriation for 1968 for "Vietnam costs". P.L. 90-500, 82 Stat. 849, authorizing Armed Forces expenditures for 1969, in Sec. 401 authorized the use of funds "to support * * * Vietnamese and other Free World Forces in Vietnam". The 1969 Department of Defense appropriation act, P.L. 90-580, 82 Stat. 1120, Title V, contains similar language in Sec. 537(a) (1). Authorization for Armed Forces expenditures for 1970 is made in P.L. 91-121, 83 Stat. 204, which explicitly authorizes in Sec. 401(a) (1) $2,500,000,000 for use to support "Vietnamese and other Free World Forces in Vietnam". The 1970 Department of Defense appropriation act, P.L. 91-171, 83 Stat. 469, Title VI, Sec. 638(a) (1) provides that appropriations shall be available to support "Vietnamese and other free world forces in Vietnam."

* Except where the context indicates otherwise, the use of the term appropriations acts includes authorization acts.

suspension enabled the Executive to increase the number of men in uniform to meet the expanding role of our armed forces in Vietnam.

The magnitude of the operations which these Congressional acts made possible is conceded by all. The massive appropriation of funds and the conscription of troops—even absent the prior express authorization of the Joint Resolution—constitutes the authorization necessary to satisfy any requirement of "significant" Congressional assent (*Berk* v. *Laird, supra,* 429 F.2d at 305). Indeed, in *Orlando* v. *Laird, supra,* Judge Dooling found "the steady legislative support" of the war to be of "more compelling significance" than the Joint Resolution (317 F. Supp. at 1019).

2. CONGRESSIONAL RATIFICATION
(1)

Appellant concedes that the Congressional authorization for the engagement of American forces in combat, which, he contends, the Constitution mandates, is not limited exclusively to formal declarations of war. The history given in the opinion of Judge Judd compels that conclusion (317 F. Supp. at 721–23). Appellant contends, however, that in the case of Vietnam the only other acceptable alternative to a formal declaration of war is some kind of prior explicit authorization for the engagement of American troops and that all actions undertaken in the absence of such authorization are illegal.

We have already shown that the Joint Resolution would meet this test in the case of Vietnam, but the numerous appropriation acts cited would also satisfy the test. Aside from paying for and ratifying prior Executive actions, these appropriations acts also constituted a prior authorization for the actions which they continued to make possible. At every point, limitations on future use of the funds could have been imposed in order to effect an immediate withdrawal. But no such restrictions were ever passed.

In any case, even if there had never been a Joint Resolution and even if every penny of the billions of dollars appropriated were for past due bills, the Supreme Court has made clear on many occasions that "Congress may . . . do by ratification what it might have authorized." *Ex Parte Endo,* 323 U.S. 283, 303, n.24 (1944). The principle is supported in numerous decisions. Among them are some involving military action undertaken by the President without prior authorization.

In *Wilson* v. *Shaw,* 204 U.S. 24 (1907), the President acquired land for the purpose of constructing the Panama Canal. The President's action was not undertaken in the manner which Congress had prescribed. In holding that subsequent action on the part of Congress ratified the President's action, the Supreme Court held in language particularly apposite here (204 U.S. at 32):

> *A short but sufficient answer is that subsequent ratification is equivalent to original authority.* The title to what may be called the Isthmian or canal zone, which, at the date of the act, was in the Republic of Colombia, passed by an act of secession to the newly formed Republic of Panama. The latter was recognized as a nation by the President. A treaty with it, ceding the canal zone, was duly ratified. 33 Stat. at L. 2234. Congress has passed several acts based upon the title of the United States, among them one to provide temporary government, 33 Stat. at L. 429; another, fixing the status of merchandise coming into the United States from the canal zone, 33 Stat. at L. 843; another, prescribing the type of canal, 34 Stat. at L. 611. *These show a full ratification by Congress of what has been done by the Executive. Their concurrent action is conclusive upon the courts. We have no supervising control over the political branch of the Government in its action within the limits of the Constitution.* [Emphasis added.]

In the *Prize Cases,* 67 U.S. (2 Black) 635 (1862), the Supreme Court had occasion to rule on the propriety of a blockade undertaken by President Lincoln at the outset of the Civil War and prior to any express Congressional authorization. In the course of its opinion the Supreme Court observed (67 U.S. at 670):

> If it were necessary to the technical existence of a war, that it should have a legislative sanction, *we find it in almost every act*

passed at the extraordinary session of the Legislature of 1861, which was wholly employed in enacting laws to enable the Government to prosecute the war with vigor and efficiency. And finally, in 1861, we find Congress *"ex majore cautela"* and in anticipation of such astute objections, passing an act "approving, legalizing, and making valid all the acts, proclamations, and others of the President, &c., as if they had been issued and done under the previous express authority and direction of the Congress of the United States. [Emphasis added.]

The Supreme Court continued (67 U.S. at 671):

Without admitting that such an act was necessary under the circumstances, it is plain that if the President had in any manner assumed powers which it was necessary should have the authority or sanction of Congress, that on the well known principle of law, *"omnis ratihabitio retrotrahitur et mandato equiparatur,"* this ratification has operated to perfectly cure the defect. In the case of *Brown* vs. *United States,* (8 Cr., 131, 132, 133,) Mr. Justice Story treats of this subject, and cites numerous authorities to which we may refer to prove this position, and concludes, "I am perfectly satisfied that no subject can commence hostilities or capture property of an enemy, when the sovereign has prohibited it. But suppose he did, I would ask if the sovereign may not ratify his proceedings, and thus by a retroactive operation give validity to them?"

Although Mr. Justice Story dissented from the majority of the Court on the whole case, the doctrine stated by him on this point is correct and fully substantiated by authority.

The objection made to this act of ratification, that it is ex post facto, and therefore unconstitutional and void, might possibly have some weight on the trial of an indictment in a criminal Court. But precedents from that source cannot be received as authoritative in a tribunal administering public and international law. [Emphasis added.]

In the same opinion the Supreme Court cited the ratification of the Mexican War by Congress after the President had engaged American troops. The Supreme Court noted that the act which recognized *"a state of war existing by the act of the Republic of Mexico"* not only provided for the future prosecution of the war, "but was itself a ratification of the Act of the President in accepting the challenge without a previous formal declaration of war by Congress.'' (67 U.S. at 668).*

Ratification has also been found in appropriations legislation. As the District Court noted, there is no constitutional distinction between appropriations legislation and other acts of Congress. In *Ludecke* v. *Watkins,* 335 U.S. 160 (1947), the issue was whether the President had the authority to deport enemy aliens pursuant to the Alien Enemy Act of 1798 after the conclusion of actual hostilities, where the Alien Enemy Act specifically provided such authority only during the course of ''a declared war between the United States and any foreign nation. * * *''

The Supreme Court, in sustaining the President's power to deport an enemy alien after the termination of hostilities, noted that (335 U.S. 173, n. 19) :

> [Congress] has recognized that the President's powers under the Alien Enemy Act of 1798 were not terminated by the cessation of actual hostilities by appropriating funds ''* * * for all necessary expenses, incident to the maintenance, care, detention, surveillance, parole, and transportation of alien enemies and their wives and dependent children, including transportation and other expenses in the return of such persons to place of bona fide residence or to such other places as may be authorized by the Attorney General. * * *'' 61 Stat. 279, 292. ''And the appropriation by Congress of funds for the use of such agencies stands as confirmation and ratification of the action of the Chief Executive. *Brooks* v. *Dewar,* 313 U.S. 354, 361.'' *Fleming* v. *Mohawk Wrecking and Lumber Co.,* 331 U.S. 111, 116; see also *Isbrandtsen-Moller Co.* v. *United States,* 300 U.S. 139.†

---

* A similar act of ratification took place in 1914. President Wilson seized the Mexican port of Vera Cruz in 1914 as an act of reprisal, in order, he said, to "enforce respect" for the government of the United States. The two Houses of Congress adopted separate resolutions in support of President Wilson's action but the Senate did not complete action on its resolution until after the seizure of Vera Cruz. *National Commitments, supra,* p. 14.

† The Court need not tarry long with appellant's attempt to distinguish this established case law. He suggests that decisions involving ratification by appropriation all involved some form of prior Congressional authorization where subsequent appropriations only provided confirmation of the Executive's interpretation of the prior legislation. Accepting appellant's suggestion as true, it is plain, as has been demonstrated, that the President consistently relied upon the Joint Resolution as the source of his authority to dispatch troops to battle

The only limitation on the doctrine of ratification, where the ratifying acts do not expressly ratify the particular executive conduct, is that the circumstances surrounding the Congressional action must clearly indicate Congress was aware of the particular Executive conduct and, in the case of appropriation acts, that its appropriation was making possible the continued Executive conduct. See e.g. *Greene* v. *McElroy,* 360 U.S. 474 (1959). The issue there was whether regulations promulgated by the Secretary of Defense for the issuance of security clearances had been ratified by Legislative appropriation. The regulations had been promulgated without the authorization of Congress or the President and did not accord with the most elementary standards of fairness.

In an effort to sustain the validity of these procedures, the Secretary of Defense argued that Congress had ratified the procedures by appropriating funds to finance a program under which reimbursement for lost wages would be made to employees of government contractors who were temporarily denied, but were later granted security clearance. The only description made to Congress of the procedures promulgated by the Secretary of Defense was a general statement of the vaguest sort indicating that regulations of an unspecified nature had been promulgated. The description in the words of the Supreme Court "hardly constituted even notice to the Committee [which approved the appropriation] of the nature of the hearings afforded" under the promulgated procedures (360 U.S. at 505, n.30). Under these circumstances the Court held that the appropriation in question "could not constitute a ratification of the hearing procedures, for the procedures were in no way involved in the special reimbursement program" (360 U.S. at 505). *Cf. Youngstown Sheet & Tube Co.* v. *Sawyer,* 343 U.S. 579, 585 (1952), where the Supreme Court in striking down the President's seizure of the steel mills noted that there was no express legislative authorization: "[N]or is there any act of Congress * * * from which such a power can fairly be implied."

The decision in *Ex Parte Endo,* 323 U.S. 283 (1944), is pred-

in Vietnam. There is thus far more present here than "Congressional appropriations standing alone * * * " (See p. 178).

icated on similar reasoning. There the issue was whether Congress had ratified the detention of admittedly loyal Japanese-Americans by the War Relocation Authority. In declining to infer ratification from Congressional appropriation the Supreme Court observed (323 U.S. at 303 n. 24):

> Congress may of course do by ratification what it might have authorized. *Swayne & Hoyt* v. *United States,* 300 U.S. 297, 301–302. And ratification may be effected through appropriation acts. *Isbrandtsen-Moller Co.* v. *United States,* 300 U.S. 139, 147; *Brooks* v. *Dewar,* 313 U.S. 354, 361. But the appropriation must plainly show a purpose to bestow the precise authority which is claimed. We can hardly deduce such a purpose here where a lump appropriation was made for the overall program of the Authority and no sums were ear-marked for the single phase of the total program which is here involved. Congress may support the effort to take care of these evacuees without ratifying every phase of the program.

In the present case, the "conflict in Vietnam was not something hidden in department regulations" (317 F. Supp. at 728). Not only was Congress fully aware of the purpose for which its appropriations were being used, but specific sums were and continue to be "ear-marked" for the support of the President's dispatch of troops to battle in Vietnam. By language which can hardly be more explicit, Congress authorized the use of funds for men and materiel which they knew to be destined for use by the armed forces in Vietnam. These acts clearly and unequivocally demonstrate Congressional ratification of the President's actions.

Appellant refers to the reasons given by some members of Congress who voted for these appropriations. These statements are simply irrelevant. In determining whether Congress by its actions ratified the President's acts, the only issue is whether the Congressional acts relied upon, by their effect, if not their express language, authorized and made possible the continued conduct of the war by the President. Disclaimers voiced by various Congressmen that their votes for appropriations not be construed as approval of the Executive's policy in Vietnam can not override the fact that, knowing for what purpose the Executive proposed to use the monies appropriated, the members of Congress voted for the appropriations acts. As the Supreme Court observed in *Soon Hing* v. *Crowley*, 113 U.S. 703, 710–11 (1884):

> And the rule is general with reference to the enactments of all legislative bodies that the courts cannot inquire into the motives of the legislators in passing them, except as they may be disclosed on the face of the acts, or inferrible from their operation, considered with reference to the condition of the country and existing legislation. The motives of the legislators, considered as the purposes they had in view, will always be presumed to be to accomplish that which follows as the natural and reasonable effect of their enactments. *Their motives, considered as the moral inducement for their votes, will vary with the different members of the legislative body. The diverse character of such motives, and the impossibility of penetrating into the hearts of men and ascertaining the truth, precludes all such inquiries as impracticable and futile.* (Emphasis added.)

Judge Judd aptly applied this view to the instant case, when he said (317 F. Supp. at 724):

> Whatever the comments of individual Congressmen, the act nevertheless gave Congressional approval to military expenditures in Southeast Asia. That some members of Congress talked like doves before voting with the hawks is an inadequate basis for a charge that the President was violating the Constitution in doing what Congress by its words had told him he might do.

History and decisional law therefore support the District Court's legal conclusion that Congress could properly ratify the Executive's use of the armed forces and could place this ratification in appropriations legislation.

(2)

Appellant raises a number of arguments, discussed below, to support an assertion that "if Congress is held to exercise its war power merely by appropriating money to salvage an Executive-initiated military operation, the restrictions inherent in Article I, Section 8, Clause 11, are completely emasculated" (App. Br.

p. 58).* The assertion fails because the fact is that the founding fathers granted Congress the means to enforce the "inherent restrictions" in Clause 11. As Judge Dooling observed in the *Orlando* opinion (317 F. Supp. at 1018):

> The Constitution does not simply make the power to declare war a legislative power, it makes the related powers over the military, their provision and their governance equally matters of legislative concern, and extends the legislative power to calling up the militia to repel invasion and even to the granting of letters of marque, a species of authorized predation seemingly of a dimension to concern the Executive rather than to involve the legislative process. The systematic vesting of control over the means and the determination of the occasion of belligerency in the Congress makes inevitable that no combat activity of magnitude in size and duration can continue without affirmative and systematic legislative support.

See also: *Davi* v. *Laird,* 318 F. Supp. 478 (W.D. Va. 1970).

Indeed, recent events—culminating in the passage of funds to support combat activities in Vietnam, but prohibiting any military expeditions by United States ground forces to Laos or Thailand (Dept. of Defense Appropriations Act, *supra,* §§ 838, 843)—illustrate the point made by Judge Dooling. The opponents of the restrictions on funds for military operations in Cambodia, Laos and Thailand were forced to accept restrictions or get no appropriations whatever. As the Chairman of the House Appropriations Committee stated (Cong. Rec., Daily Issue, Dec. 29, 1970, H12495):

> In the conference with the Senate today, when we considered the use of American ground combat troops in Cambodia, the House was compelled, in order to get a conference agreement, to strike out this proviso [permitting the use of troops in Cambodia and Thailand under certain circumstances] which the House supported originally, and which the House conferees would have continued to support. We yielded in order that a conference report might be placed before the House today for consideration.

---

* Most of these arguments would also apply to any form of ratification of Executive employment of military force although, as shown above, such ratifications have been historically and legally recognized.

This statement also illustrates the fact that, contrary to appellant's suggestion that the "onus" is on the anti-war forces to marshal a majority to stop the President, the burden is always on the President to obtain a majority to appropriate the money needed to make the conduct of the war possible and under conditions he deems advisable. These recent events are likewise a sufficient answer to appellant's suggestion that a Presidential veto of such a restriction would ultimately require a two-thirds vote of Congress to stop military involvement, whereas a simple majority may defeat a declaration. The suggestion simply ignores the reality of the Legislative process. The Executive is always beholden to the Congress for the funds necessary to engage in a war; a veto of an appropriations bill restricting the use of funds as a practical matter means no appropriations at all rather than an unrestricted appropriation.

Appellant's contention that the Executive can place Congress under irresistible pressure to appropriate funds to "support our boys" is also specious. Congress can readily overcome such an argument by the Executive by appropriating only such funds as may be necessary to stage an immediate, safe withdrawal. And, as for appellant's contention that Congressional assent can be coerced by executive initiative (the *"fait accompli"* theory), Judge Dooling's response is pertinent (317 F. Supp. at 1019):

> That, however, is simply a charge of Congressional pusillanimity. Such evidence * * * could only disclose the motive and could not disprove the fact of authorization. The Constitution presents the Congress with the opportunity for it, but it cannot compel the making of unpopular decisions by members of Congress.

Adoption of any particular formula for registering Congressional approval will not insure Congressional responsibility,* while imposition of any such requirement would severely restrict

---

* Appellant claims that if the Congress is not precluded from authorizing military action through appropriations legislation and other combat-related legislation, the electorate will not be able to hold members of the Congress accountable for their legislative stance for or against such military action. In fact, however, the positions taken by Congressional candidates with respect to our military involvement in Vietnam have been vital issues in Senatorial and House elections almost from the beginning. Also, there is no evidence that the founding fathers desired to restrict Congress to a formal declaration of war as

the discretion of the Congress in an area where it is most necessary. For that reason, Judge Judd correctly concluded that even if the general question of whether there had been Congressional approval is a justiciable one, for the Judiciary to dictate the manner or language of the authorization would involve it in a political question (317 F. Supp. at 728–29). The manner and form of the authorization may involve questions of policy of the greatest magnitude. Vital considerations of international politics and our relationships with other countries are involved. See *United States* v. *Sisson,* 294 F. Supp. 511, 514–15 (D. Mass. 1968). These considerations may well influence both the mode and the language of Congressional approval. Thus, Congress should not be limited in its choice of the forms its approval may take.

The manner in which our armed forces are employed is certainly a matter committed by the Constitution jointly to the Executive and Legislative Departments, and once there is any indication of Congressional assent to the Executive's use of the armed forces, the Court's inquiry should terminate. For as the Supreme Court said, in *Wilson* v. *Shaw, supra,* 204 U.S. at 32;

> Their concurrent action is conclusive upon the courts. We have no supervising control over the political branch of the Government in its action within the limits of the Constitution.

(3)

Judge Dooling in his *Orlando* opinion concluded that: "the reality of the collaborative action of the executive and the legislative required by the Constitution has been present from the earliest stages." (317 F. Supp. at 1019; see also: *United States* v. *Sisson, supra,* 294 F. Supp. at 514 [Wyzanski, J.].) Though some members of Congress and others, having later found our involvement in Vietnam to be unwise, now charge that President Johnson's employment of the armed forces in Vietnam was an act of usurpation, the record establishes that he acted with the consent of the Congress and in full accord with the requirements of the Constitution.

opposed to any other mode of legislative approval, in order to render the members of Congress more accountable to the people.

Conclusion

The judgment below should be affirmed.

February 12, 1971

> Respectfully submitted,
> EDWARD R. NEAHER,
> *United States Attorney,*
> *Eastern District of New York.*

ROBERT A. MORSE,
  Chief Assistant United States Attorney,
DAVID G. TRAGER,
EDWARD R. KORMAN,
JAMES D. PORTER, JR.,
  Assistant United States Attorneys
    of Counsel.

Extracts from Solicitor General's Brief, Massachusetts v. Laird, U.S. Supreme Court†

Original Jurisdiction Should Be Declined Because the Issue Presented Is Non-Justiciable

This Court should decline to accept jurisdiction for the additional reason that the issue sought to be raised in this case is a

† The United States Attorney in *Berk* and *Orlando* submitted the government's Supreme Court brief in *Massachusetts* v. *Laird* to the Second Circuit

non-justiciable political question, *Baker* v. *Carr*, 369 U.S. 186;
Powell v. *McCormack, supra; Georgia* v. *Stanton*, 6 Wall. 50;
Luther v. *Borden*, 7 How. 1, and fails to meet the general criterion of justiciability stated in *Powell* v. *McCormack*, 395 U.S.
486, 516–517.

A. GENERAL CONSIDERATIONS OF JUSTICIABILITY

This Court has recently stated that the general test of justiciability is whether " 'the duty asserted can be judicially identified and its breach judicially determined,' and whether protection for the right asserted can be judicially molded." *Powell* v.
McCormack, supra, 395 U.S. at 517; *Baker* v. *Carr, supra*, 369
U.S. at 198. In the instant case, it is doubtful whether the asserted duty of Congress to participate in the war-making process
can be judicially identified; if it (18) can be identified, nonetheless a breach of that duty cannot be judicially determined; nor
can protection for Massachusetts' asserted right be judicially
molded.

1. IT IS AT LEAST UNCERTAIN WHETHER THE ASSERTED DUTY OF CONGRESS TO PARTICIPATE IN THE WAR-MAKING PROCESS CAN BE JUDICIALLY IDENTIFIED.

Massachusetts' initial contention is that the commitment of
American troops to hostilities must be authorized by Congress.
The Constitution confers the power "[t]o declare War" on Con-
gress, Art. I, Sec. 8, para. 11, and this Court early referred to
the power to make war as legislative in character. *E.g., Bas* v.
Tingy, 4 Dall. 37, 38; *Talbot* v. *Seeman*, 1 Cranch 1; but see
Little v. *Barreme*, 2 Cranch 170, 177. Those cases, however, also
recognized that not all hostilities need be formally declared.
" [H]ostilities may subsist between two nations, more confined in
its nature and extent; being limited as to places, persons and

Court of Appeals since many of the same points were raised in both cases.
Footnotes have been renumbered. Brackets are in original brief. Cross references to material reproduced in this book have been changed to reflect paging
of this book.

things; and this is more properly termed imperfect war; because not solemn, and because those who are authorized to commit hostilities act under special authority, and can go no further than to the extent of their commission." 4 Dall. at 40 (Washington, J.).

Under what circumstances congressional authority is required for such "limited" wars is open to debate. On the whole, the early cases might appear to state that such authority was required. But subsequent opinions, dealing with hostilities initiated by the opposing party, either assumed or held that such authority was *not* required. Thus, in *Montoya* v. *United States*, 180 U.S. 261, this Court characterized Indian Wars, fought so far as appears entirely on executive authority, as a type of limited war for which a declaration of war was not required; the question of congressional authorization was never examined. And in the *Prize Cases*, 2 Black 635, 668, this Court specifically held that no congressional action was required to authorize the blockades proclaimed by President Lincoln at the outset of the Civil War:

> If a war be made by invasion of a foreign nation, the President is not only authorized[1] but bound to resist force by force. He does not initiate the war, but is bound to accept the challenge without waiting for any special legislative authority. And whether the hostile party be a foreign invader, or States organized in rebellion, it is nonetheless a war, although the declaration of it be *"unilateral."* * * * *"* * * A declaration of war by one country only, is not a mere challenge to be accepted or refused at pleasure by the other." [Emphasis in original.]

The Court specifically held that the question in that case, whether the insurrection had advanced to a state of civil war, was one to be decided *by the President,* and that the Court was bound by his decision. While noting that congressional authority was not wanting if it were required, the Court specifically refused to reach that issue. *Id.* at 670–671.

---

[1] The Court was referring to Acts of Congress of February 28, 1795, and March 3, 1807, authorizing the President to call out the militia and use the military and naval forces of the United States in case of invasion by foreign nations, and to suppress insurrection against the government of a state or of the United States. 2, Black at 668. These statutes constituted neither a declaration of war nor an authorization of specific, limited hostilities.

Recognition of executive power to repel attacks without specific congressional authorization directly influenced the wording of the war power clause. See 2 Farrand, *Records of the Federal Convention*, pp. 318–319. The draft Constitution first submitted to the delegates gave Congress the power "[t]o make war." Mr. Pinkney objected to vesting this power in the whole Congress on the grounds its proceedings were "too slow". He urged that the power to make war be vested in the Senate. Mr. Butler, on the other hand, said that the same objections to vesting the power in the legislature would also apply against vesting it in the Senate; he was for vesting the power in the President, "who will have all the requisite qualities, and will not make war but when the Nation will support it." Responding to these objections to vesting the power "to make war" in Congress, Mr. Madison and Mr. Gerry moved to insert the word "declare" instead of "make" in the draft, "leaving to the Executive the power to repel sudden attacks." The amendment was adopted by the Convention, and "to make war" was replaced by "to declare war".

It soon became apparent that the President's power to repel sudden attacks was not confined to the territory of the United States. In 1801 President Jefferson, who supported a restricted view of the powers of the Presidency, on his own authority sent the American fleet into the Mediterranean, where it engaged in a naval battle with the Tripolitan fleet. In a message to Congress Jefferson construed his authority under the Constitution as permitting him to engage in defensive—but not offensive—operations without Congressional authorization. 11 Annals of Cong. 12 (1801).[2] He had taken the action, he said, because Tripoli "had come forward with demands unfounded either in right or in compact, and had permitted itself to denounce war, on our failure to comply before a given day." The style of the demands "admitted but one answer", and so Jefferson had sent American vessels of war into the Mediterranean "with orders to protect our commerce against the threatened attack." A Tripolitan cruiser engaged in battle an American ship, and was captured

---

[2] See also *Youngstown Co.* v. *Sawyer*, 343 U.S. 579, 642, n. 10 (Jackson, J., concurring) ; Note, *Congress, The President, and the Power to Commit Forces to Combat*, 81 Harv. L. Rev. 1771, 1772–1782 (1968).

"after a heavy slaughter of her men." However, "[u]nauthorized by the Constitution, without the sanction of Congress, to go beyond the line of defence, the vessel, being disabled from committing further hostilities, was liberated with its crew." Jefferson then asked that Congress authorize future "measures of offence" so as to "place our force on an equal footing with that of its adversaries". (*Id.* emphasis added.)

Others took a less restrictive view. Alexander Hamilton, while agreeing that no congressional sanction was necessary for defensive operations even beyond the territory of the United States, believed that the President's power to act under the Constitution without Congressional authority extended to an action to repel aggression from another nation, because a state of war "is completely produced by the act of one [nation]—it requires no concurrent act of the other." 7 Works of Alexander Hamilton 746 (J. Hamilton ed. 1851). The "plain meaning" of the Constitutional grant of power to Congress to declare war, according to Hamilton, was that:

> it is the peculiar and exclusive province of Congress, *when the nation is at peace* to change that state into a state of war; whether from calculations of policy, or from provocations, or injuries received: in other words, it belongs to Congress only, *to go to War.* But when a foreign nation declares, or openly and avowedly makes war upon the United States, they are then by the very fact *already at war,* and any declaration on the part of Congress is nugatory; it is at least unnecessary. * * * [*Id.* at 746–747; emphasis in original.]

Both sides of the debate recognize a dividing line between the authority of the President, acting alone, and the authority of Congress. Ordinarily, one might believe that the judicial function permitted both resolution of the debate—that is, a determination how extensive a conduct of hostilities the authority to repel permits—and a decision into which category a particular conflict falls. There are, however, substantial reasons to doubt whether that is a judicially manageable task.

As is well enough known, the doctrine of executive response has been extended well beyond this country's borders, to protect

American persons and property wherever found. *E.g., Durand v. Hollins,* 8 Fed. Cas. 111 (CC S.D.N.Y.); Memorandum of the Legal Advisor of the Department of State, 75 Yale L. J. 1085 (1966); *Amicus Curiae* Brief on Behalf of the Lawyers Committee on American Policy Toward Vietnam. The determination to station troops in South Vietnam, a friendly nation, was as much a matter for executive judgment as was Jefferson's decision to send the fleet into the international waters of the Mediterranean.[3] The troops and American property being there, it is at least proper to defend them against attack (Jefferson) if not to take all expedient measures to deal with the aggressor (Hamilton). That in turn calls for decision whether the executive actions taken were strictly ''defensive'' measures, or whether the opposing forces were properly identified as ''the aggressor.'' [4] In the one case, the Court would have to develop standards which are simply unreal in the face of the exigencies of battle; in the other, it would be delving into questions which—like the recognition of a foreign state, p. 39 *infra*—are suitable only to political decision.

What looks at the outset to be a typical issue suitable for judicial resolution thus appears on closer inspection to be doubtful in the extreme. The recent magnitude of the hostilities cannot be the test; they did not attain that magnitude overnight. The question of executive against congressional authority would have to be resolved at each stage of its development in the light of the circumstances existing at that stage. At that level, we submit, it is at least uncertain whether the maturing of the asserted congressional duty to participate in authorizing the hostilities can be judicially identified.

[3] "Certainly it is not the function of the Judiciary to entertain private litigation—even by a citizen—which challenges the legality, the wisdom, or the propriety of the Commander-in-Chief in sending our armed forces abroad or to any particular region." *Johnson* v. *Eisentrager,* 339 U.S. 763, 789.

[4] Cf. Stone, *Aggression and World Order* (Berkeley, 1958). This Court would not be called upon to decide who is "the aggressor" in the sense an international tribunal might be asked to resolve that issue. The question here is whether, as a matter of domestic legality, the Court can question the characterization of that issue already made by another branch of government. Cf. pp. 30, 38 *infra*.

2. BREACH OF THE DUTY ASSERTED CANNOT BE DETERMINED BY THIS COURT.

Assuming it could be decided that a congressional duty to authorize the hostilities has matured, it could not be judicially determined whether Congress has breached that duty. For Massachusetts quite properly does not assert that in order to fulfill its constitutional obligation Congress must pass a formal declaration of war. Instead Massachusetts' brief seems to recognize that the power to "declare War" conferred upon Congress by Article I, Sec. 8 of the Constitution, contains within it the power to determine when and how to declare war. See Br. p. 70.

Indeed, the Constitution does not require Congress to authorize American participation in hostilities only through a formal declaration. *Bas.* v. *Tingy, supra,* 4 Dall. 39–40, 43–45. Any such requirement would impose unworkable limitations on the nation's conduct of its foreign affairs. As Judge Wyzanski noted in *United States* v. *Sisson,* 294 F. Supp. 511, 515 (D. Mass.), one reason why a formal declaration of war in Indochina might not have been sought is that "[a] declaration of war expresses in the most formidable and unlimited terms a belligerent posture against an enemy." Another reason may be that a declaration of war in Vietnam would have "international implication of vast dimensions," and would "produce consequences which no court can fully anticipate." *Ibid.*[5] Whatever the reasons, it would be very undesirable for Congress to be limited to authorizing a war effort through formal declaration, and it is not so limited.[6]

---

[5] A contrary conclusion has been reached, erroneously in our view, by Judge Sweigert in the Northern District of California. *Mottola* v. *Nixon,* Civ. No. 70-943, decided September 9, 1970. Compare *Berk* v. *Laird,* Civ. No. 70-C-697 (on remand), E.D.N.Y., decided September 16, 1970; the government is having the *Berk* opinion printed and will submit it shortly as a supplement to this brief.

[6] The brief of Massachusetts and the amicus Constitutional Lawyers' Committee on Undeclared War urge that the constitutional vesting of the power to declare war in Congress was designed to give Congress, not the President, the power to initiate combat hostilities, and that Congress should not be placed in the position of having to approve military hostilities which have already been begun. However, in only two wars in American history, at most, has Congress been able to authorize war prior to commencement of actual hostili-

It hardly needs belaboring that Congress has acted consistently, from the beginning of hostilities in 1965 and in very substantial ways, in support of the American effort in Indochina.[7] As Massachusetts' complaint points out, the annual direct cost of that effort increased from $1,700,000,000 for fiscal year 1965 (Complaint, p. 5), to over $19,000,000,000 for fiscal year 1967 (*id.*, p. 6) and over $30,000,000,000 is now being spent annually (*id.*, p. 3). According to the complaint the United States has currently spent a total of over $110,000,000,000 (*id.*, p. 3). The number of American troops in Vietnam has increased from 23,000 at close of 1964 (*id.*, p. 4), to over 500,000 in 1968, and approximately 400,000 are still there (*id.*, pp. 7–8). The funds used to conduct the hostilities were appropriated by Congress, frequently with specific reference to Vietnam,[8] the manpower used in combat was made available by Congress' extension of the draft.[9] In sum, as Judge Wyzanski remarked in *Sisson, supra,*

ties. The Mexican War was begun by executive action in April, 1846 (See President Polk's Message to Congress of May 11, 1846, 15 Cong. Globe, 29th Cong., 1st Sess. 783 (1846)), which Congress ratified on May 13, 1846 (9 Stat. 9–10). See the *Prize Cases,* 2 Black 635, 668. In the Civil War, the South had occupied Fort Sumter, and President Lincoln in April, 1861, had instituted military activities in response, all prior to Congressional authorization of the war in August, 1861 (12 Stat. 326). See the *Prize Cases, supra.* American participation in World War I began with a Congressional declaration that Germany, through "repeated acts of war," had "thrust a state of war upon the United States, which Congress formally recognized (40 Stat. 1). And in World War II, the Congressional declaration of war (55 Stat. 795–797) followed the Japanese attack on Pearl Harbor. Thus, of the six declared wars in American history (War of 1812, Mexican War, Civil War, Spanish-American War, World War I, and World War II), in only the War of 1812 and the Spanish-American War can it be said that Congress was not faced with recognizing the *fait accompli* of actual hostilities. When one adds the many military actions involving American troops which were never declared as war, or otherwise preceded by specific congressional directive, it becomes apparent that Congress has almost invariably been in the approving rather than the initiating role. See *Background Information on the Use of United States Armed Forces in Foreign Countries,* Committee Print for the House Committee on Foreign Affairs, 91st Cong., 2d Sess.
[7] *E.g.,* The Southeast Asia Resolution (Gulf of Tonkin), P.L. 88-408, 78 Stat. 384; see *Berk* v. *Laird,* 317 F. Supp. 715 (E.D.N.Y.) (See p. 116).
[8] See p. 85.
[9] The Military Selective Service Act of 1967, P.L. 90-40, 81 Stat. 100, 50 U.S.C. (App. Supp. V) 451, *et seq.* Until June 1969, Congress also authorized the President to call up the reserves for use in the war. P.L. 89-687, Title I, 80 Stat. 981; P.L. 90-500, Title III, 82 Stat. 850.

294 F. Supp. and 514, ''What the court thus faces is a situation in which there has been joint action by the President and Congress, even if the joint action has not taken the form of a declaration of war.''

The question then becomes whether this observable congressional involvement is sufficient to meet any constitutional requirement of legislative concurrence. While if put to the issue we would argue that it is sufficient,[10] here we suggest that the question cannot be judicially determined. We propose two bases for that conclusion.

First, the same considerations which make plain that Congress is not limited to a formal declaration of war as its sole means of authorizing American participation in combat, also lead to the conclusion that no particular form of authorization is necessary. Like the decision to declare war, decisions regarding the form and substance of congressional enactments authorizing hostilities are determined by highly complex considerations of diplomacy, foreign policy and military strategy inappropriate to judicial inquiry. For this Court to impose formal requisites of action would be to straitjacket the nation in ''this vast external realm,'' *United States* v. *Curtiss-Wright* Corp., 299 U.S. 304, 319, in which flexibility of action in dealing with other sovereigns is essential.

Given that in this respect the Congress shares power with the Executive in directing state affairs, their mutual action ought not to be hindered by judicial inquiry or intrusion.[11] See *Chicago*

[10] Cf. *Brooks* v. *Dewar,* 313 U.S. 354; *Isbrandtsen-Moller Co.* v. *United States,* 300 U.S. 139, 147; *Fleming* v. *Mohawk Co.,* 331 U.S. 111, 116; *Ludecke* v. *Watkins,* 335 U.S. 160, 173, n. 19, recognizing the well-established principle that Congress through appropriation acts may ratify actions taken by the executive department. Such a ratification occurs if the appropriation "plainly show[s] a purpose to bestow the precise authority which is claimed", *Ex Parte Endo,* 323 U.S. 283, 303, n. 24. The series of statutes appropriating funds for use of the armed forces in Vietnam, clearly bestow such authority for American military participation in Vietnam, as Congress time and again in these statutes specified that the funds were to be used by the armed forces for "support [of] Vietnamese and other free world forces in Vietnam." Compare the *Prize Cases,* 2 Black 635, 670.

[11] The scope of possible intrusion is revealed by the three-page proposed "manageable standard" suggested by the American Civil Liberties Union and the Civil Liberties Union of Massachusetts, *amici curiae,* Br. pp. 12–14. That

& *Southern Air Lines* v. *Waterman SS. Corp.*, 333 U.S. 103, 111;
Coleman v. *Miller*, 307 U.S. 433, 454; *Oetjen* v. *Central Leather
Co.*, 246 U.S. 297, 302; *Pauling* v. *McNamara*, 331 F.2d 796
(C.A.D.C.), certiorari denied, 377 U.S. 933; See also *Youngstown Co.* v. *Sawyer*, 343 U.S. 579, 635–637. That is, the question
how, or in what form, to authorize hostilities is an essentially
political one. Unless in some extreme case—unlike this one—
Congress has done nothing whatever which could be interpreted
as authorizing a war, or has explicitly placed itself in conflict
with the Executive, the judicial branch cannot determine whether
or not its actions satisfactorily demonstrate that "this nation
has 'made up its mind in an adequate way.' " (Mass. Br. p. 70).

Second, any inquiry into the motives or practical freedom of
Congress in enacting apparently authorizing legislation is also
foreclosed. Massachusetts' case rests on the proposition that all
present legislative expressions of support for American participation in the hostilities can be dismissed as coerced on the
ground that "as a practical matter, Congressmen have no alternative but to support our fighting men" (Br. p. 84).

> But it is idle to suggest that the Congress is so little ingenious
> or so inappreciative of its powers, including the power of im-
> peachment, that it cannot seize policy and action initiatives at
> will, and halt courses of action from which it wishes the na-
> tional power to be withdrawn. * * * [Evidence of] a charge of
> Congressional pusillanimity * * * and its extent and validity
> are not to be supposed, could only disclose the motive and could
> not disprove the fact of authorization. The Constitution presents
> the Congress with the opportunity for it, but it cannot compel
> the making of unpopular decisions by the members of Con-
> gress. * * *

Orlando v. *Laird*, Civ. No. 70 C 745, E.D.N.Y., decided July 1,
1970, slip op., pp. 16–18; see also Jones, *The President, Congress
and Foreign Relations*, 29 Cal. L. Rev. 565, 577 (1941); Corwin,
The President: Office and Powers, 210–211 (1941). The inquiry
which Massachusetts proposes—and which would be required to

standard was properly rejected as unmanageable, for the reasons given above,
in *Berk* v. *Laird, supra*, p. 116.

impugn the statements repeatedly made by Congress in the cited legislation, n. 14 *supra*—is in itself an assault upon the dignity of a coequal and independent branch, and for that reason should not be undertaken. See *Field* v. *Clark,* 143 U.S. 649, 672–673; *Baker* v. *Carr,* 369 U.S. 186, 214–215.

In this respeot the issue here is quite different from that in *Green* v. *McElroy,* 360 U.S. 474, on which Massachusetts relies. There, the Court was concerned whether Congress had authorized executive action—the establishment of an industrial security program—which omitted "traditional safeguards of due process" in its dealings with individuals. 360 U.S. at 506–508. Such a program raised serious constitutional doubts, which the Court was unwilling to face in the absence of a clear congressional judgment that that particular feature was essential. But there is no doubt here that Congress has used language authorizing American participation in the hostilities; the issue is whether, in view of supposed influences on its freedom of action, that language should be given operative force. The question of authorizing that participation is not one which it could rationally be believed Congress overlooked; it is the subject of daily debate, and a pivotal issue in election campaigns.

3. EFFECTIVE JUDICIAL RELIEF CANNOT BE ORDERED IN THIS CASE.

Even assuming that this Court could find a congressional duty to authorize American participation in Vietnam and determine its breach, the Court could not mold effective "protection" for the right Massachusetts asserts. Massachusetts seeks (1) a declaration that the United States' present participation in the Vietnam hostilities is unconstitutional, and (2) an injunction enjoining the Secretary of Defense from (a) increasing the present level of the United States troops in Indochina and (b) from ordering any inhabitant of Massachusetts to Vietnam absent effective congressional action (Complaint, p. 12).

At the outset, it is clear that injunctive relief could not properly be granted. If the Secretary of Defense were enjoined from sending Massachusetts citizens to Vietnam, the result would be to place an additional burden on citizens of others states. Even if it were otherwise appropriate to broaden the requested injunction to cover citizens of all states, such an injunction would, in effect, mandate the withdrawal of all United States forces from Vietnam within a one-year period, the standard tour of duty of an American soldier in Vietnam. As the President has repeatedly emphasized in his ongoing dialogue with Congress, announcement of a total withdrawal within a short, definite period of time could entail disastrous diplomatic, political and military consequences for the United States.

Even assuming an injunctive remedy could be devised with sufficient flexibility to prevent military and political disaster (in plaintiff's words, within a "reasonable time," see Br., p. 34), this Court would face insurmountable enforcement difficulties. Judicial supervision of a withdrawal from Vietnam would entail unthinkable complexities and a possible confrontation of massive scope. The Court might have to set up its own office of military affairs and supervise the vast and intricate process of military disengagement. It might have to provide officials to carry on diplomatic discussions with the North Vietnamese and other governments. Entirely aside from practical difficulties, any such steps would constitute a serious breach of the "fundamental division of authority and power established by the Constitution * * *" which "precludes judges from overseeing the conduct of foreign policy or the use and disposition of military power * * *" *Luftig* v. *McNamara,* 373 F.2d 664, 665–66 (6 C.A.D.C.).[12] See also *Velvel* v. *Johnson,* 287 F.Supp. 846 (D. Kans.), affirmed, 415 F.2d 236 (C.A. 10), certiorari denied, 396 U.S. 1042; *Simmons* v. *United States,* 406 F.2d 456, 460 (C.A. 5), certiorari denied, 395 U.S. 982; *Ashton* v. *United States,* 404 F.2d 95 (C.A. 8), certiorari denied, 394 U.S. 960;

---

[12] The President has already embarked on a course of action designed to terminate our involvement in Vietnam combat. Over 100,000 United States troops have been withdrawn and the President has announced his intent to withdraw an additional 150,0000 troops by April 20, 1971. The President's Interim Report to the Nation, June 3, 1970, Weekly Compilation of Presidential Documents, Vol. 6, No. 23, p. 721, June 8, 1970. The President has pledged "to end the war in a way that will promote peace rather than conflict throughout the world." *Id.,* p. 724.

United States v. *Sisson, supra;* compare *Berk* v. *Laird,* C.A. 2, No. 35,007 decided June 19, 1970 (on preliminary injunction) with *Berk* v. *Laird, supra* n. 11 (on remand).

The possibility that Congress would remedy any deficiency in authorization by further acts presents questions equally unsuitable for judicial consideration. One may readily suppose that Congress would continue to act in conjunction with the Executive, through the appropriation of funds, the authorization of manpower and other cooperative measures. On the basis of such congressional action, taken after the Court's decree that American participation in the hostilities is unconstitutional, it might well be contended that Congress has ratified the combat effort. If the government were then to bring an action to modify a declaratory judgment or to dissolve an injunction ordered by this Court, or if the government were to raise the subsequent congressional authorization as a defense to an enforcement action for violation of the Court's decree, this Court would once again confront the non-justiciable questions of foreign policy and congressional motive involved in an evaluation and congressional expressions concerning American participation with hostilities.

In these circumstances, a declaratory judgment would be inappropriate. In *Powell* v. *McCormack, supra,* this Court spoke in broad terms about the availability of a declaratory judgment in the absence of other relief and regardless ''of whether other forms of relief are appropriate.'' 395 U.S. at 518. In *Powell,* however, the Court was adjudicating the well-defined rights of one man in a situation in which it was by no means certain that those rights could not be vindicated in further judicial proceedings as a result of the declaratory judgment. In the instant case, Massachusetts asserts a right claimed in behalf of millions of citizens to end the American presence in Vietnam. The judiciary could do no more than to announce the right. ''[N]o principle of constitutional law has been more firmly established or constantly adhered to, than * * * that this Court has no jurisdiction in any case where it cannot render judgment in the legal sense of the term; and when it depends upon the legislature to carry its opinion into effect or not, at the pleasure of Congress.''

Gordon v. *United States,* 117 U.S. 697, 704. Compare *Jaffe, Judicial Control of Administrative Action* 490–494 (1965).

B. MASSACHUSETTS' COMPLAINT REQUIRES THIS COURT TO DECIDE NON-JUSTICIABLE POLITICAL QUESTIONS

We believe it clear on the above analysis that the claims Massachusetts presents and the relief it seeks are not of the type which admit of judicial resolution. That analysis can be restated in terms of the six standards which this Court stated in *Baker* v. *Carr,* 369 U.S. 186, 217, denote the presence of a non-justiciable political question:

> Prominent on the surface of any case held to involve a political question is found a textually demonstrable constitutional commitment of the issue to a coordinate political department; or a lack of judicially discoverable and manageable standards for resolving it; or the impossibility of deciding without an initial policy determination of a kind clearly for nonjudical discretion; or the impossibility of a court's undertaking independent resolution without expressing lack of the respect due coordinate branches of government; or an unusual need for unquestioning adherence to a political decision already made; or the potentiality of embarrassment from multifarious pronouncements by various departments on one question.

Each of the six is ''inextricable from the case at bar.'' *Ibid.*[13]

1. A TEXTUALLY DEMONSTRABLE CONSTITUTIONAL COMMITMENT OF THE ISSUE TO A COORDINATE POLITICAL DEPARTMENT.

As shown above, pp. 24–32, the power of Congress ''To declare War'' includes a power to determine, free of judicial interference, the form which its authorization of hostilities will take. The power of the President, pp. 18–24, includes the power to repel attacks on American citizens and property, wherever

[13] Compare Finkelstein, *Judicial Self-Limitation,* 37 Harv.L. Rev. 338 (1924); Weston, *Political Questions,* 38 Harv. L. Rev. 296 (1925); Finkelstein, *Further Notes on Judicial Self-Limitation,* 39 Harv. L. Rev. 221 (1925).

located, and to determine when such attacks have occurred.[14] And Congress and the President, together, control the nation's conduct in "the vast external realm" in which this Court repeatedly has stated it cannot interfere. *Curtiss-Wright Corp., supra,* 299 U.S. at 319; cases cited, p. 29 *supra.* Acceptance of any one of these propositions indicates a "textually demonstrable constitutional commitment of the issue to a coordinate political department." Certainly, this Court should not undertake to decide when and how war should be declared, or that more limited steps cannot first be taken without such a declaration.

2. A LACK OF JUDICIALLY DISCOVERABLE AND MANAGEABLE STANDARDS FOR RESOLVING THE ISSUE.

For the reasons shown above, it is clear that judicial standards do not exist for determining whether Congress has done "enough" to authorize American participation in hostilities for which its authorization might be required; and, it is at least doubtful whether such standards exist for determining whether congressional authorization is required for hostilities which begin by attacks on American citizens or property. The search for such standards would involve the Court in inquiries which, in themselves, are inappropriate for the judicial branch by requiring it to question the judgment, honesty, or motives of a coordinate branch. The question is one as to which only Congress can effectively determine whether power was delegated or not, or necessary or not.

[14] See *Martin* v. *Mott,* 12 Wheat. 19, 29–30:

> If it be a limited power, the question arises, by whom is the exigency to be judged of and decided? Is the President the sole and exclusive judge * * * or is it to be considered as an open question * * * ? We are all of opinion, that the authority to decide whether the exigency has arisen, belongs exclusively to the president, and that his decision is conclusive upon all other persons. We think that this construction necessarily results from the nature of the power itself, and from the manifest object contemplated by the act of congress. The power itself is to be exercised upon sudden emergencies, upon great occasions of state, and under circumstances which may be vital to the existence of the Union. A prompt and unhesitating obedience to orders is indispensible to the complete attainment of the object. * * *

See also *Johnson* v. *Eisentrager,* 339 U.S. 763, 789.

3. THE IMPOSSIBILITY OF DECIDING WITHOUT AN INITIAL POLICY DETERMINATION OF A KIND CLEARLY FOR NON-JUDICIAL DISCRETION.

Characterizing the issue as "simply whether the executive has the constitutional authority to send inhabitants of Massachusetts to participate in the Vietnam war" (Br. 31), Massachusetts insists that this implicates no policy determinations but only questions of law. Behind that apparently straightforward issue, however, lie others, necessary to its decision, which would involve the judiciary in matters of policy. Thus, assuming it was the executive only that acted, it would be necessary to decide whether the American participation in the hostilities is "defensive" or not, whether the opposing forces are "the aggressor," and other issues of like import. These are issues the President may decide in committing American troops to battle; they are matters for transparent importance to our posture in foreign affairs. To permit the President's decision to be subject to judicial review could prejudice the most important matters of state. *Martin* v. *Mott, supra; Durand* v. *Hollins, supra.*

In addition, as we have seen, there has in fact been affirmative congressional involvement at all stages of the hostilities. How Congress couches the authorization which it confers is itself, for the reasons already set out, pp. 24–32 *supra,* a policy determination of a kind not meet for judicial re-examination. This is archetypally a decision "of a kind for which the Judiciary has neither aptitude, facilities nor responsibility * * *." *Chicago & Southern Air Lines* v. *Waterman S.S. Corp.,* 333 U.S. 103, 111.

4. THE IMPOSSIBILITY OF A COURT'S UNDERTAKING INDEPENDENT RESOLUTION WITHOUT EXPRESSING LACK OF RESPECT DUE COORDINATE BRANCHES OF GOVERNMENT.

We have already shown how the inquiry Massachusetts proposes into the effectiveness of the congressional authorizing statutes would, necessarily, entail great disrespect to that branch. It should be apparent that the same disrespect would be inherent in any attempt to go behind the various statements of the Executive which bear both on its authority to act and the nation's posture in world affairs—for example, whether North Vietnam has been the aggressor, or whether there have been sudden attacks, in the various situations which have led to the further involvement of American troops. *Field* v. *Clark, supra; Luther* v. *Borden, supra,* 7 How. at 43.

5. UNUSUAL NEED FOR UNQUESTIONING ADHERENCE TO A POLITICAL DECISION ALREADY MADE.

This suit challenging the legality of the use of American troops in Vietnam is not a case that merely "touch[es] foreign relations." *Baker* v. *Carr, supra,* 369 U.S. at 211; it involves a direct challenge to the Executive's conduct of those relations. An analogy may be found in the cases which refuse to examine the decision of the executive as to recognition of a foreign state. *E.g., Banco Nacional de Cuba* v. *Subbatino,* 376 U.S. 398, 410; *National City Bank* v. *Republic of China,* 348 U.S. 356, 358; *Ricaud* v. *American Metal Co.,* 246 U.S. 304; *Guaranty Trust Co.* v. *United States,* 304 U.S. 126, 137–138; *United States* v. *Pink,* 315 U.S. 203. This matter of recognition of foreign governments "strongly defies judicial treatment". *Baker* v. *Carr, supra,* 369 U.S. at 212. Irreparable damage in the conduct of American foreign policy would obviously be caused if the Executive recognized one foreign government, and the Judiciary another.

Similarly, here, the adverse consequences upon this nation's foreign relations would be immense if the decision to commit troops in support of the government in South Vietnam were to be subject to judicial challenge. No friendly nation could remain assured of American military assistance in the case of aggression until there had been a judicial test in this country of the legality of American assistance. The credibility of American promises to its allies through the world would be debased. Surely, therefore, our presence in Vietnam is a matter which presents the strongest kind of situation of "unusual need for unquestioning adherence to a political decision already made." *Baker* v. *Carr, supra,* 369 U.S. at 217.

6. THE POTENTIALITY OF EMBARRASSMENT FROM MULTIFARI-
OUS PRONOUNCEMENTS BY VARIOUS DEPARTMENTS ON ONE
QUESTION.

In no field more than foreign affairs have the courts exhibited
a strong concern for avoidance of determinations which will
cause embarrassment to the Executive. *E.g., Ex Parte Peru,*
318 U.S. 578 (judicial inquiry into claim of sovereign immunity concerning Peruvian vessel precluded by position of State
Department) ; *Mexico* v. *Hoffman,* 324 U.S. 30 (judicial inquiry
into claim of sovereign immunity concerning Mexican vessel permissible where it does not conflict with State Department position) ; *Banco Nacional de Cuba* v. *Sabbatino, supra* (court will
not inquire into validity of internal act of foreign state). In
Banco Nacional de Cuba v. *Sabbatino, supra,* discussing issues of
international law, this Court observed that ''the less important
the implications of an issue are for our foreign relations, the
weaker the justification for exclusivity in the political branches.''
376 U.S. at 428. Conversely the more important the implications
of an issue are for our foreign relations, the stronger the justification for judicial abstinence. There are few present issues with
more important implications for American foreign policy than
our efforts in Vietnam. Any conclusion by this Court question-
ing the legality of this government's action in Vietnam—particularly if, as appears necessary, it entailed the re-examination of
official statements and acts—could only cause the most extreme
embarrassment to this nation in its present and future conduct
of foreign affairs. It would, as well, be an unprecedented instance of judicial action in a field far removed from the area of
special judicial competence.

Conclusion

In sum, we submit that the constitutionality of the American
military presence in Vietnam is a non-justiciable issue which
cannot be decided by this Court. This conclusion follows from

each one of the six tests of whether an issue presents a nonjusticiable political question, and from the general test of justiciability. *Baker* v. *Carr, supra; Powell* v. *McCormack, supra.* This in no way means, however, as Massachusetts would have this Court believe, that the grant of power to Congress in Article I, Sec. 8 "To declare War" is thereby rendered meaningless. As this Court has recognized, there are certain provisions of the Constitution which are to be enforced exclusively by the political departments of the Government. *Baker* v. *Carr, supra; Luther* v. *Borden, supra.* This does not mean that they are unenforceable; simply that they are unenforceable through judicial means.

The Congressional power "To declare War" is virtually a self-enforcing provision of the Constitution. For Congress possesses the "constitutional arms for its own defense" from executive encroachment. Federalist No. LXXIII, Vol. 2, p. 71 (1914 ed.). A President has great responsibilities, and many instances in our history show that these responsibilities are supported by adequate powers. Within the very widest limits, the President should not be hemmed in by the prospect of judicial supervision in the exercise of these powers. Indeed, this is the essence of Executive authority, exercised by one of the three great and coordinate branches of the government. Despite his considerable powers, however, no President has the ability to engage this country in prolonged hostilities without the support of Congress. A President violates the constitutional powers of Congress in this area at his peril—and Congress is the best judge of whether there has been a violation. This is an issue that should be resolved by the Congress and Executive, and not by the Judiciary.

Extracts from Consolidated Reply Brief, Berk and Orlando, Second Circuit Court of Appeals

Point I

The repeal of the Gulf of Tonkin Resolution leaves no doubt that there has been no Congressional authorization of the Vietnam War.

Since the submission of appellants' main briefs in this case, Congress has repealed the Gulf of Tonkin Resolution. An amendment to the Foreign Military Sales Act (P.L. 91-672, 84 Stat. 2053, January 12, 1971) states:

> Sec. 12. The joint resolution entitled "Joint resolution to promote the maintenance of international peace and security in Southeast Asia," approved August 10, 1964 . . . is terminated effective upon the day that the second session of the Ninety-first Congress is last adjourned.

The President signed the act on January 12, 1971.

The repeal of the Gulf of Tonkin resolution is highly significant in this action. Repeal makes clear that either the resolution never had the significance claimed for it or, if it did, then that authorization is now withdrawn. Either way, the resolution can no longer be considered as meaningful in this action.

The government devotes a substantial part of its brief [pp. 192–197] to prove that the Tonkin Gulf Resolution was the linchpin of the Executive's constitutional authority to wage war. If that is so, then its repeal is an event of immense constitutional moment, stripping the Executive of whatever authority he previously drew from that resolution.[1]

The government seeks to disparage the effect of repeal by stating that the war may legally continue since "Congress has expressly refused to order the withdrawal of American forces from Vietnam by any specified date." [p. 201] However, as shown in appellant Berk's main brief (hereinafter "Berk brief"), the Constitution does not place a burden on Congress to stop the war. The entire constitutional scheme is to the contrary—it makes clear that without proper authorization from Congress no war can constitutionally begin or continue. Accepting the government's argument in this case that Tonkin was such an authorization, any pretense that the Constitution is still being complied with is now gone.

But the government does not take only one position with respect to Tonkin. Although it now argues in court that the resolution was constitutionally significant, the State Department told Congress precisely the opposite. . . .

In addition, an administration spokesman, Senator Dole, said after repeal: "As I said at the time I offered the amendment to effect repeal, the Gulf of Tonkin Resolution is inappropriate to today's realities in Southeast Asia . . . The Tonkin Gulf Resolution has never been used by President Nixon, and he has no intention of using it. Indeed, he has made it clear that he has never relied on it in the conduct of American policy in Vietnam. In any event, I think it has been superfluous, and it is superfluous." 116 *Cong. Rec.* S 21850 (daily ed. January 2, 1971.)

By presenting one version of Tonkin to the courts and another

[1] See, e.g. remarks of Senator William Fulbright: "One of the most unheralded events of American constitutional history occurred on January 12, 1971, when President Nixon signed into law a bill, which, among other things, repealed the Gulf of Tonkin Resolution. With that tarnished, contested and thoroughly unlamented act of Congress went the last compliance with . . . that clear provision of the Constitution which says that the power to initiate war belongs to Congress, not the President." 117 *Cong. Rec.* S 887 (daily ed. Feb. 5, 1971). See also remarks of Rep. Paul N. McCloskey: "what possible conclusion can be drawn from the repeal of the resolution save that Congress expressly intended to terminate the President's authority to 'prevent further aggression,' 'assist' South Vietnam, and most certainly, to terminate his authority to wage offensive warfare in Laos and Cambodia." 117 *Cong. Rec.* H 794 (daily ed. Feb. 18, 1971)

to the Congress, the government has attempted the impossible task of portraying the passage of Tonkin as the functional equivalent of a declaration of war while simultaneously viewing the repeal of Tonkin as a meaningless gesture. Such a hybrid view of Tonkin establishes it as an irrevocable grant of authority to the Executive to wage war. If repeal is not sufficient to terminate the power which Tonkin is alleged to have conveyed to the Executive, what more must Congress do to extricate the nation from war?

The varying steps which Congress took with respect to Tonkin show that the original resolution was limited to an expression of unity in the face of what happened in the Tonkin Gulf in August 1964. Congress was expressing its approval of Executive response to what the State Department called "a crisis situation in the affected area." . . . In August, 1964 the President had asked for a resolution "expressing the unity and determination of the United States" in seeking peace in Southeast Asia, and he received such a resolution.[2] It expressed the willingness of the United States "to take all necessary steps, including the use of armed force" to assist SEATO members, but it did not by its own terms authorize or empower the President to initiate a major war. Limited in scope, purpose and aim, the Tonkin Resolution was publicly denigrated by both President

[2] The background of the resolution was described as follows by the Senate Foreign Relations Committee in a report cited and relied upon by the appellees:

> "In the case of the Gulf of Tonkin resolution, the Senate responded to the Administration's contention that the effect of the resolution would be lost if it were not enacted quickly. . . . In order, therefore, to avoid the delay that would arise from a careful analysis of the language of the resolution and the further delay that would arise if the resolution had to go to a Senate-House conference to reconcile differing versions, the Foreign Relations Committee and the entire Senate speedily approved the resolution in the language in which it had already been adopted by the House of Representatives. The prevailing attitude was not so much that Congress was granting or acknowledging the executive's authority to take certain actions but that it was expressing unity and support for the President in a moment of national crisis and, therefore, that the exact words in which it expressed those sentiments were not of primary importance."

Senate Report No. 797, 90th Cong. 1st Sess. November 20, 1967, p. 20.

Johnson who originally asked for it and President Nixon who said he did not need it. . . .

Congressional statements relating to the repeal show that this was indeed the view of the legislative body also. The House Conference Report on the repeal (H. Rep. No. 91-1805, December 31, 1970, 116 *Cong. Rec.* H 12609, daily ed. December 31, 1970) noted: ''The managers on the part of the House accepted the Senate language [providing for repeal of Tonkin]. Recent legislation and Executive statements make the 1964 resolution unnecessary for the prosecution of United States foreign policy.'' *Ibid.* at H 12610.

If the Tonkin resolution is now considered ''unnecessary,'' ''inappropriate,'' and ''superfluous'' by both Executive and Congress, how can it be considered the original legal authorization of the war? Appellees' attempt to promote the Gulf of Tonkin Resolution as the basis of the Executive's constitutional authority to wage war in Vietnam while simultaneously attemping to dismiss its repeal as a meaningless gesture is untenable.

Point II

> *Congressional appropriations of funds for the military do not constitute authorization or ratification of the Vietnam War.*

With the repeal of the Gulf of Tonkin resolution, the government is reduced to relying exclusively on the military appropriations bills passed over the last six years as authorization of the Vietnam war. However, in doing so it totally ignores the constitutional text and history and it evades the key constitutional question; whether appropriations bills whose language in no way *explicitly* authorizes or ratifies any military action can nevertheless be held *implictly* to do so. And the government refuses to examine the crucial distinction between Congressional power to *start* a war and its obligation to *stop* one.

The government spends most of its argument about appropriations on points with which appellant has no quarrel. It cites a series of cases for the proposition that Congress may ratify what it might have initially authorized . . . , and other cases for the proposition that Congress may confirm Executive construction of a prior, ambiguous legislative act through appropriation acts.[3] . . . Finally it says that Congressional ratification depends on its awareness of the particular Executive action under scrutiny. . . .

But these issues are not crucial or significant in the present case. We are not faced with a situation, as in the Mexican War, the Civil War or the Panama Canal cases, where Congress explicitly and definitively ratified Executive action after it had been taken. If Congress now declared war or passed an explicit resolution ratifying Executive action in Southeast Asia, the cases cited by the government might have some relevance. But Congress has done precisely the opposite in repealing the Tonkin resolution. Nevertheless, the government seeks to squeeze a far fetched inference out of money bills which cannot bear the weight put on them.

A. STATUTORY LANGUAGE

The government claims that "By language which can hardly be more explicit, Congress authorized the use of men and materiel which they knew to be destined for use by the armed forces in Vietnam." . . . There were three separate formulas used to appropriate money for Vietnam:

1. For transfer by the Secretary of Defense, upon determination by the President that such action is necessary in connection with military activities in southeast Asia, to any appropriation available to the Department of Defense for military functions, to be merged with and to be available for the same purposes and for the same time period as the ap-

[3] In a footnote . . . , the Government makes no attempt to dispute appellant's argument that the cases relied upon for this point all involved pre-existing Congressional authorization found in another statute. . . . In short no case has been cited for the proposition that appropriations acts standing alone could ratify Executive action—whether Congress was aware of the conduct in question or not.

propriation to which transferred, $700,000,000, to remain available until expended. (P.L. 89-18, 79 Stat. 109, May 7, 1965)

2. Sec. 401. (a) Funds authorized for appropriation for the use of the Armed Forces of the United States under this or any other Act are authorized to be made available for their stated purposes in connection with support of Vietnamese and other free world forces in Vietnam, and related costs, during the fiscal years 1966 and 1967, on such terms and conditions as the Secretary of Defense may determine. (P.L. 89-367, 80 Stat. 36, March 16, 1966)

3. Sec. 401. The Congress hereby declares—

(1) its firm intentions to provide all necessary support for members of the Armed Forces of the United States fight- in Vietnam;

(2) its support of efforts being made by the President of the United States and other men of good will throughout the world to prevent an expansion of the war in Vietnam and to bring that conflict to an end through a negotiated settlement which will preserve the honor of the United States, protect the vital interests of this country, and allow the people of South Vietnam to determine the affairs of that nation in their own way; and

(3) its support for the convening of the nations that participated in the Geneva Conferences or any other meeting of nations similarly involved and interested as soon as possible for the purpose of pursuing the general principles of the Geneva accords of 1954 and 1962 and for formulating plans for bringing the conflict to an honorable conclusion. (P.L. 90-5, 81 Stat. 5, March 16, 1967)

The first formula falls far short of the government's claim that it contains language "which can hardly be more explicit." Vietnam is not even mentioned. By discussing "military activities in Southeast Asia," does the bill authorize an American invasion of Indonesia, or Burma, or Singapore? Would it permit an atomic attack on southern China which certainly lies "in Southeast Asia?" Clearly the language lacks the precision one would hope for in an authorization of war.

The second formula is hardly much better. On its face it simply permits military support of Vietnamese and other forces in

Vietnam. But such support can be by shipment of weapons only. There is nothing in the language which explicitly authorizes American forces themselves to be used. The vague formula found in this law is often used in foreign assistance laws where actual use of American troops is not contemplated. Thus the Foreign Assistance Act of 1961 (P.L. 87-195, 75 Stat. 424, September 4, 1961) authorized the President "to furnish military assistance * * * to any friendly nation, the assisting of which the President finds will strengthen the security of the United States." (Sect. 503). Using the government's interpretation of the appropriations acts, these words would permit the President to begin a war anywhere he chose at any time as long as he could find a "friendly nation" to assist. Clearly Congress had no such thought in mind.

The third formula was used only once and its legislative history is described in detail in [the affidavit submitted below (see pp. 99–105)]. As the affidavit shows, the law was meant to have no substantive significance.

B. CONGRESSIONAL RESPONSIBILITY TO START A WAR

The government's brief is like Hamlet without the prince. Although a vital constitutional question is at issue, neither the text of the Constitution nor the constitutional debates, nor the framers' intention concerning the war power is examined by the government. This is understandable since there is no question that the founding fathers did not intend to grant the Executive the power to wage war without explicit authorization by Congress. They never intended that Congress's power to declare war meant only that it had the burden of stopping a war after it had begun. And they certainly never intended that such a vital power could be exercised through the passage of appropriations bills which contain not one word authorizing military action.

To avoid the problem of the constitutional text and constitutional history, the government engages in a sleight-of-hand. Instead of looking for Congressional authorization (which was clearly not present in Vietnam), the government finds such authorization in Congress's failure to stop the war. In other words if Congress does not authorize Executive action which is illegal without such authorization, the required authority will be found in Congressional silence. In short, inaction becomes action.

Thus the government says "At every point, limitations on future use of funds could have been imposed in order to effect an immediate withdrawal. But no such restrictions were ever passed." . . . In this view the failure to pass restrictions on Executive action becomes authority for that action.

The distinction between taking affirmative action and failing to take restrictive action is central to every area of the law and was certainly known to the framers of the Constitution. If they thought that the nation would be sufficiently protected against the dangers of Executive-initiated war in this way, then why did they not give the President the power to declare war and Congress the power to stop military action if they did not like it? But this is clearly not what the Constitution says nor what it means.

No matter how the government characterizes its appropriations argument, it still places the onus on Congress to stop the war after the Executive has started it. But why should Congress be forced to place restrictions in an appropriations bill? What section of the Constitution requires it? What section of the Constitution gives the President the right to put Congress in that position? The government cites no such constitutional clause because there is none.

Congress has firmly and unequivocally rejected the proposition that its passage of appropriations bills is a satisfactory exercise of its war powers . . . :

Senator Alan Cranston: . . .

> Given the current debate over this country's Vietnam policy, one can hardly say that Congress has granted precise authority to wage war in Indochina. Whenever appropriations for the war come up for a vote, supporters claim that we cannot abandon our boys who are fighting there. Many Congressmen vote for the appropriations for that reason. Other Congressmen vote for the military appropriations bill so that our forces can be withdrawn safely from Vietnam at the earliest possible date.

To say that a Congressman ratifies the continuation and expansion of the Vietnam war when he votes for appropriations to protect American servicemen as they are withdrawn is a cruel deceit. It makes as much sense to argue that the Department of the Interior could grant leases to drill in the Santa Barbara Channel in the absence of explicit congressional authorization and relying only on congressional passage of the general appropriations for the Department of the Interior's ongoing activities. 116 *Cong. Rec.* S 11818, daily ed. July 21, 1970.

Congressman Claude Pepper: . . .

And the other thing is that the President can say, "Very well. I am going to use my authority as Commander in Chief. I want to send the troops out to X, Y, Z area, wherever it may be. If you don't want to furnish them ammunition, you let them stand out there and be shot. I will tell you, Mr. Congressman, it is your decision whether you want to supply them or not." Is that a fair circumstance under which Congress should have an opportunity to exercise its best judgment of what the people want and have a right to? Is that a fair occasion for Congress to exercise its proper authority?

I think we ought in some way or another to get away from the idea that if we don't like what the Executive is doing when he employs our military forces then we just don't pay them or don't supply them or don't furnish them other essential requirements. . . .

Only the most superficial understanding of the practicalities of American Government could allow anyone to construe congressional appropriations for the military as real approval or consent to the prosecution of the current conflict. Each time a military appropriation comes before the House, I review in my own mind the many objections I have to our continued involvement in Vietnam and our more recent expansion of the war into Cambodia. However, the stress of repetition makes it no more possible for me to cast my vote against sending the best equipment we have to our troops than would have been possible when I first began to have doubts. Imagine the monumental crisis in our Government if the Congress should take such an action.

Then I refer there to the action of President Roosevelt, who sent the fleet around the world. He evidently had some doubt about whether Congress would authorize that expense, so he sent them to the other side of the world and then he told Congress, If you want them back, provide the money to get them back. That is sort of the same problem that we have.

"Congress, the President and the War powers," *Hearings before House Committee on Foreign Affairs June, July, August 1970,* 91st Cong. 2d Sess. p. 369.

C. LEGISLATIVE HISTORY

In its discussion of legislative history the government again tries to prove a point which has no relevance to the issues in this case. Appellant would agree that if Congress had passed a declaration of war, the motives of each legislator as he voted for such a declaration would be irrelevant. But that is not the case here.

It is in the context of a set of vague and ambiguous Congressional actions that appellant has submitted its materials on the legislative history. Appellant will not repeat its earlier analysis of the passage of these bills. . . . [See p. 85.] Suffice to say that from the very start the ranking members of Congress who were responsible for sponsoring the bills in question made clear that the military spending bills ''could not properly be considered as determining foreign policy, as ratifying decisions made in the past, or as endorsing new commitments.'' (Statement of Senator Richard Russell, 112 *Cong. Rec.* 3135). The history of these bills completely dissipates the notion that they were intended to ratify or authorize the war in Vietnam.

Point III

The issues involved in the instant case are justiciable.

The government again raises the argument that this action involves a non-justiciable political question. However this Court settled that matter in its decision of June 19, 1970, 429 F.2d 302:

History makes clear that the congressional power "to declare War" conferred by Article I, section 8, of the Constitution was intended as an explicit restriction upon the power of the Executive to initiate war on his own prerogative which was enjoyed by the British sovereign. Although Article II specifies that the President "shall be Commander in Chief of the Army and Navy of the United States" and also vests the "executive power" in him and requires that he "take Care that the Laws be faithfully executed," these provisions must be reconciled with the congressional war power. * * * Since orders to fight must be issued in accordance with proper authorization from both branches under some circumstances, executive officers are under a threshold constitutional "duty [which] can be judicially identified and its breach judicially determined." Baker v. Carr, *supra,* 369 U.S. at 198, 82 S. Ct. at 700.

* * *

Although the rule has long been that the alleged "illegality" of a war may not be raised as a defense to prosecution for refusal to submit to induction into the armed forces, United States v. Mitchell, 369 F.2d 323 (2 Cir. 1966), cert. denied, 386 U.S. 972, 87 S. Ct. 1162, 18 L.Ed.2d 132 (1967); United States v. Bolton, 192 F.2d 805 (2 Cir. 1951), this court indicated in *Bolton* that "any question as to the legality of an order sending men to Korea to fight in an 'undeclared war' should be raised by someone to whom such an order has been directed." 192 F.2d at 806 (dictum). The rule should be the same for a soldier ordered to Vietnam under allegedly similar circumstances. 429 F.2d at 305–306.

The only basis for a finding of non-justiciability, this court said, was the inability to suggest "a set of manageable standdards" to determine what "specified joint legislative-executive action is sufficient to authorize various levels of military activity." 429 F.2d at 305. Appellant has developed such a standard which neither the court below nor the government has disputed. Furthermore, with respect to a major war such as the court below found to be present in Vietnam, everyone agrees— including this court, the lower court and the government—that the Executive cannot wage such a war alone. Thus the only element lacking to foreclose dismissal on political question grounds has been filled.

The Solicitor General's brief in *Massachusetts* v. *Laird,* 39 LW 3196 (1970) (attached as an appendix to appellees' brief [See p. 214]) in no way affects this court's holding. The Solicitor

General argued, first, that it is uncertain whether Congressional authority under the war power can be judicially identified. Second, he states that the breach of Congressional duty to participate in the war-making process cannot be justicially determined. And thirdly, effective relief cannot be judicially molded.

The simple answer to the Solicitor General's claim is that neither Judge Dooling nor Judge Judd in their decisions below had any difficulty in identifying the duty of Congress to participate in the war-making process and determining that question in the context of the Vietnam war. Whether their conclusions were right or wrong, they certainly were able to apply traditional judicial tools to examine Congressional action, to inquire behind the form of legislation to determine its proper scope and force and to test that action against the Constitution. The hypothetical problems of examining wars at other times and in other places are not present in this case.

As for the claim that effective relief cannot be judicially molded, the orders of only two individuals are involved and judicial power has often been exercised to block or change military orders. See *Feliciano* v. *Laird,* 426 F.2d 424 (2d Cir. 1970), *Donham* v. *Resor,* 436 F.2d 751 (2d Cir. 1971), *Smith* v. *Resor,* 406 F.2d 141 (2d Cir. 1969), *Schonbrun* v. *Commanding Officer,* 403 F.2d 371 (2d Cir. 1968), cert. den. 394 U.S. 929 (1969).

But this court need not even proceed that far. Declaratory relief alone can be afforded. See *Powell* v. *McCormack,* 395 U.S. 486, 517 (1969). A mandate can be delayed for a long period of time to allow Congress and the President to act.

Thus, none of the reasons offered by the Solicitor General afford any basis for denying judicial inquiry into the vital constitutional questions at stake.

Conclusion

For the foregoing reasons, it is respectfully prayed that the judgment of the District Court be reversed and that a judgment be issued declaring that appellees are without authority to order

appellant to Vietnam and/or ordering his return from Vietnam
to the United States.

Respectfully submitted,

> LEON FRIEDMAN, ESQ.
> BURT NEUBORNE, ESQ.
> NEW YORK CIVIL LIBERTIES UNION
>> 84 Fifth Avenue
>>> New York, New York 10010

> THEODORE C. SORENSEN, ESQ.
>> 345 Park Avenue
>>> New York, New York 10022

> NORMAN DORSEN, ESQ.
> N. Y. U. SCHOOL OF LAW
>> 40 Washington Square South
>>> New York, New York 10012

> KAY ELLEN HAYES, ESQ.
>> 1 Chase Manhattan Plaza
>>> New York, New York 10005

> A. LAWRENCE TOOMBS
> STEVEN J. HYMAN
> KUNSTLER, KUNSTLER & HYMAN
>> 511 Fifth Avenue
>>> New York, N. Y.
> *Attorneys for Plaintiff-Appellant* *

Of Counsel:
  MARC LUXEMBERG, ESQ.

---

* Attorneys for the plaintiff gratefully acknowledge the assistance of Messrs.
Arthur Eisenberg and Edwin J. Oppenheimer, Jr., staff members of the New
York Civil Liberties Union and candidates for admission to the bar, for their
invaluable assistance in the preparation of this brief. Attorneys for plaintiff
also acknowledge the research of Mr. Martin Guggenheim, student, New
York University School of Law.

The Second Circuit Decision

In view of the elaborate legal briefs submitted to the appellate court, and the able oral arguments of Norman Dorsen and Leon Friedman, the decision of the Second Circuit on April 20, 1971, came as a great disappointment.

The first half of the opinion concisely restated the legal arguments presented by the parties. The appeals court reiterated the rejection of the president's-inherent-authority argument and embraced the mutual-participation test suggested by the District Courts. The court then accepted the conclusion of the District Courts that congressional authorization of the war could be inferred from the systematic enactment of military appropriations acts. Curiously, however, after correctly summarizing plaintiffs' contentions in the first half of its opinion, the court apparently misconstrued them during the critical second half. As the major justification for its refusal to require explicit congressional authorization of a war, the appeals court recited the practical disadvantages which would flow from a requirement that all major military operations by authorized by a formal declaration of war. However, plaintiffs had repeatedly informed the court that they did not contend that a formal declaration of war was necessary to authorize major military operations. Plaintiffs' contention was, rather, that whatever form of congressional authorization was ultimately chosen by Congress (whether a declaration of war or a resolution), it should be couched in an explicit, formal, manner.

Decision in Berk and Orlando, Second Circuit Court of Appeals

ROBERT P. ANDERSON, *Circuit Judge:*

Shortly after receiving orders to report for transfer to Vietnam, Pfc. Malcolm A. Berk and Sp. E5 Salvatore Orlando, enlistees in the United States Army, commenced separate actions in June, 1970, seeking to enjoin the Secretary of Defense, the Secretary of the Army and the commanding officers, who signed their deployment orders, from enforcing them. The plaintiffs-appellants contended that these executive officers exceeded their constitutional authority by ordering them to participate in a war not properly authorized by Congress.

In Orlando's case the district court held in abeyance his motion for a preliminary injunction pending disposition in this court of Berk's expedited appeal from a denial of the same preliminary relief. On June 19, 1970 we affirmed the denial of a preliminary injunction in *Berk* v. *Laird,* 429 F.2d 302 (2 Cir. 1970), but held that Berk's claim that orders to fight must be authorized by joint executive-legislative action was justiciable. The case was remanded for a hearing on his application for a permanent injunction. We held that the war declaring power of Congress, enumerated in Article I, section 8, of the Constitution, contains a ''discoverable standard calling for *some* mutual participation by Congress,'' and directed that Berk be given an opportunity ''to provide a method for resolving the question of when specified joint legislative-executive action is sufficient to authorize levels of military activity,'' and thereby escape application of the political question doctrine to his claim that congressional participation has been in this instance, insufficient.

After a hearing on June 23, 1970, Judge Dooling in the district court denied Orlando's motion for a preliminary injunction on the ground that his deployment orders were constitutionally authorized, because Congress, by "appropriating the nation's treasure and conscripting its manpower," had "furnished forth the sinew of war" and because "the reality of the collaborative action of the executive and the legislature required by the Constitution has been present from the earliest stages." *Orlando* v. *Laird,* 317 F. Supp. 1013, 1019 (E.D.N.Y. 1970).

On remand of Berk's action, Judge Judd of the district court granted the appellees' motion for summary judgment. Finding that there had been joint action by the President and Congress, he ruled that the method of congressional collaboration was a political question. *Berk* v. *Laird,* 317 F. Supp. 715, 728 (E.DN.Y. 1970).

The appellants contend that the respective rulings of the district court that congressional authorization could be expressed through appropriations and other supporting legislation misconstrue the war declaring clause, and alternatively, that congressional enactments relating to Vietnam were incorrectly interpreted.

It is the appellants' position that the sufficiency of congressional authorization is a matter within judicial competence because that question can be resolved by "judicially discoverable and manageable standards" dictated by the congressional power "to declare War." See *Baker* v. *Carr,* 369 U.S. 186, 217 (1962) ; *Powell* v. *McCormack,* 395 U.S. 486 (1969). They interpret the constitutional provision to require an express and explicit congressional authorization of the Vietnam hostilities though not necessarily in the words, "We declare that the United States of America is at war with North Vietnam." In support of this construction they point out that the original intent of the clause was to place responsibility for the initiation of war upon the body most responsive to popular will and argue that historical developments have not altered the need for significant congressional participation in such commitments of national resources. They further assert that, without a requirement of express and explicit congressional authorization, developments committing the nation to war, as a *fait accompli,* became the inevitable adjuncts of presidential direction of foreign policy, and, because military appropriations and other war-implementing enactments lack an explicit authorization of particular hostilities, they cannot, as a matter of law, be considered sufficient.

Alternatively, appellants would have this court find that, because the President requested accelerating defense appropriations and extensions of the conscription laws after the war was well under way, Congress was, in effect, placed in a strait jacket and could not freely decide whether or not to enact this legislation, but rather was compelled to do so. For this reason appellants claim that such enactments cannot, as a factual matter, be considered sufficient congressional approval or ratification.

The Government on the other hand takes the position that the suits concern a non-justiciable political question; that the military action in South Vietnam was authorized by Congress in the "Joint Resolution to Promote the Maintenance of Internal Peace and Security in Southeast Asia"[1] (the Tonkin Gulf Resolution) considered in connection with the Seato Treaty; and that the military action was authorized and ratified by congressional appropriations expressly designated for use in support of the military operations in Vietnam.

We held in the first *Berk* opinion that the constitutional delegation of the war-declaring power to the Congress contains a discoverable and manageable standard imposing on the Congress a duty of mutual participation in the prosecution of war. Judicial scrutiny of that duty, therefore, is not foreclosed by the political question doctrine. *Baker* v. *Carr, supra; Powell* v. *McCormack, supra.* As we see it, the test is whether there is any action by the Congress sufficient to authorize or ratify the military activity in

[1] The two district judges differed over the significance of the Tonkin Gulf Resolution, Pub. Law 88-408, 78 Stat. 384, August 10, 1964, in the context of the entire course of the congressional action which related to Vietnam. Judge Judd relied in part on the Resolution as supplying the requisite congressional authorization: Judge Dooling found that its importance lay in its practical effect on the presidential initiative rather than its constitutional meaning.

Although the Senate repealed the Resolution on June 24, 1970, it remained in effect at the time appellants' deployment orders issued. Cong. Record S. 9670 (June 24, 1970). The repeal was based on the proposition that the Resolution was no longer necessary and amounted to no more than a gesture on the part of the Congress at the time the executive had taken substantial steps to unwind the conflict, when the principal issue was the speed of deceleration and termination of the war.

question. The evidentiary materials produced at the hearings in the district court clearly disclose that this test is satisfied.

The Congress and the Executive have taken mutual and joint action in the prosecution and support of military operations in Southeast Asia from the beginning of those operations. The Tonkin Gulf Resolution, enacted August 10, 1964 (repealed December 31, 1970) was passed at the request of President Johnson and, though occasioned by specific naval incidents in the Gulf of Tonkin, was expressed in broad language which clearly showed the state of mind of the Congress and its intention fully to implement and support the military and naval actions taken by and planned to be taken by the President at that time in Southeast Asia, and as might be required in the future "to prevent further aggression." Congress has ratified the executive's initiatives by appropriating billions of dollars to carry out military operations in Southeast Asia [2] and by extending the Military Selective Service Act with full knowledge that persons conscripted under that Act had been, and would continue to be, sent to Vietnam. Moreover, it specifically conscripted manpower to fill "the substantial induction calls necessitated by the current Vietnam buildup." [3]

[2] In response to the demands of the military operations the executive during the 1960s ordered more and more men and material into the war zone; and congressional appropriations have been commensurate with each new level of fighting. Until 1965, defense appropriations had not earmarked funds for Vietnam. In May of that year President Johnson asked Congress for an emergency supplemental appropriation "to provide our forces [then numbering 35,000] with the best and most modern supplies and equipment [brackets in original decision]." 111 Cong. Rec. 9283 (May 4, 1965). Congress appropriated $700 million for use "upon determination by the President that such action is necessary in connection with military activities in Southeast Asia." Pub. L. 89-18, 79 Stat. 109 (1965). Appropriation acts in each subsequent year explicitly authorized expenditures for men and material sent to Vietnam. The 1967 appropriations act, for example, declared Congress' "firm intention to provide all necessary support for members of the Armed Forces of the United States fighting in Vietnam" and supported "the efforts being made by the President of the United States . . . to prevent an expansion of the war in Vietnam and to bring that conflict to an end through a negotiated settlement . . . ." Pub. L. 90-5, 81 Stat. 5 (1967).

The district court opinion in *Berk* v. *Laird,* 317 F. Supp. 715 (E.D.N.Y. 1970), sets out relevant portions of each of these military appropriation acts and discusses their legislative history.

[3] In H. Rep. No. 267, 90th Cong., 1st Sess. 38 (1967), in addition to extending the conscription mechanism, Congress continued a suspension of the

There is, therefore, no lack of clear evidence to support a conclusion that there was an abundance of continuing mutual participation in the prosecution of the war. Both branches collaborated in the endeavor, and neither could long maintain such a war without the concurrence and cooperation of the other.

Although appellants do not contend that Congress can exercise its war-declaring power only through a formal declaration, they argue that congressional authorization cannot, as a matter of law, be inferred from military appropriations or other war-implementing legislation that does not contain an express and explicit authorization for the making of war by the President. Putting aside for a moment the explicit authorization of the Tonkin Gulf Resolution, we disagree with appellants' interpretation of the declaration clause for neither the language nor the purpose underlying that provision prohibits an inference of the fact of authorization from such legislative action as we have in this instance. The framers' intent to vest the war power in Congress is in no way defeated by permitting an inference of authorization from legislative action furnishing the manpower and materials of war for the protracted military operation in Southeast Asia.

The choice, for example, between an explicit declaration on the one hand and a resolution and war-implementing legislation, on the other, as the medium for expression of congressional consent involves "the exercise of a discretion demonstrably committed to the * * * legislature," *Baker* v. *Carr, supra* at 211, and therefore, invokes the political question doctrine.

Such a choice involves an important area of decision making in which, through mutual influence and reciprocal action between the President and the Congress, policies governing the re-

permanent ceiling on the active duty strength of the Armed Forces, fixed at 2 million men, and replaced it with a secondary ceiling of 5 million. The House Report recommending extension of the draft concluded that the permanent manpower limitations "are much lower than the currently required strength." The Report referred to President Johnson's selective service message which said, "* * * that without the draft we cannot realistically expect to meet our present commitments or the requirements we can now foresee and that volunteers alone could be expected to man a force of little more than 2.0 million. The present number of personnel on active duty is about 3.3 million and it is scheduled to reach almost 3.5 million by June, 1968 if the present conflict is not concluded by then." H. Rep. No. 267, 90th Cong., 1st Sess. 38, 41 (1967).

lationship between this country and other parts of the world are formulated in the best interests of the United States. If there can be nothing more than minor military operations conducted under any circumstances, short of an express and explicit declaration of war by Congress, then extended military operations could not be conducted even though both the Congress and the President were agreed that they were necessary and were also agreed that a formal declaration of war would place the nation in a posture in its international relations which would be against its best interests. For the judicial branch to enunciate and enforce such a standard would be not only extremely unwise but also would constitute a deep invasion of the political question domain. As the Government says, "* * * decisions regarding the form and substance of congressional enactments authorizing hostilities are determined by highly complex considerations of diplomacy, foreign policy and military strategy inappropriate to judicial inquiry." It would, indeed, destroy the flexibility of action which the executive and legislative branches must have in dealing with other sovereigns. What has been said and done by both the President and the Congress in their collaborative conduct of the military operations in Vietnam implies a consensus on the advisability of *not* making a formal declaration of war because it would be contrary to the interests of the United States to do so. The making of a policy decision of that kind is clearly within the constitutional domain of those two branches and is just as clearly not within the competency or power of the judiciary.

Beyond determining that there has been *some* mutual participation between the Congress and the President, which unquestionably exists here, with action by the Congress sufficient to authorize or ratify the military activity at issue, it is clear that the constitutional propriety of the means by which Congress has chosen to ratify and approve the protracted military operations in Southeast Asia is a political question. The form which congressional authorization should take is one of policy, committed to the discretion of the Congress and outside the power and competency of the judiciary, because there are no intelligible and objectively manageable standards by which to judge such actions. *Baker* v. *Carr, supra,* at 217; *Powell* v. *McCormack, supra,* at 518.

The judgments of the district court are affirmed.

IRVING R. KAUFMAN, *Circuit Judge* (concurring):

In light of the adoption by Congress of the Tonkin Gulf Resolution, and the clear evidence of continuing and distinctly expressed participation by the legislative branch in the prosecution of the war, I agree that the judgments below must be affirmed.

When the opinion of the Second Circuit in the *Berk* and *Orlando* cases was made available to members of Congress, it produced a storm of criticism. Even supporters of the war in Vietnam expressed their consternation at the opinion, which placed Congress in the position of having approved the war in Vietnam without knowing it.

Congressional Comments on Orlando Opinion

[June 2, 1971]

MR. HATFIELD: As the Senator from Arkansas probably remembers, we had a recent court case entitled *Orlando* versus *Laird,* which was decided by the United States Court of Appeals on April 20, 1971. This was on an appeal from a lower District Court's action to challenge the constitutionality of the Vietnam War. * * *

MR. FULBRIGHT: Mr. President, will the Senator yield?

MR. HATFIELD: I yield.

MR. FULBRIGHT: There were two points in the case the Senator just referred to. I take it from what the Senator said that the court did not accept the view that a Commander in Chief, the President could do as he pleased. As the Senator emphasized, Congress, by authorizing the draft and appropriating the money exercises constitutional responsibility.

The Court did not say, did it, that as Commander in Chief he can wage the war any way he likes? Did it say that?

MR. HATFIELD: No.

MR. FULBRIGHT: I am glad to hear that. The Court, then, is not in complete agreement with the Secretary of State, or Mr. Katzenbach, or Mr. Acheson in their theory that Congress has no business in foreign relations and that the war power is obsolete. The Court did not agree with them, did it?

MR. HATFIELD: No.

MR. FULBRIGHT: I am glad to hear that. 117 *Cong. Rec.* S. 8044 (daily ed. June 2, 1971).

[June 4, 1971]

MR. FULBRIGHT: It was the first time my attention was called to that case [Orlando], which, it seems to me, is extremely significant. As I indicated the other day, as a long-time principle, I was not convinced that a purely voluntary professional army was in the long-term interests of the country. I had until this matter was brought up, tentatively decided to vote for an extension of the draft. But I think this case is extremely significant. At least, it is to me. It is the first time such a decision has been brought to my attention. I think this is the first time the court has held as it did in this case, * * *

What this means is that if I vote to extend the draft under the present circumstances of the war in Vietnam, I am thereby endorsing the carrying on of that war. This has really caused me grave concern these last 2 days, since I got the full copy of the decision which I have inserted into the RECORD.

I am bound to say I do not like to think that by voting for the draft, which we have had on many occasions prior to the Vietnamese war, the court would infer from that action that I am thereby endorsing the policy which we are now following in Vietnam.

That inference is utterly inconsistent with what I and others have been trying to do in attempting to assure that the war-making power resides in the Congress. I had never dreamed of not voting money for the Defense Department, which is a general appropriation. We all know we have to have a Defense Department, and I certainly am not going to vote to have no Defense Department. But in this case, we do not need the draft for this specific purpose. We have had the draft, in times past, when I did approve of the policy which required it.

But with this kind of interpretation by the Court, I find it very difficult to reconcile a vote for extension of the draft at this time. That does not mean that at some future time, and under different circumstances, I would not vote for the draft. I am inclined to think that the infusion of civilian manpower into the Armed Forces is a good thing and consistent with the democratic process.

. . .

I have said to the Senator from Mississippi that, over the long term, as a matter of principle, I am not sold on a professional army, but I am also not sold on the war in Vietnam, as the Senator knows. I do not like to cast a vote that in the words of the court, looks like an endorsement of that war.

MR. STENNIS: Mr. President, will the Senator yield?

MR. FULBRIGHT: I yield.

MR. STENNIS: By the way, that is not a Supreme Court decision; it is a Court of Appeals decision.

MR. FULBRIGHT: The Court of Appeals of the Second Circuit.

MR. STENNIS: With all deference to the Court, that is a mere dictum, I have to say—an incidental thought there—because this is a manpower bill for all of our forces, as the Senator knows, and we could not possibly have anything except a remnant of the services, particularly in this sudden transition, unless we could pass the bill.

I appreciate greatly the Senator's sentiment. I have bottomed my argument on the point that this is not manpower just for the war—as some persons think it is—but the main thrust is for our defense here at home.

MR. FULBRIGHT: But is not the Senator disturbed about this interpretation that when we vote for this measure, we are in effect endorsing and authorizing the war? Why did we repeal the Gulf of Tonkin resolution? This raises a very serious constitutional question about which the Senator from Mississippi and

I were in complete agreement, and I refer to the commitment resolution, dealing with the role of Congress in taking this country into a war. The Senator, I believe, is as concerned about that as I am, and I think this puts a very serious light on it.

I do not think there is anything as important to the country as the cessation of this war at the earliest possible time. I have already committed myself publicly to support the Hatfield-McGovern amendment, which is a direct attack upon this issue through cutting off appropriations.

It would seem to me that if the opinion of this court, which is a circuit court of appeals, is the doctrine that it be followed, I would find myself embarrassed if I were to vote for the extension of the draft under the circumstances.

Has the Senator from Mississippi read this entire case, by the way? I have put it in the RECORD.

MR. STENNIS: Mr. President, if the Senator will yield, I know of it. But the court did not point out, now, how we could maintain our services, our ICBM's, our Polaris submarines, our nuclear carriers, without manpower of some kind. *When you vote for a bill, there are a lot of ingredients in it, and for the Court to single out that this vote is an endorsement of the war, it seems to me, misses the mark and is too broad by any standard.* (Emphasis added [by authors].)

. . .

MR. FULBRIGHT: What would be the Senator's attitude toward an amendment to the effect that a manpower bill is not to be construed as an endorsement of any particular war? That, so far as such a legislative act can be interpreted, in this case extending the drafting of men for the army, is not to be interpreted as this Court apparently did interpret it.

MR. STENNIS: Mr. President, I do not know that we could cover a point like that by legislative mandate. It is an argumentative matter, as the court argued it was, and I argued it was not.

To be frank, I do not think it is proper subject matter for an amendment, but it is a matter of common sense that we would be left defenseless if we had to literally follow the court's reasoning. And I think we had better leave it on that ground.

MR. FULBRIGHT: Is that the equivalent of the Senator saying the court was wrong in the way it interpreted the matter.

MR. STENNIS: With all deference, yes.

MR. FULBRIGHT: I appreciate that statement, and I also think I agree with the Senator. This question of dealing with a constitutional question by legislative act is always rather difficult. However, the courts do use their powers of interpretation and inference in saying that such and such is the inference that Congress intended; and they use these measures, in effect, to read Congress' mind, or to infer that this is what Congress had in mind.

I certainly want to make it clear that I did not have that in mind when I have supported draft bills in the past. It never occurred to me that support was related to an endorsement of a specific conflict.

I have the same feeling about appropriations. I agree with the Senator from Mississippi that we have to have a military establishment, but I do not like this idea that thereby we endorse everything the Military Establishment does, or every policy of the President. This seems to me to be a distortion of the constitutional provision of the war powers. It strikes me that way and I wanted to put that into the RECORD, so that at least it can be considered further. 117 *Cong. Rec.* S. 8322–23 (daily ed. June 4, 1971).

[June 22, 1971]

THE PRESIDING OFFICER: The Senate will be in order. The clerk will state the proposed modification.

The assistant legislative clerk read as follows:

At the end of the bill add the following new section:

SEC. 302. Nothing in this or any other Act shall be deemed to constitute an authorization for conduct of military hostilities in Southeast Asia pursuant to the war powers of Congress as specified in article I, section 8 of the Constitution unless specifically authorized . . .

MR. JAVITS: Mr. President, this is an amendment which was brought on by court decisions. What the amendment tries to do is to negative the court opinion that, either by passing the draft or military appropriations bills, Congress has given the President an authority, in conducting the war in Vietnam, over, above, or beyond whatever he otherwise has.

Let us remember, as it stands now, the President says he is depending upon his authority as Commander in Chief to liquidate a war which he found when he took office. He justifies his authority for everything, including Cambodia and Laos, on that ground. Nonetheless, Mr. President, we must also bear in mind that we have terminated the Gulf of Tonkin resolution. That resolution, however it may have been arrived at, whatever may have been the debate here, whatever may have been the representations made to the Senate at the time it was passed, was enacted and did give a broad mandate of authority to the President.

THE PRESIDING OFFICER: The Senator's time has expired.

MR. JAVITS: I yield myself 5 additional minutes.

Now that the Tonkin Gulf resolution is off the books, the question is, What is the constitutional power of the President in respect to conducting the Vietnam war?

This question has been tested in two cases, one in the Circuit Court of Appeals for the Second Circuit, the other in the U.S. District Court for the District of Massachusetts.

The difficulty which we have been put into by these court decisions, Mr. President, is that they turned on the following issue: The issue was whether or not this was a political question, so that the court would refuse jurisdiction.

The court said the method by which Congress would give the President the authority to act in respect of the Vietnam war was political, and it would not deal with it. But the court said whether or not Congress gave the President authority was a legal question, and it would deal with that.

The court decision found an implied authority given by the Congress to the President from the fact that Congress had extended the selective service law, and had appropriated the money to carry out military operations in Southeast Asia.

The opinion has already been put in the RECORD. It is well known. It was the subject of a very distinguished colloquy between Senator Stennis and Senator Fulbright. Senator Stennis said then quite properly—I thoroughly agree with him, and I think it is worth quoting—

When you vote for a bill, there are a lot of ingredients in it; and for the court to single out that this vote is an endorsement of the war, it seems to me misses the mark and is too broad by any standard.

Then Senator Stennis said that he thought the lower courts were wrong—that is, the Circuit Court of Appeals and the District Court—about the decision they made that this was implied authorization. * * *

MR. STENNIS: I yield myself 8 minutes, or so much thereof as I may use.

Mr. President, I commend the Senator from New York for the substance as well as the tone of the remarks he has made with respect to this amendment. Frankly, it is a matter that has troubled me from the beginning. . . .

One reason why I would not want the amendment to come to a vote—and this is with great deference to the author—is that there is no way to word an amendment of this type without leaving confusion of a different kind, because this would move in on the Constitution. With great deference to the court, I do not think any court, unless it is the Supreme Court of the United States, can change the Constitution by merely a conclusion, especially one that just goes to one point that was in many bills, such as the Selective Service Act and the appropriation bills that had already been passed. * * *

So I think it would be unfortunate for us to try now to refute a court—and it is not the highest court in the land—as to the question of a war authorization. I do not think we are called on to refute them. With great deference, I think that, as a whole, they erred, that they reached the wrong conclusion, and put the cart before the horse, if I may express it that way, or magnified the question they were deciding into one affecting the entire Selective Service Act. * * *

MR. JAVITS: Mr. President. I have listened to the Senator from Mississippi with the greatest care. I realize and I hope that the courts will realize, the position into which they have placed us all. If we read the Court opinion, it is as bad for the affirmative as it is bad for the negative, and if there are going to be implications from adopting something, then there will be implications from rejecting something. So that the Senator is right when he says that this is a problem of great responsibility.

In order to help us, I am going to ask the Senator the following, and I hope he will understand the sense in which I ask it.

Mr. President, I feel we should not, at this time, press it upon this measure.

As I read the colloquy which the Senator from Mississippi had with the Senator from Arkansas (Mr. Fulbright), it really does not exactly meet the point, as he phrased the question. I think it is important to see whether the legislative history could be made crystal clear that no implication can or should be read into the passage of the Selective Service Act which could represent an implied congressional authorization of the Vietnam war. * * *

Is there anything in this act, if it becomes law, which may be deemed to constitute an authorization for the conduct of military hostilities in Southeast Asia pursuant to the war powers of Congress as specified in Article I, section 8 of the Constitution?

MR. STENNIS: I can certainly say to the Senator that, in my estimation, and as I interpret the Constitution, there are no provisions in the bill that would authorize the war in Vietnam as provided in article I, section 8 of the Constitution.

MR. JAVITS: Would the Senator let me—

MR. STENNIS: May I add this—I think that so far as the bill is concerned, we are not trying directly to authorize or to terminate that war, not yet.

MR. JAVITS: Or to imply any authority which has not been otherwise given?

MR. STENNIS: No. I think it does not imply any additional authority. Now it carries with it the manpower that will be used in Vietnam in connection with the war. There's no doubt about that. And the money bill that follows, presumably in the future, some of that money will be used for the war, as the Senator already knows. But there is no grant authority in the bill. So far as the war is concerned, we are not doing any more than we are compelled to do, as I see it, to keep up our military forces. * * *

MR. JAVITS: Mr. President, I asked the Senator from Mississippi, as the manager of the bill: Is there anything in this act which could be deemed to constitute an authorization by the Congress for the conduct of military hostilities in Southeast Asia pursuant to the war powers of Congress as specified in article I, section 8 of the Constitution?

MR. STENNIS: Mr. President, according to the interpretation of the Senator from Mississippi on article I, section 8, I do not think there is anything in the bill that would authorize the conduct of the war in Southeast Asia. . . .

MR. EAGLETON: I would like to ask the Senator an additional question.

I assume the Senator from Mississippi does not regard this bill, which provides for the conscription of young men to serve in the Armed Forces to provide for the national defense, as authority for the President to use them in any other way than the Constitution states. For instance, if young men are sent into Indochina war, does not Congress have to authorize such hostilities in accordance with the Constitution?

MR. STENNIS: My answer to that question is yes. Yes, that is correct. . . .

MR. JAVITS: Mr. President, I believe we all certainly agree that this is a matter of such delicacy, involving a responsibility beyond that of an individual Senator, that it is prudent on this record not to press the amendment at this time. I reserve the right, based upon a reading and consideration of the whole record and any other amendment which may be offered to this bill, to urge this or some other revised version of the amendment on some other occasion before the time for consideration of amendments is up.

I withdraw the amendment. 117 *Cong. Rec.* S. 9685, 9686, 9687, 9688 (daily ed. June 22, 1971).

PART FIVE

Appeal to the Supreme Court

The final action in the *Berk* and *Orlando* cases was an appeal to the Supreme Court. Although the court had refused to hear the *Mora* case in 1967 and had voted 6 to 3 not to accept the first Massachusetts case challenging the war, there was still hope that it would hear the cases coming from the Second Circuit.

In the first place, the cases were the only actions which had actually ruled on the legal issues of the war on their merits. Since the District of Columbia Circuit had said in a 1966 case that the courts should not get into the problems at all, the Second Circuit's willingness to rule on the merits created a conflict among the lower federal courts on an important legal issue—a situation which by itself often justifies Supreme Court review. Secondly, the war was apparently winding down, and any order that the court issued would not take effect until the spring of 1972, when it would have a minimum impact on the actual conduct of this war, but exert important influence on the future state of the law. Thirdly, the decision of the Supreme Court in *The New York Times* case involving publication of the Pentagon papers indicated that the justices were taking a new look at the problems of executive authority under the war powers. Justice Douglas had said, in an opinion, joined by Justice Black, "The Constitution by Article I, Sect. 8 gives Congress, not the President, power 'to declare War.' Nowhere are Presidential wars authorized." Justice Stewart wrote, with Justice White concurring, ". . . of course, Congress alone can declare war. This power was last exercised almost 30 years ago at the inception of World War II." Even Justices Harlan and Blackmun and Chief Justice Burger suggested that "Constitutional considerations forbid 'a complete abandonment of judicial control' in the area of foreign relations." Since only four votes were necessary to bring a case to the Supreme Court and three votes had already been cast to take the Massachusetts case, a hope existed that a fourth vote might be available to bring the cases up.

By the time the appeal to the Supreme Court was filed, Berk had been discharged from the army and Orlando had returned from Vietnam. In order to insure that technicalities would not preclude Supreme Court review, two new plaintiffs, each with current orders to report to Vietnam, were added, Douglas Kaplan and Ernest daCosta.

The request for review restated the legal issues presented to the lower court and, in addition, attempted to persuade at least four members of the court that the welfare of the nation would be served by resolving once and for all the issue of the war's legality.

Extracts from ACLU Petition for Review in the Supreme Court †

Preliminary Statement

There is little doubt that the Vietnam War is the most disturbing and troublesome issue of our times. It has divided and agitated American society not only because a great many citizens now question the wisdom of our efforts in Southeast Asia, but be-

† Footnotes have been renumbered.

cause the legality and constitutionality of American military involvement in Vietnam is in serious question. Millions of Americans feel that we have become embroiled in Vietnam through procedures which have failed to satisfy constitutional norms. Thus they view the struggle in Vietnam not as the lawful expression of the nation's will but as an unlawful exercise in naked power. . . .

. . .

Reflecting Senator Ervin's perception that much of the divisiveness flowing from the war in Vietnam stems from the war's questionable legal basis, virtually every political figure in the nation has offered an opinion on the war's legality. Charges of "Executive usurpation," "Congressional pusillanimity," "Constitutional crisis" fly back and forth in the Congress and on the editorial pages throughout the nation. Many state legislatures have passed or are considering special laws to protect their citizens from service in Vietnam with a view to obtaining a court test of the war. (See *The New York Times*, May 2, 1971, p. 40.) Until the Second Circuit spoke in the *Berk* and *Orlando* cases, there was silence from the one organ of government vested with responsibility to speak authoritatively on the proper allocation of constitutional responsibility between the Executive and the Congress—the Federal judiciary.

The silence of the courts on this issue meant that soldiers— like the petitioners herein—who had been ordered to go to Vietnam to risk their lives in what they claimed was an illegal war had no forum to hear their complaints. For the federal courts to avoid their responsibility of hearing the constitutional complaints of the citizens most directly affected by the Executive's actions is to deny the very purpose for which they were instituted.[1]

The silence of the courts on the issue of the Executive's authority to wage war in Vietnam has not led to any resolution, or

[1] James Madison stated when he introduced the Bill of Rights into Congress: "independent tribunals of justice will consider themselves in a peculiar manner the guardians of those rights [in the Bill of Rights]: they will be an impenetrable bulwark against every assumption of power in the Legislative or Executive; they will be naturally led to resist every encroachment of rights expressly stipulated for in the Constitution by the declaration of rights." 1 *Annals of Congress*, 1st Cong., 1st Sess. 439.

to any hope of resolution, of the problem by the other branches of government. The Executive continues to flirt with the concept of inherent authority to wage war. The Congress cannot fashion a legislative response because of widespread disagreement as to the meaning of Article I, Section 8 and its impact upon Executive power. Thus, the nation may be doomed to repeat its Vietnam agony wntil a definitive rule is established by the body who alone can say the last word: this Court.

I.

> *The conflicts among the lower courts and among the co-ordinate branches of government as to the jurisdiction of the federal courts to review the Executive's war powers and the constitutional standards to be applied require a definitive resolution of the issues involved.*

The current state of the law relating to the meaning of Article I, Section 8, clause 11 of the Constitution and the ability of the courts to review the constitutional reach of the Executive's war power is in conflict and remains totally unsatisfactory.

First, a basic disagreement has arisen between the Circuits as to the justiciability of a contention that no Congressional authorization exists for the waging of the Vietnam war.

The Second Circuit, and both District Court judges below, rejected the government's contention that challenges to the legal sufficiency of the Executive's waging of war in Vietnam posed non-justiciable issues.[2] The Second Circuit's view of jurisdiction

[2] Judge Dooling held that the issues are justiciable:

". . . determining whether or not a political decision has been taken by the appropriate set of governmental acts inescapably presents a purely judicial question when the existence or nonexistence of a valid political authorization as the source of a particular command is drawn in question by one directly affected by it in his individual liberty as a citizen. * * * [If a court decides against the government] [brackets in original brief], the only consequence can be resumption of conformity to constitutional norms of political conduct to achieve, dilute, deflect or reverse the desired political objectives." 317 F. Supp. at 1016.

This view has been recently confirmed by three members of this Court in *New York Times Co.* v. *United States,* 39 LW 4879 (June 30, 1971). Justice

has been adopted by a District Court in the Northern District of California. *Mottola* v. *Nixon,* 318 F. Supp. 538 (N.D. Cal. 1970).

The District of Columbia Circuit has reached a diametrically opposed jurisdictional position in *Luftig* v. *McNamara,* 373 F.2d 664, 665–666 (D.C. Cir. 1967), *cert. den.* 387 U.S. 945 (1967). The District of Columbia Circuit's jurisdictional position has been accepted by District Courts in Massachusetts and Virginia, *Massachusetts* v. *Laird,* No. 71-419-W (D. Mass. June 1, 1971); *Davi* v. *Laird,* 318 F. Supp. 478 (W.D. Va. 1970).

Among those courts reaching the merits of the challenges to the war in Vietnam, equally contradictory results have occurred. Judge Dooling found that the Gulf of Tonkin Resolution lacked compelling significance as authority to wage war in Vietnam. 317 F. Supp. at 1019. Judge Judd disagreed. 317 F. Supp. at 723. The Second Circuit cited the Tonkin Gulf Resolution as authority for the war, but ignored the fact of its repeal in January 1971. Finally, the District Court in *Mottola* stated that the Tonkin Gulf Resolution ''falls far short of a declaration of war, or even of implied authorization for the kind of all out full scale war subsequently launched by the President in Vietnam.'' 318 F. Supp. at 544.

Moreover, recent disclosures of the highly questionable circumstances which surrounded the adoption of the Tonkin Gulf Resolution in 1964 further cloud its legal effect. See The New York Times, *The Pentagon Papers* 234ff. (Bantam ed. 1971).

The Second Circuit below relied primarily on the appropriation of funds for the Vietnam war and the extension of the draft as constitutionally sufficient manifestations of Congressional as-

Harlan said in dissent (Chief Justice Burger and Justice Blackmun concurring):

> "I agree that, in performance of its duty to protect the values of the First Amendment against political pressures, the judiciary must review the initial Executive determination to the point of satisfying itself that the subject matter of the dispute does lie within the proper compass of the President's foreign relations power. Constitutional considerations forbid 'a complete abandonment of judicial control.' Cf. United States v. Reynolds, 345 U.S. 1, 8 (1953)" 39 LW at 4892.

Certainly the judiciary must examine the direct use of the war power by the Executive to satisfy itself that "the subject matter of the dispute lies within the proper compass of the President's foreign relations power." In this vital area there cannot be a "complete abandonment of judicial control."

sent to the war. However, this ground was explicitly rejected by the *Mottola* court. 318 F. Supp. at 543.

More important, that ground of the Second Circuit's decision was severely criticized on the floor of the Senate by the Chairmen of both the Foreign Relations Committee and the Armed Services Committee, who expressed consternation at the court's opinion. 117 *Cong. Rec.* S8320–23 (daily ed. June 4, 1971). . . .

This exchange on the floor of Congress reflects the great division that exists between the coordinate branches of government on the reach and meaning of the war power clauses of the Constitution. The Executive has consistently maintained that it possesses "inherent authority" to prosecute large scale military operations in the absence of Congressional authorization by virtue of its control of the nation's foreign policy and its role as Commander-in-Chief of its armed forces. See generally, Brief of the Solicitor General in *Massachusetts* v. *Laird*, No. 42 Orig., October Term, 1970, pp. 18–24; televised interview of President Richard M. Nixon on July 1, 1970 reported at 117 *Cong. Rec.* S8761 (daily ed. June 10, 1971). See also 116 *Cong. Rec.* S9598, 9591 (daily ed. June 23, 1970); 116 *Cong. Rec.* S21850 (daily ed. January 2, 1971).[3]

Members of Congress have categorically rejected the existence of inherent Executive authority to wage war and have severely criticized the Second Circuit's ruling that Congressional approval of the Vietnam war may be implied from the passage of appropriations bills and the extension of the draft. An amendment was introduced into the Senate to negative the Second Circuit's opinion in *Orlando* but it was then withdrawn as unnecessary. See 117 *Cong. Rec.* S9685–89 (daily ed. June 22, 1971). . . . See in addition to the debates noted above, remarks of Senator Alan Cranston, 116 *Cong. Rec.* S11818 (daily ed. July 21,

[3] All the courts that have examined the matter have firmly rejected the idea that the President could wage a war of Vietnam dimensions without the authorization of Congress. The Second Circuit noted: "If the executive branch engaged the nation in prolonged foreign military activities without any significant congressional authorization, a court might be able to determine that this extreme step violated a discoverable standard calling for some mutual participation by Congress in accordance with Article I, section 8." *Berk* v. *Laird,* 429 F.2d at 305. See also Judge Dooling's opinion in *Orlando,* 317 F. Supp. at 1016; Judge Sweigert's opinion in *Mottola,* 318 F. Supp. at 541.

1970); Appendix p. 39a. Senator George S. McGovern, 116 *Cong. Rec.* S11987 (daily ed. July 23, 1970); . . . Senators Mark Hatfield and J. William Fulbright, 117 *Cong. Rec.* S8044 (daily ed. June 2, 1971). . . . See also statement of Senator Richard Russell, 112 *Cong. Rec.* 3135 (February 16, 1966). . . .

The Executive itself has taken inconsistent positions on the legal basis of the Vietnam War. The State Department represented to Congress that the Gulf of Tonkin resolution was unnecessary for the prosecution of the war. See Letter from H. G. Torbert, Jr., Acting Assistant Secretary of State for Congressional Relations to Senator J. William Fulbright. Quoted in Senate Report No. 91-872, 91st Cong., 2d Sess. 20, 23 (1970).

Despite these disclaimers, the government has urged *in every single case in which the issue has arisen* that the Gulf of Tonkin Resolution was a constitutional basis for the war—even after its repeal.

The inevitable result of the inconsistent positions concerning the constitutional basis for the war is to perpetuate the national confusion over its legality and to intensify the bitterness of the national debate over its continuation. Indeed, the only point that has clearly emerged from the welter of conflicting opinions over the legal basis for the war is that unless and until this Court clarifies the constitutional allocation of powers between the Congress and the Executive in the area of war and peace, confusion and uncertainty must plague any future consideration of the war in Vietnam by the political branches of government.

. . .

Conclusion

As noted above, the fact that this Court has not spoken on the legality of the Executive's steps in Vietnam has led to endless confusion by all the branches of government and among the people as to the meaning of the war power clauses. A denial of review in this case will perpetuate that confusion. Until constitutional responsibility is firmly fixed by this Court, the nation will continue to question the constitutional legitimacy of any military action that the government takes in the future.

The political arms of the government can readily adjust to any determination this Court makes and assign appropriate duties and responsibilities. As Judge Dooling said below: "the only consequence can be resumption of conformity to constitutional norms of political conduct to achieve, dilute or reverse the desired political objectives." 317 F. Supp. at 1016.

The consequences of continued silence by this Court on Vietnam can only be confusion, unrest, and continued uncertainty about any future military action. The nation requires a final answer to these questions which have so troubled and perplexed our society.

For the reasons set forth above the petition for certiorari should be granted.

————————

On October 12, 1971, in a brief unsigned order, five members of the Supreme Court denied Orlando's petition and refused to review the legality of the Vietnam war. Justices Douglas and Brennan dissented.

Ironically, a total of four justices of the Supreme Court—the number required to secure review—had voted to review the war's legality, but review was finally denied because the votes were not cast at the same time. Justice Douglas had urged review of the war's legal basis since the *Mitchell* case in 1966. Justice Stewart had brilliantly outlined the legal issues raised by the war and had joined Justice Douglas in voting for review in the *Mora* case. Justice Harlan, scholarly and cautious, had joined Justice Stewart in voting to permit Massachusetts to argue its challenge to the war's legality in *Massachusetts* v. *Laird*. The addition of Justice Brennan, a fourth justice, to the pro-review wing of the court in *Orlando* should have clinched the matter and brought the issue before the Court for ultimate resolution.

However, just as factors outside the legal process, such as the invasion of Cambodia in June 1970, had undoubtedly influenced the Second Circuit's landmark decision in the first *Berk* appeal, extraneous factors combined to block the issue of the war's legality from reaching the Supreme Court in October 1971.

First, the makeup of the court had shifted during the pendency of the *Orlando* petition for review. The death of Justice Black and the illness-induced resignation of Justice Harlan had hurt Orlando's chances for review. Justice Harlan's resignation not only cost the pro-review forces a possible vote (Justice Harlan had cast an equivocal vote for review in *Massachusetts* v. *Laird*) but removed one of the court's most scholarly and courageous justices, who could be counted upon to vote his conscience even in the most politically sensitive of cases. Justice Black's death removed the court's leading "strict constructionist" from the bench. Famous for his often literal interpretations of the Constitution, Justice Black was capable of ruling that the phrase "Congress shall . . . declare War" meant exactly what it says.

Second, the Executive was publicly proclaiming its intention to wind down the war. Substantial numbers of American troops had been withdrawn from combat, and, although the weekly toll of dead and wounded continued, the intensity of American combat participation had undoubtedly decreased. Thus, the pressure for judicial action was significantly less than it had been in June 1970, when the Second Circuit decided the first *Berk* appeal.

Third, it was widely believed that secret negotiations involving Vietnam were occurring, and the court was sensitive about taking any action which might disturb such negotiations, if any.

Finally, after a period of paralysis, Congress appeared, in October 1971, more willing to shoulder its constitutional responsibilities and to re-assert its control over the Executive's war power. Thus, the repeal of the Gulf of Tonkin Resolution, the passage of the National Commitments Resolution by the Senate in June 1970, the passage of the Mansfield and Cooper-Church Amendments by the Senate, and the introduction of many war-powers resolutions in Congress demonstrated that even without judicial intervention, Congress would no longer tolerate the usurpation of its war power by the Executive.

Whether any or all of these factors induced Justice Stewart to reverse himself and to vote against review is, of course, conjecture. For whatever reasons, however, five of the seven sitting justices declined to rule on the war's legality and left unresolved the issue of how this nation goes to war.

PART SIX

Conclusion

In the traditional sense, Berk and Orlando "lost" their attempt to end the war in Vietnam through the courts. It would be a mistake, however, to evaluate the impact of the *Berk* and *Orlando* cases from so narrow a perspective; for, from both a legal and a practical standpoint, the cases were extremely effective.

First, the principle of judicial review of Executive warmaking was explicitly recognized for the first time by the courts. No longer could a president ignore the Constitution and launch the nation into war without fear of a judicial check upon his actions. Indeed, had the *Berk-Orlando* precedent existed in the early days of the Vietnam war, it is doubtful whether President Johnson would have dared to engage in dramatic escalation without seeking the explicit approval of Congress. Given the historic role of judicial review as the primary method of enforcing the Constitution, its introduction into the area of Executive warmaking is a constitutional event of the highest magnitude.

Second, the myth of inherent presidential authority to wage war was utterly destroyed. The grandiose view of the Executive's inherent power to wage war was rejected categorically by every judge who passed upon it. The inherent-power argument was so lacking in intellectual justification that it was able to flourish only in the absence of judicial review. As soon as it came under judicial scrutiny, it was laughed out of court.

Third, Congress was put on notice that it could no longer avoid its constitutional responsibilities by abdicating them. *Berk* and *Orlando* established without question that primary congressional responsibility for war and peace was firmly embedded in the Constitution, and that Congress could not avoid its responsibilities simply by deferring to the Executive. The cases had established that congressional involvement in presidentially initiated hostilities was inevitable—in the form of appropriations bills. Thus, whether Congress wished it or not, the *Berk* and *Orlando* courts had created a Rubicon which future congressmen would have to cross. No longer could critics of a war be dissuaded from debating its merits during the appropriations process by assurances that paying the bills for a war did not constitute its approval.

Finally, the *Berk* and *Orlando* cases emerged as a catalyst in spurring Congress to take effective action to insure that the tragedy of Vietnam can never be repeated.

Beginning in January 1971, many senators and congressmen introduced legislation to restrict the war powers of the president. Senator Robert Taft of Ohio introduced a resolution on January 27, 1971, calling for the president to convene Congress immediately after he has ordered American troops to combat so that he may secure specific legislative authorization for his orders. Senator Jacob Javits of New York recommended in February 1971 that the president be permitted to commit American forces to repel attacks on American territory or to comply with existing treaty commitments, but that he must return to Congress for explicit authorization if military hostilities continue beyond thirty days. Senator Thomas Eagleton of Missouri went even further. His bill would not allow any existing treaty to trigger a presidential war. His proposal also contained a specific provision that "authorization to commit the Armed Forces of the United States to hostilities may not be inferred from legislative enactments, including appropriations bills, which do not specifically include such authorization." Even Senator John Stennis, chairman of the Senate Armed Services Committee and a hawk on Vietnam, introduced his own war-powers measure, also requiring "specific statutory authority" before the president could begin a war. He said on the floor of the Senate: ". . . we must return to the original safeguard before our Nation can be committed to a state of actual war with any nation; that is, the Congress, representing the people must so declare." †

In the House of Representatives similar measures were introduced. A series of hearings were held by the Foreign Relations Committees of both houses in which distinguished scholars, lawyers, and other legislators supported the need for explicit control of the president's power to wage war. Legislative leaders in Congress, including the Republican minority leader, Senator Hugh Scott, endorsed the principle of the various bills.

The reason for the new consensus in Congress was the recognition of the terrible mistakes that had been made in Vietnam, mistakes that could have been avoided by a more careful reading of the Constitution by the Executive branch. By starting and waging a major war in Vietnam without the express authorization of Congress, Presidents Johnson and Nixon both insured widespread dissent and unrest. Congress had finally come to realize that constitutional responsibility for war and peace had to be firmly fixed by explicit legislation, or the legitimacy of any future military action by the government would be put into serious question. As Senator Stennis said when he introduced his resolution: ". . . we have . . . learned that unless this course is followed [of having Congress explicitly authorize war] the people as a whole do not feel committed; they do not and cannot have a full sense of personal commitment and personal obligation." That realization by the congressional leaders made them extremely eager to pass some war-powers legislation regardless of opposition by the Executive department.

Thus, even though, in the narrowest sense, Malcolm Berk and Salvatore Orlando "lost" their cases, their courage in bringing the issue into the courts allowed the nation to win an important legal victory.

† 117 *Cong. Rec.* S 6615 (daily ed. May 11, 1971).

Index